"Bringing together the rich and long ....m and worker self-management with the digital economy of the twenty-first century, Scholz's timely and groundbreaking new book provides both in-depth analysis and practical steps to make the Internet economy truly work for all who most rely on it."

Zeynep Tufekci, writer at *The New York Times*, Berkman Center for Internet and Society at Harvard University, professor at The University of North Carolina at Chapel Hill

"Trebor Scholz has written a unsparing and bracing critique of platform capitalism. Moreover, he's developed a blueprint for transcending it: a tough-minded platform cooperativism that eschews the utopianism of 'sharing economy' bromides. Anyone concerned about the future of work should read this book."

Frank Pasquale, author of *The Black Box Society*

"Based on years of research and cooperation, Uberworked and Underpaid passionately and sharply tracks down the dark side of the 'sharing economy,' that is the reduction of labor to a cheap and disposable commodity, without protections or benefits. Against such hyper-precarization, Scholz believes in the possibility of autonomous self-organization of digital work. Posing platform cooperativism against crowd fleecing and the on-demand service economy, Scholz's book is an invaluable contribution to a much needed reinvention of a socialism for the twenty-first century."

Tiziana Terranova, author of *Network Culture: Politics for the Information Age*

Uberworked and Underpaid

For Suvarnaprabha

Uberworked and Underpaid

How workers are disrupting the digital economy

Trebor Scholz

polity

First published in 2017 by Polity Press

Polity Press
65 Bridge Street
Cambridge CB2 1UR, UK

Polity Press
350 Main Street
Malden, MA 02148, USA

ISBN-13: 978-0-7456-5356-3
ISBN-13: 978-0-7456-5357-0(pb)

A catalogue record for this book is available from the British Library.

Library of Congress Cataloging-in-Publication Data

Names: Scholz, Trebor, author.
Title: Uberworked and underpaid : how workers are disrupting the digital economy / Trebor Scholz.
Description: Cambridge, UK ; Malden, MA : Polity Press, 2017. |
    Includes bibliographical references and index.
Identifiers: LCCN 2015037155| ISBN 9780745653563 (hardback) |
    ISBN 9780745653570 (pbk.)
Subjects: LCSH: Information technology–Economic aspects. | Information technology–Social aspects. | Social media–Economic aspects. | Labor. | Electronic commerce–Social aspects. | Internet industry.
Classification: LCC HC79.I55 S3565 2016 | DDC 331.7/6138433–dc23 LC record available at http://lccn.loc.gov/2015037155

Typeset in 10.5 on 12 pt Sabon
by Toppan Best-set Premedia Limited
Printed and bound in the United Kingdom by Clays Ltd, St Ives PLC

For further information on Polity, visit our website: politybooks.com

Contents

Contents

Acknowledgments

This book is based on years of research, taking into consideration work from the arts, law, technology studies, and the social sciences. It is informed by many exchanges with participants at the Digital Labor Conferences that I have convened at The New School in New York City since 2009.

I enjoy critical thought wherever I can find it, which meant that while writing this book I focused not only on printed matter but also on mailing lists, e-books, jounalistic accounts, and blog essays. I couldn't have written Uberworked and Underpaid without the conversations on the Institute for Distributed Creativity mailing list, which I founded in 2004. Many of its members offered commentary and prodded me into starting this project. This book, then, reflects what I learned about digital labor.

Some readers may search the pdf of this book and will be most interested in a particular chapter. Therefore, in the process of writing, I aimed for each chapter to hold up on its own, also outside of the context of the entire book.

This book greatly benefited from many discussions. I would like to thank those who invited me to present and test the ideas and arguments for this book through lectures at the Massachusetts Institute for Technology, Harvard University, Warsaw's Center for Contemporary Art, Yale University, Transmediale, Re:publica, Schloss Solitude, Carnegie Mellon University, University of Cologne, Georgetown University, McGill, and universities in Berlin, Chiang Mai, Athens, Uppsala, Mexico City, and Hong Kong. I am especially grateful to the Centre for Innovation Law and Policy at the University of Toronto for inviting me to deliver the Grafstein Lecture in March of 2014 and to Hampshire College for asking me to present the 8th Erick Schocket Memorial Lecture a year later.

Many people helped to shape the ideas by offering helpful comments on the manuscript. First of all, my New School colleague McKenzie Wark, along with various undisclosed academic reviewers, deserves special thanks for persuading Polity Press to give this book a chance. Thank you also to my editor at Polity, Elen Griffiths, for helping me to make this a better book.

I owe gratitude to The New School, and Eugene Lang College in particular, for sustaining my cross-disciplinary practice as a scholar-activist, cultural catalyst, and educator. My faculty colleagues across the university, at Lang, Media Studies, and Parsons, have been extraordinarily congenial and supportive of my work, for which I would like to thank them as well.

At the University of Maryland School of Law, I would like to thank Frank Pasquale for his unceasing invaluable input and enduring friendship. He kept me going; I owe him much. At Cornell University's School of Industrial and Labor Relations, I would like to thank Jefferson Cowie for his enthusiastic comments. Fred Turner read and commented on earlier versions of this book. (I hope that it reads more like a waterfall now.) At Leuphana Universität, many thanks to Mercedes Bunz, for her graceful comments and encouragement. At Ryerson University, I would also like to thank Henry Warwick for his support of the project. My gratitude goes out also to Rochelle LaPlante, Winifred Poster, David Carroll, Antonio A. Casilli, Orit Halpern, Karen Gregory, Samuel Tannert, Nathan Schneider, Natalie Bookchin, and Roger Brishen.

During my sabbatical in 2012–13, the Institute for Cultural Inquiry (ICI) in Berlin hosted me in its magnificent quarters through a guest fellowship. Thank you, Christopher Holtzey, director of the ICI, and Corinna Haas, ICI's librarian.

I would like to extend a special thanks to my smart and wonderfully quirky New School students for their curious questions and useful input, in particular those who participated in my seminars on digital labor in 2011 and 2014. I hope that this book will help them to navigate their own work lives with greater critical awareness.

Life during the time of writing this was filled with speaking engagements at conferences and the work of chairing The Politics of Digital Culture series at The New School. There have been many convivial meetings, much time preparing for class and teaching, and advising.

On a personal note, these past years were also about raising my two daughters Rosa and Emma with my partner in life, the artist Jenny Perlin. They make me proud in more ways than I can name. I was only able to take on the bleak realities of digital labor because of their giggles and loving embrace.

Author's Note

Please note that some citations do not have page numbers. The reason
for this omission is that they are based on ebooks, not print books.
Text passages can, however, be easily found through simple searches.

Introduction: Why Digital Labor Now?

No one would have believed, in the first decade of the twenty-first century, that the ideological bubble of the "sharing economy" would deflate so quickly, or that workers, labor advocates, programmers, and activists would soon start to build structures for democratic ownership and governance on the Internet. It is likely that we will look back to this era and understand it as a turning point for both the nature of work and our lifestyles.

The title of this book purports to be about the "sharing economy" but it goes beyond that. In fact, it starts off with an atlas of sites of digital work – from on-demand work to in-game labor, and finishes with proposals for ways in which workers and their allies can start to take back the digital economy.

Fairly compensated digital work with reliable hours holds considerable potential for low-income immigrants and those living in geographically remote or economically precarious regions. Such digital work could also provide a decent income for the more than 650,000 people[1] who are released from prison each year, struggling to find a well-paying job. People who care for a child or a sick relative or those who have phobias or other restrictions that do not allow them to leave their homes could also benefit. Half of all Americans earn less than $30,000 a year; they cannot afford to pay for basic needs like housing, food, healthcare, childcare, or utilities.[2] Unemployment among black Americans is twice as high as that among white Americans. And for Latinos, the situation is only slightly better. Women are often hit the hardest by unemployment. Digital labor could play a positive role for these groups, offering them more flexibility and sparing them some of the hardships associated with traditional workplaces.

The overall burden of the debt crisis and changing work regimes means that for millions of Americans, a paycheck is increasingly unlikely to include legal protections or benefits. If we acknowledge that this trend is unlikely to be reversed in favor of a 40-hour work-week with a regular paycheck, the question becomes: what are good alternatives for the one third of the workforce that is not traditionally employed?

One proposal on the table is for portable benefits for workers who have several employers. Another suggestion is to build democratically governed service platforms and online marketplaces owned and oper-ated by those who most rely on them. A network organized around what I have called "platform cooperativism" could rival firms like Amazon or Uber. Cities could build and operate their own platforms for short-term rentals, and inventive unions could protect workers in the platform economy.

These "platform co-ops" already exist today; they demonstrate that society can positively develop a moral vision of digital work that does not tolerate surveillance, surreptitious extraction, and exploitation.

Loconomics,[3] for instance, is a freelancer-owned cooperative where members-freelancers own shares, receive dividends, and have a voice in running the company. Loconomics offers massages and other serv-ices that are locally in demand. Membership in Loconomics costs $29.95 per month and there is neither a bidding process nor a markup. The founders started testing the Loconomics app in the San Francisco/ Bay Area in the spring of 2016 and will now expand it to other cities.

Stocksy[4] is an artist-owned cooperative for stock-photography. The co-op is based on the idea of profit sharing and co-ownership with the artists who are contributing photos to its platform. Artists can apply to become members and, when accepted, license images, receiv-ing 50 percent commission on sales and profit sharing at the end of the year. The objective of the cooperative is to create sustainable careers for its members.[5]

These are just two examples – and many more are to follow – but their very existence shows that platform cooperatives can offer a clear alternative to the individualist ethos of the "sharing economy." But platform co-ops are only still emerging and so far, despite their poten-tial, it appears that the magic of digital work and growth of the sharing economy could be more harmful for low-income workers than any other technological development of the past four decades. Currently, digital labor appears to be the shiny, sharp tip of a gar-gantuan spear of neoliberalism made up of deregulation, economic inequality, union busting, and a shift from employment to low-wage temporary contracts.

In his book *Average is Over*, the conservative economist Tyler Cowen introduces us to one possible endgame for this trend. Soon, he predicts, there will be a superclass, a "hyper-meritocracy" of 10 to 15 percent of the population that will make over $1 million per year.[6] For the bottom 85 percent, he envisions an annual income along the lines of $5,000–10,000. Cowen takes Mexico as an example where "lodging [for the poor] is satisfactory, if not spectacular, and of course the warmer weather helps."[7] In Cowen's vision, there's nothing that we can do to avert a future in which a tiny hyper-meritocracy of Americans enjoy fantastically interesting lives while the rest slog along, tranquilized by free Internet and low-paying gigs. On Cowen's planet, Leftoverswap.com would rule and Uber would be celebrated for honoring schoolteachers who drive for UberX after hours to put food on the table.

The following scenarios of digital work highlight its darker side. Take Boston native Jennifer Guidry, for instance. Guidry strings together several gigs, trying to make a full-time living.[8] Guidry, a woman in her mid-thirties, is driving for upstarts like Lyft, Uber, and Sidecar. Sometimes her day starts with drop-offs at the airport in the early morning while her family is still asleep. When her children are at school, she assembles furniture and tends gardens. However, all of these gigs still don't add up to a living wage, the work is unpredictable, and she does not have employer-paid health insurance or a pension plan.

Low-wage and part-time jobs have dominated the global financial recovery; Guidry is only one of 53 million Americans who scrape by despite earning several incomes from multiple jobs. It takes skill and time to constantly track down new gigs; the on-demand economy requires perma-youth, flexibility, and perpetual health.

A 2015 study by Jonathan Hall (Uber) and Alan Krueger (Princeton University) showed that Uber drivers in 20 cities are netting about $17.50 an hour, which, following accounts from drivers, comes out to anywhere between $10 and $13 an hour after subtracting the cost of insurance, gasoline, auto payments, and maintenance.[9] While some drivers appreciate the flexible hours, they realize that with increasing competition, their wages are likely to sink. In the absence of binding standards (e.g., price per mile), the working conditions for these drivers, classified as "independent contractors" instead of "employees," can (and do) change arbitrarily.

In this book, rather than analyzing the "sharing economy" in isolation, I am considering it alongside practices like crowd work. Kristy Milland, for example, turned to Amazon Mechanical Turk (AMT) in

2005. Like many others, she started working with AMT to supplement her income, but five years later, after her husband lost his job, she started to work up to 17 hours a day to take care of bills and pay off the debt that they had accrued.

For novice workers on the Mechanical Turk platform, the pay can range between $2 and $3 an hour, which is also the average hourly rate on CrowdFlower and other companies in the sector. In 2010, speaking to young tech entrepreneurs, CEO of CrowdFlower Lukas Biewald, shared that "[b]efore the Internet, it would be really difficult to find someone, sit them down for 10 minutes and get them to work for you, and then fire them after those 10 minutes. But with technology, you can actually find them, pay them the tiny amount of money, and then get rid of them after you don't need them anymore."[10]

While in Brazil and France regulators have punished "sharing economy" businesses that violate labor laws, such behavior is largely tolerated in the United States; "disruptive" business practices are understood as an integral part of the economic playbook.[11]

Milland writes that the people who commission work on Mechanical Turk often "don't realize that there is a living, breathing human on the other end of the connection who needs to feed their children, pay medical bills, or ensure their home doesn't go into foreclosure."[12]

In addition to Milland and Guidry, there are the Yelp and Amazon reviewers who fuel for-profit sites with their free labor. Until recently, Harriet Klausner was Amazon's top book reviewer. A retired librarian, Klausner reads two books a day. Her profile shows the grand sum of 31,014 reviews (and counting); book reviewing is her career, she states. While Klausner is not paid, she is respected among her fellow reviewers, major newspapers have written features about her, and, not unlike professional literary critics, she has a degree of power. Klausner's opinion can help or hinder the careers of young novelists. She is not the only one who spends her space time in this way. Every day, one billion people in advanced economies have between two billion and six billion spare hours among them.[13] Capturing and monetizing those hours is the goal of platform capitalism. A manager of volunteers for the telecommunications company Verizon explains how he recruits the enthusiasm of the "voluntariat": "If handled adeptly, [volunteers] hold considerable promise. ... You have to make an environment that attracts [them], because that's where the magic happens."[14]

About This Book

This book was written for the people who feel stuck in this economy, who don't have the time to write about it, and who are looking for a future of work that they can wholeheartedly embrace. Part I comprises four chapters; it introduces and discusses sites of paid and uncompensated digital work; it aims to draw a dotted line around the term "digital labor," and it spells out the concept of crowd fleecing, which distinguishes what is happening on labor platforms like Uber from traditional exploitation.

In the first chapter, I examine the sites and size of the rapidly growing digital labor segment of the workforce. This is the beginning of a much-needed typology of digital labor, starting here with paid digital work, that identifies central discussions relevant to these emerging forms, namely that of worker rights under platform capitalism, the myth of choice and flexibility, the illegality of many sites and practices under Federal labor law, the short-termism of Silicon Valley, the materiality of this work, historical precursors for an ecosystem of digital work, and the question of decent digital labor.

Drawing on the work of Andre Gorz, Mike Davis, Erin Hatton, Frank Pasquale, and Susan Buck-Morss, I reveal, in great detail and with a rich set of examples ranging from crowd work to on-demand service labor; what is lost in the transition from employment to contingent contract work. How are workers supposed to plan their lives and think ahead when the ground is constantly shifting? I pay particular attention to Amazon Mechanical Turk and Uber because these companies have become emblematic of platform capitalism; they provide templates for the society-wide reorganization of work.

Beyond technology, other factors that impact the role of the labor platforms discussed in this chapter include: a lack of regulation, the decline of labor unions, the society-wide reorganization of work, and publicly traded stockholder companies driven by growth imperatives and the fiduciary duty to maximize profits. This chapter sets the stage for the discussions in Part II of the book.

Chapter 2 is a continuation of the typology begun in the first chapter. It is an introduction to sites of unpaid digital work, such as data labor – the surreptitious capture of value from quotidian online activities – hope labor, gamification, and geospatial labor. In this chapter I refer to work by Julian Kücklich, Ross Perlin, Gary Shteyngart, Golan Levin, Arlie Russell Hochschild, Jonathan Crary, Tiziana Terranova, and Franco "Bifo" Berardi. I explain that free labor per se is not the main culprit; it is what I call "crowd fleecing," the growth imperative, and the fiduciary duty of the stockholder corporation to maximize profits that should be questioned and restricted.

Chapter 2 concludes with a discussion of Universal Basic Income. The practices described here cannot thrive when half of the population of the United States can barely sustain itself. Specifically, I argue for a version of Universal Basic Income that is globally implemented and paid at sustenance level. Anything below that would still put workers in the position of having to scramble for additional income; it would merely become a subsidy for large corporations.

In chapter 3, building on the work of Karl Marx, Raymond Williams, Dallas Smythe, Michael Hardt and Antonio Negri, Mario Tronti, Maurizio Lazzarato, Paolo Virno, Christian Fuchs, and Lewis Hyde, I pinpoint omissions in the current discussion about digital labor.

The fluidity of the use of the term "digital labor" makes a rigorous definition less interesting than a reflection about this constantly changing conversation. In order to productively talk about digital work, all involved have to overcome disciplinary narcissism and political differences and start looking for a common language and understanding. Coming out of the previous two chapters, chapter 3 is seeking a useful vocabulary to address digital labor. After all, how can we reshape what we are unable to articulate?

Digital labor is everything but "immaterial;" it is a sector of the economy, a set of human activities that is predicated on global supply chains of material labor; it is about human activities that have economic value and are performed through a range of devices on highly monopolized platforms in real time on a truly novel and unprecedented scale.

Despite the recognition that too much play seeps into what we consider as work, I argue against the surrender of the language of labor.

By letting go of the language of labor we would lose associations with the history of organized labor and related struggles and movements. Not talking of labor depoliticizes the discussion by disconnecting it from traditional labor practices as well as the accomplishments, sacrifices, and lessons learned from this history.

Chapter 3 also emphasizes the materiality of digital labor and clarifies my use of terms like "work" and "labor." I am also throwing into question concepts like immaterial labor and Virno's claim of total financialization of the everyday.

Finally, this chapter introduces the concept of the "produser factory," where social participation goes hand-in-hand with value extraction. Considering the four billion people who are not connected to the Internet, there are still large zones of non-work and time not captured by Mark Zuckerberg's dreams of Facebook access for all. So far, there is still a fence around the "produser factory."

In chapter 4, I propose that the term exploitation is in fact inadequate to describe the sites of value extraction that I introduced in the first two chapters. This debate is not a contribution to the more technical exchange about exploitation among Marxist economists, but rather, at the onset, a collection of perspectives on exploitation from scholars such as Byung-Chul Han, Adam Arvidsson, Geert Lovink, Mark Andrejevic, Brian Holmes, Nicholas Carr, and Alan Wertheimer,

I introduce the concept of "crowd fleecing" to describe a discontinuity between traditional and contemporary forms of exploitation such as crowd work. Where to draw the line between what is fair and legal and what is cruel and what should not be tolerated? The concept of crowd fleecing can help provide a framework for the economic exploitation and mistreatment of unprecedented numbers of globally distributed, mostly anonymous, invisible solo workers, each synced and available in real time to a small number of platform owners. Crowd fleecing is a result of the reorganization of work marked by temporal uncertainty that supplants the model of employment. Here, I ask how can it be that a rich country like the United States tolerates unfair labor practices like the ones on Mechanical Turk, CrowdFlower, and 99Designs.

At the end of chapter 4, I identify practices that should be prioritized in terms of media attention, labor advocacy, and regulatory intervention.

Many people understand the complex problems with the current shift of labor markets to the Internet but few think there is anything that they can do about it. This book is for them. It is also written in honor of Stéphane Hessel who reminded us that "the worst possible outlook is indifference that says 'I can't do anything about it; I will just get by.' Behaving like that deprives you of one of the essentials of being human: the capacity and freedom to feel outraged."[15]

The book is also for my students who are often told that their careers will look like self-driving cars heading toward Armageddon. It is for all who are looking for an introduction to the broader discussion of digital labor and platform cooperativism.

The second part of this book, comprising three chapters, provides a contrast to Tyler Cowen's vision for the future of work based on democratic values, mutualism, and cooperativism. It is about a future of digital work in which we would want our children to participate. What would have to change for that to happen? This book encourages readers to think about how to protect themselves against exploitation on power hubs like Uber and Facebook, how to form and run platform cooperatives like Loconomics or Fairmondo, and how to inspire others with their work.

The last three chapters propose a range of pathways for action, solidarity, and ways in which the digital economy can be made more just, especially for its most vulnerable contributors.

In chapter 5, I show that technological development outpaces regulatory efforts by the government and that current labor law inadequately reflects the development of distributed digital work on the ground, thereby leaving an ever-growing segment of the working population unprotected. The chapter confronts the legal gray zones of digital labor by discussing whether workers are statutory employees or independent contractors. Here, I introduce the idea of portable benefits for contingent workers, a modification to Tim Berners-Lee's "Magna Carta of the Web," and French proposals to tax Internet companies like Amazon and Facebook based on the value that French citizens generate on those sites.

Chapter 6 is about escape, tactical refusal, and withdrawal. How we can break off and switch off? How can we "bomb the cloud" and disengage, or "unthink" data labor? How can we own the cloud? This chapter proposes selective engagement and the possibility of cutting loose from data labor. Who needs to see one billion faces anyway? Can we leave Facebook or Google and promote thorny conversations and slowly growing friendships? What does disengagement from the Internet or even an unthinking of its logic really mean? It's about a society where, as Geert Lovink put it, a tweetless life is constructed as not living. These are a false dichotomy. Life is not about either being connected or being unplugged. It is not about signing my life away to platform capitalism or simply giving it a pass.

As an additional strategy when thinking about resistance to platform capitalism, I suggest to not forget about the electoral process and also to remember the physical infrastructures of platform owners. Where are the protests, for instance, at Amazon's headquarters in Seattle?

Chapter 7 serves as a preemptive strike against an Uber-ized future that might be; it provides readers with actionable advice. I reflect on the importance of electoral politics, inventive unions, new forms of guilds; social media and design interventions. At the center of this chapter, however, is the proposal for what I call "platform cooperativism." This term can be briefly described as follows:

- First, it is about cloning the technological heart of Uber, Task Rabbit, Airbnb, or UpWork. Platform cooperativism creatively embraces, adapts, or reshapes technologies of the sharing economy, putting them to work with different ownership models. It is in this sense that platform cooperativism is about structural change, a transformation of ownership models.

- Second, platform cooperativism is about solidarity, sorely missing in an economy driven by a distributed and mostly anonymous workforce: the interns, freelancers, temps, project-based workers, and independent contractors. Platforms can be owned and operated by inventive unions, cities, and various other forms of cooperatives such as worker-owned, produser-owned (produceruser – produser), multi-stakeholder, co-ops.
- Third, platform cooperativism is built on reframing concepts like innovation and efficiency with an eye toward benefiting all, not just sucking up profits for the few. I propose ten principles of platform cooperativism that are sensitive to the critical problems facing the digital economy right now. Platform capitalism is amazingly ineffective in watching out for people.

The Digital Labor Conferences

The Digital Labor Conferences at The New School in New York City have been central to this book. In research areas like Internet & Society, such gatherings play a crucial role as publications take a long time to surface while technology changes rapidly. Importantly, all the digital labor conferences highlighted both practitioners and scholars.

The urgency to discuss the climate change of digital labor and pathways to a sustainable future for workers is no longer in question. But that was not always so.

When I started these conferences I was intrigued by people cheerfully contributing to social networking services. They performed their new identities seemingly without hesitation, offered up their personal data, and put in hour after hour of their time. As a writer, activist, professor at a progressive university, I have a commitment to academic research, and practices like organizing, protests, and interventions. This combination of scholarship and practice led me to inaugurate this series of digital labor conferences.

The Internet as Playground and Factory[16] in 2009 felt like the Woodstock of digital labor at the time; it was a historical gathering of researchers, artists, and legal scholars; the focus was mainly on digital labor/"playbor." Over 2,000 researchers, through a mailing list called the Institute for Distributed Creativity, discussed digital labor over a period of nine months leading up to the event. While the event was extremely well received, some scholars were openly skeptical of the term "digital labor," the research area as a whole, and also the unashamed disciplinary agnosticism of the event. Despite the widely-read and cited volume based on the conference,[17] it took six years, countless conferences, publications, festivals, seminars, articles, exhibitions, and of course, the proliferation of Uber, Amazon, and Google as templates of work, until "digital labor" was accepted as a serious area of inquiry.[18]

Events after that, especially in 2014, focused far less on data labor; what some have called "Facebook" labor – and increasingly on crowd fleecing, exploitation of paid digital work, the possibilities for worker solidarity and inventive unions given the rapid shift of labor markets to the Internet.

In 2015, the Platform Cooperativism: The Internet, Ownership, Democracy event[19] came out of my proposal for a change of ownership of labor platforms like Uber. In "Platform Cooperativism vs. The Sharing Economy," written in 2014, I argued that service platforms like Uber could be owned and operated by worker cooperatives or unions.[20] 2015 was also a seminal year for policy workshops, research papers, working groups, and op-eds about the future of work, mainstreaming the discourse about worker rights in the digital economy.

I wrote the book you are reading now alongside these conferences, critically chronicling the discourse and sites of work and interviewing countless speakers while also contributing my own analysis and proposals.

In *The Flight From Reality in the Human Sciences*, Ian Shapiro argues for a problem-driven approach to framing of the research methodology. "Normative theorists," he writes, "spend too much time commenting on one another, as if they were themselves the appropriate objects of study."[21] Shapiro makes the case for starting with a problem in the world, next coming to grips with previous attempts that have been made to study it, and then defining the research task by reference to the value added. This theoretical enterprise does not only identify what is wrong with what is currently being done across the various sites of digital labor, it engages with activists, workers, designers, developers, and policy makers to discuss how it might be improved and to then move in that direction.

Part I

Part I

1

Waged Labor and the End of Employment

It seems inevitable, doesn't it? The traditional relationship of employer and employee stands like a lone tree, a relic of the past. In the twenty-first century, "flexible workers" – the Uber drivers, baristas, crowd workers, fast-food cooks, models, and adjunct professors – all supposedly carry the torch of choice and autonomy high above their heads, bringing light to the monotonous world of formal jobs. "Think Outside the Boss," the slogan goes. Continued employment with social security and legally regulated norms is no longer the rule. Digitization is making work increasingly dense. Casual work, part-time or freelance, is the new normal. Full-time jobs are fragmented into freelance positions, turning workers into "micro-entrepreneurs" who are competing under conditions of infinite labor supply. Increasingly, companies retain a small number of core employees, making up the rest with temporary contract laborers. It echoes from all corners: don't romanticize employment. And it's true: employment is a relatively young and by all means flawed relationship but it would be a mistake to give up on the protections and benefits that come with employment. Digital labor is instrumental in the process of dissolving direct employment, thereby creating low-wage futures for millions of people. Just like the railroad industries of the past, "sharing economy" platforms are changing the world of work. As the horse is already out of the barn, proponents argue, we might as well embrace this new working world.

Ryan Bingham, the antihero and central character of the 2009 film *Up in the Air* makes this argument almost irresistibly. Ryan (played by George Clooney) is a hired gun, a corporate consultant whose sole job it is to tell people that they are being fired. In fact, this is his company's business: stepping in when corporations want to lay off their workers, telling them that they are being "let go." Firing people for a living allows Ryan to enjoy a lifestyle of executive business class travel and luxurious hotels. Bingham's standard line when facing the soon-to-be-unemployed is "anybody who ever built an empire, or changed the world, sat where you are now. And it is because they sat there that they were able to do it." Bingham's spiel about opportunity and innovation echoes the rhetoric of Silicon Valley; you might even say that it prepares the newly unemployed for the digital economy.

The rhetoric of the enterprising individual is meant to make people feel optimistic about a "liberation" from career and employment and a forced entry into the world of entrepreneurship. Just check in with your "inner entrepreneur" and "do what you love!" Reid Hoffman, cofounder of LinkedIn, begins his book *The Start-Up of You* by channeling Ryan Bingham: "All humans are entrepreneurs." All jobs that are solid melt into freelance labor while Silicon Valley exports its playbook to the rest of the world. Hoffman points to "our ancestors in the caves" who invented their own rules for living:

> *They were founders of their own lives. In the centuries since then we forgot that we are entrepreneurs. We've been acting like labor.*

On the other hand, the author Bob Black, the scholar Kathi Weeks, or the anarchist CrimethInc Ex-Workers' Collective, distance themselves from the obsession with work altogether. "The carrot is just a stick by other means," as Black put it.[1] Their stance does not stop at a rejection of employment; it is a rejection of the demeaning system of domination at work altogether; it's a call to slow down the engines of productivity.

The platform economy helps to facilitate an overall shift away from salaried employment. "Did anyone ever like having a boss, irritating colleagues, or long hours, anyway?," supporters of the extractive economy ask. The spokespeople for the extractive "sharing economy," on the other hand, glorify independent work, choice, opportunity, and autonomy. Burn the heavy briefcase, the two-bedroom house, the car payments; *humans are meant to be lions*. Bingham puts it so convincingly:

> *I see people who work at the same company for their entire lives. They clock in, they clock out, and they never have a moment of happiness. You have an opportunity here.*

This dream of flexible work, of an opportunity for a better life, spurs many of the contemporary labor practices that I introduce in this chapter.

1) Toward a Typology of Digital Labor

As part of this typology of paid digital labor, I closely examine practices like crowdsourcing, paid in-game labor, and content farming. I ask which forms of paid digital labor shaped the terrain of unregulated digital work. I caution that the templates of work introduced by companies like Uber and Amazon Mechanical Turk can lead to a regime of work that is even worse than previous systems of labor.

Ultimately, this typology can lead to a broader understanding of the landscape of digital labor practices necessary for careful and network-savvy regulation. Such typology, read alongside chapter 7, can clarify which tendencies are worth advancing while at the same time calling out practices and companies that need regulatory attention and punishment for violations of the Fair Labor Standards Act. In the absence of worker protections for the most vulnerable workers, we face the threat of a crushing regime of digital work.

My perspective on digital work is informed by four conferences that I convened between 2009 and 2016. This research is grounded in the review of studies coming out of fields like sociology, political science, labor law, and media theory. The writing is informed by news accounts and interviews with workers, labor advocates, cooperativists, historians, venture capitalists, activists, artists, civic technologists, designers, and union representatives. While this chapter emphasizes the perils of digital labor, I conclude with a vision of decent digital work. In chapter 7, you'll find a proposal for what I call platform cooperativism.

Throughout this chapter, I show how digital labor platforms and "new vectors of the production of wealth," as the French economist Yann Moulier Boutang put it,[2] have made contemporary work more intensive (dense), while restructuring labor markets on a global scale. Time becomes even more central as an instrument of oppression.

One new quality of contemporary labor online is the vast scale of a global, on-demand labor force available in real time. The virtual hiring hall UpWork,[3] for example, claims to have 10 million workers; the grand sum of real-time work hours ingested by this globally operating company is unprecedented. Netscape co-founder Marc Andreessen claimed that his software is eating the world and indeed, today, there is a pronounced power asymmetry between the class of platform owners, that holds all four aces and the workers who hold none, as David Graeber puts it.

What can this chapter accomplish and what are its limitutions? The examples offer a freeze-frame perspective haunted by technological obsolescence; think about the quick succession with which Google discontinued *Google Wave, Google Knol, Google Reader, Google Glasses, and Google+*. Amazon introduced HomeServices, Amazon Flex, and Handmade at Amazon, while oDesk acquired Elance and rebranded it as Upwork. TaskRabbit changed its *modus operandi*, its "pivot" in industry parlance, from one day to the next. Uber can alter its agreements with drivers with the click of a button. The constant reshuffling of labor markets makes it hard to offer a stable inventory of these practices.

What follows in the next two chapters, broken down into paid (chapter 1) and unpaid (chapter 2) digital work, is a proposal for a typology of digital work that is crucial for the discussion about the future of work. While such typology, grounded in historical and political observations, is necessary, it has also clear limitations. What I place in one category, for instance, isn't always comfortably contained in that grouping. There are fluid boundaries between these categories; even the distinction between paid and unpaid labor is not always so clear. In *Labor in the Global Digital Economy*, the British labor scholar Ursula Huws establishes categories of digital work. Huws argues that it is impossible to assign a type of worker to each category to extrapolate their class belonging, for instance. Some workers engage in several different kinds of labor, both simultaneously and over the course of their lives, she writes. They are crossing these simple categories. Even in one household, one finds relatives who carry out quite different kinds of labor. Further complicating the picture, there are workers like Jennifer Guidry, mentioned in the introduction to this book. Workers like Guidry are "multi-homing," which means that they are, for instance, toiling for Uber in the morning and assembling furniture for TaskRabbit in the afternoon.

The typology that I am presenting here, clearly, cannot be comprehensive. The area of content moderation, workers filtering out inappropriate content submissions on social media, for instance, is not addressed extensively here. It deserves more attention. As the cooperative models that I am introducing in chapter 7 are just emerging, I did not include them here.

To understand that such typology cannot be comprehensive, you only have to follow the litany of the news cycle; in any given month, new platforms enter this landscape. I pay a good amount of attention to Amazon Mechanical Turk (AMT) while focusing less on other upstarts because AMT has became an influential template for the future of work.

Contained within the presented categories is also a geography of digital work; I am really discussing different social groups: specific labor platforms and ways of working that are experienced differently by individuals in different cultures. But despite these cautionary notes, lumping all of these labor practices together as "digital labor" may lead to misunderstandings as I have witnessed in many debates.

Overview

1) Toward a typology of digital labor
2) Crowdsourcing: all together now!
3) Digital labor in the shadows: Amazon Mechanical Turk
4) The ecosystem of paid digital labor
5) Ethical crowdwork? Platform cooperatives
6) Content farming
7) Competitive crowdsourcing
8) User-led innovation
9) In-game labor
10) Online labor brokerages
11) On-demand labor
12) Online personal assistance

2) Crowdsourcing: All Together Now!

Examples: *Amazon Mechanical Turk, Universal Human Relevance System (UHRS), crowdSPRING, Crowdguru, CrowdFlower, CrowdSource, ManPower, Microworkers, Samasource, Microtask, Clickworker, Shorttask, ZeroFlaws, Livework, Cloudfactory, Crowdturfing*

Today, crowdsourcing is a flourishing sector of the platform economy; it has taken off especially in industries that are built around data. The crowdsourcing sector had revenues of some $375 million in 2011 alone, a 75 percent increase on the year before. There is a clear overall upward arc in revenues ever since.

The term crowdsourcing was first used in a 2006 article by *Wired* Magazine editor Jeff Howe.[4] Since then, the crowdsource-or-perish mantra was repeated in defense of greater "democratization" of work. Don Tapscott and Anthony D. Williams write that

A new economic democracy is emerging in which we all have a lead role, [because] the economics of production have changed significantly.[5]

Some, clearly, are leading more than others when it comes to financial rewards. According to NYU Business School professor Panagiotis G. Ipeirotis, crowdwork can cost companies less than half as much as typical outsourcing.[6]

Crowdsourcing has the goal of distributing the workload from one, sometimes paid, individual to many, frequently unpaid or underpaid volunteers. Companies like Google or Amazon no longer conceive of their workforce solely in terms of full-time employees; they can count on cadres of subcontracted workers worldwide who are on standby, just one click away. Animation and software testing are both sectors that are at the forefront of crowdsourcing, drawing in workers through platforms that are often still in "public beta" stage.

Canadian business executive Don Tapscott and consultant Anthony D. Williams claim in their book *Wikinomics* that the "old, ironclad vessels of the industrial era sink under the crushing waves where smart firms connect to external ideas and energies to regain the buoyancy they require to survive."[7] Firms that make their boundaries porous to external ideas and human capital, their narrative suggests, outperform companies that rely solely on internal resources and capabilities. That, at least, is the employer-centric motto of *Wikinomics*, emphasizing the ability of crowdsourcing to lower labor costs while leaving the quality of the work itself unexamined.

Crowdsourcing indicates that companies are subcontracting tasks to large numbers of people online, to then capture the value of these "outside producers" who might perform the job more swiftly and cheaply. The productive power of the network becomes a dynamo for profits. But crowdsourcing is also employed in support of public and non-market projects. What interests me most about the thorny practice of crowdsourcing is that it simultaneously inspires unambiguous excitement about the productive potentials of the Open Web, while at the same time leading to moral indignation about the alienation and ultimate exploitation of labor. The realities of crowdsourcing exist in the gaps between the film *Sleep Dealer* and the book *Wikinomics*.

Wikipedia founder Jimmy Wales is among the outspoken critics of the term. He wrote:

> *I dislike the word "crowdsourcing" because I think it turns the whole problem of how to foster openness upside down in a bad way.*[8]

The Austrian media artist and journalist Armin Medosch observes that crowdsourcing, now arrived in the twenty-first century, is seen as hip, trendy, and popular. It is not associated with mass consumption and mass production but with participation of emancipated super-consumers.[9]

On the other hand, proponents appreciate the advantages of scale – the "big" in big data – and the efficiency of access to a global knowledge base that can be rapidly mobilized. Universities, upstarts, and new media giants like Microsoft, eBay, Google, and Amazon employ crowdsourcing to test drive their algorithms through "public betas," categorizing inventory, filling in surveys, or filtering their websites for inappropriate content. Even the Defense Advanced Research Projects Agency (DARPA), the US Army Research Lab, the CIA, and various governments make use of crowdsourcing, embracing the fact that they can set up large collaborative groups at a distance, cutting travel and office costs when performing translations and transcriptions, for instance.

"Users happily do for free what companies would otherwise have to pay employees to do," says former *Wired* editor turned drone manufacturer, Chris Anderson. It's a capitalist's dream come true. "It's not outsourcing, it's crowdsourcing. Collectively, customers have virtually unlimited time and energy; only peer production has the capacity to extend as far as the Long Tail can go."[10] Following a decade-old trend, crowdwork is globally dispersed. The crowd is no longer understood as riotous; it does not have to be feared because globally distributed individuals are avaricious, selfish, and for the very most part isolated from each other. According to Anderson, as long as people are submitting themselves, they must not find it objectionable. What is missing from this analysis is that, systemically, there is no choice for these workers.

When Armin Medosch mentioned that this practice has now "arrived in the 21st century," he might have referred to the pre-computational history of competitive crowdsourcing, dating back to Napoleon Bonaparte, who had to feed his armies during their campaigns far away from home. Napoleon put out a call for the invention of a simple technique for the preservation of food. Famously, an Englishman won the competition and received Napoleon's 12,000 Francs for his idea to replace glass jars with tin cans. An Englishman.

Next, I am exploring one example in greater depth: Amazon Mechanical Turk.

3) Digital Labor in the Shadows: Amazon Mechanical Turk (AMT)

Today, crowdsourcing firms like CrowdFlower or Microsoft's Universal Human Relevance System (UHRS) are like clandestine installations on unmapped territory; too little is known about them.

Amazon Mechanical Turk, AMT or MTurk for short, is a *public* online crowdsourcing system that was founded by Amazon.com in November 2005. Based on the Agreva technology that Amazon acquired, this de facto Internet labor brokerage is designed for corporate labor management. To participate, prospective workers, or *Turkers*, need to have access to a computer, an Internet connection, a bank account, and they need to be registered with Amazon Payments, which can be a problem for people with tax or credit problems. On its website, AMT is described as a crowdsourcing marketplace that enables computer programs to co-ordinate the use of human intelligence to perform tasks which computers are unable to execute. While AMT is profiting robustly,[11] it has – following the observations of several workers – not made significant updates to its user interfaces since its inception, and the operational staff appears to be overwhelmed and burned out.

Turkers have written and shared various browser scripts to help themselves solve specific problems. While this is a wonderful example of mutual aid among AMT workers, it is also yet another instance of how the invisible labor of Turkers remains uncompensated. While people are powering the system, MTurk is meant to feel like a machine to its end-users: humans are seamlessly embedded in the algorithm. AMT's clients are quick to forget that it is human beings and not algorithms that are toiling for them – people with very real human needs and desires.

Amazon founder and CEO Jeff Bezos makes his pet project sound quite straightforward and harmonious. MTurk, he wrote, is a marketplace where "folks who have work meet up with folks who seek work." Importantly, for workers in India, crowdsourcing can offer a good livelihood. In the US, AMT helps *some* Turkers to pay for books, chocolate, or games. They *choose* to work here; for them it is a pastime but then there are others who are trying to make a living on AMT, and for them, *systemically*, it is anything but a choice.

In *The Taming of the Shrew*, William Shakespeare quips "there's small choice in rotten apples." While we are told, manipulatively, that the free market is the locus of freedom and individual empowerment, many workers are only able to pick between various low-paying employers. Systemically, genuine choice is limited if you have to pick between a set of options, all marked by cruel underpayment.

Mechanical Turk starts to look even less positive when considering that in the case of labor conflicts, Bezos's company remains strictly hands-off, insisting that AMT is merely providing a technical system. Why would they have anything to do with the labor conflicts occurring on the platform? This would be like Apple owning the factories in Shenzhen where its iPhones are assembled, but then rejecting any responsibility for the brutal work regimes and suicides of the workers in these factories because Foxconn controls daily operations. Such deflection of responsibility is, of course, by no means new; just think of the Triangle Shirtwaist Factory fire in 1911 or the April 2013 disaster at Rana Plaza in Bangladesh. The architects of new modes of working get all the profits without having to deal with the workers. Here, employers wash their hands of responsibility before returning to work.

Behind the screen: invisible labor

Amazon's Mechanical Turk is named after a chess-playing automaton designed in 1769 by the Hungarian nobleman Wolfgang von Kempelen. A small-bodied chess player hidden in a wooden case, operated this "automaton," controlling the Turk's mechanical hands of the Turk. The spectacle of a seemingly complex, mechanized chess-playing machine, complete with a turban-wearing Turk put small technical details on display as distraction while keeping the actual human labor out of sight. The operator-worker remains quite literally hidden in the black box. The Mechanical Turk was a hit in Europe at the time with Catherine the Great, Charles Babbage, and Edgar Allen Poe coming to experience it. Amazon's Mechanical Turk pays homage to this eighteenth-century Mechanical Turk. Similar to von Kempelen's historical Turk, the customers using the AMT's services today are frequently unaware of the workers delivering the services from behind the screens.

Where the historical Turk showed off technology to draw attention away from the human laborer, today, Mechanical Turk's "crowd sorcerers" work with coolness and the spectacle of innovation to conceal the worker. In 2014, various articles appeared with head-lines like "How Crowdworkers Became the Ghosts in the Digital Machine," "On-Demand Workers: 'We Are Not Robots,'" "Amazon's Mechanical Turk workers want to be treated like humans," and "Amazon's Mechanical Turk workers protest: 'I am a human being, not an algorithm.'" The angle of many of these articles is that if employers would just understand that they are dealing with human beings (instead of algorithms), they'd pay them more fairly and treat them more respectfully. Is humanizing workers – giving crowdwork-ers a face – really enough to change the situation? Is there evidence that suggests that owners would stop exploiting workers once they recognize them as human beings?

I think of Jacob Riis' 1890 book *How the Other Half Lives* – chronicling New York City tenement slums of that era – which led to massive public reactions, leading to an improvement of indoor plumbing, sewage, and garbage collection in the tenements. Upton Sinclair's 1906 *The Jungle* is another example of an artist drawing public attention to horrid working conditions and threats to public health. Artists have the power to mobilize the public, but again, will that ultimately be enough to convince the benefactors of exploitation?

Amazon describes AMT as an "artificial artificial intelligence" service. Amazon.com's iPhone application, for example, contains an experimental feature called *Amazon Remembers*, which invites users to take a photo of a product such as a chair, pen, or book. Within anywhere between five minutes and 24 hours, the service matches the photo up to a product in the company's catalogue. The application is not based entirely on image recognition software, as it may seem at first. Once a photo has been submitted, the legwork is being done by Turkers.[12] If they can locate the product, Amazon pays the worker ten cents. If the item is not in the catalogue, workers obviously have no way of finding it and consequently don't get paid for the time they worked.

One illustration of the different ways in which workers can be embedded in software is Soylent, "a Word Processor with a crowd inside."[13] In short, this MIT project, which has stalled in its beta stage, is an add-in for Microsoft Word that "embeds" Turkers in a Word document so that they can proofread or shorten your text – just highlight text and specify what you want to get done.

Another example of "crowds as code," as Microsoft Research scholar Mary L. Gray put it, is the iPhone app vizwiz.org that allows blind users to receive rapid-fire answers to questions about their surroundings. Companies like vizwiz want "a person to act as a piece of code."[14] For Gray the "ambient workforce" fills the gap that technology cannot; they are part and parcel of innovation.

Going beyond the examples of Amazon Remembers, Vizwiz, and Soylent, Lilly Irani analyzes the importance of hiding the very real workers when it comes to attracting venture capital.

> By hiding the labor and rendering it manageable through computing code, human computation platforms have generated an industry of startups claiming to be the future of data.... Hiding the labor is key to how these startups are valued by investors, and thus key to the speculative but real winnings of entrepreneurs. Microwork companies attract more generous investment terms when investors perceive them as technology companies rather than labor companies.[15]

The more unnoticeable, cheap, and unregulated the workforce promises to be, the higher the speculative fortunes of these companies will rise, Irani writes. The impression that laborers will be forever available in abundance and inexpensive is essential for their business model.

While some think of Amazon as the Halliburton of crowdwork, many Turkers who rely on AMT for their livelihood only condemn specific subcontractors in this ecosystem and would *not* characterize their work as exploitative. Don't bite the hand that feeds you. Understandably, they would not want Mechanical Turk to close shop. Instead, Turkers like Kristy Milland would like to refashion the reputation of Mechanical Turk as a workplace for extreme discount labor into one that pays fairly.

The digital infrastructure that Amazon has put in place together with its terms of use, choreograph rote, often repetitive, and potentially exploitative interactions. I have dedicated an entire chapter in this book to the question of second-degree exploitation, what I call "crowd fleecing." It's digital black box labor, to use Frank Pasquale, who reflects on the cultural meaning of the black box in his book *The Blackbox Society*:

> The term "black box"...can refer to a recording device, like the data-monitoring systems in planes, trains, and cars. Or it can mean a system whose workings are mysterious; we can observe its inputs and outputs, but we cannot tell how one becomes the other. We face these two meanings daily: tracked ever more closely by firms and government, we have no clear idea of just how far much of this information can travel, how it is used, or its consequences.[16]

In an online system like Amazon Mechanical Turk or CrowdFlower, it is mysterious where the labor is coming from or who is requesting it and what they are intending to do with it. With the workers being tucked away, the inner workings of these labor ecosystems are kept under wraps as trade secrets. The concealed workforce is not reflected in business plans, which only include direct employment. Thanks to this concealed labor pool, it is now possible to build a large company while keeping the number of salaried employees small.

Listening to workers

Some time before scholars and the media started to take notice of the dark underbelly of digital labor, filmmakers such as Alex Rivera and media artists like Aaron Koblin and Jeff Crouse pointed to hidden laborers, problematic contract law, and the politics of data labor.

The American filmmaker Alex Rivera sensed these dynamics already many years ago. In 2009, I started off the "Internet as Playground and Factory" conference with the sci-fi thriller "Sleep Dealer" by Rivera, which he had released just a few months prior to this international gathering at The New School in New York City. The film goes back to the Internet artwork *Cybraceros* that Rivera created in 1997, which contained the idea of telepresent migrant workers. The realities of crowdsourcing haunt *Sleep Dealer*, a film that offers a near future vision of globalized digital labor. *Sleep Dealer* is a dystopian fable of globalization that describes a world in which borders have become insurmountable, immigration has come to a standstill, and digital networks permeate everything. The protagonist of the film, Memo Cruz (Luis Fernando Peña), is a would-be migrant who lives in Mexico but works in the United States. In a *Matrix*-like scenario, Memo, working in an *infomaquila*, plugs into a telepresence system to direct a robot at a construction site in the United States. He can dispatch his labor through nodes implanted in his arms, thereby allowing him to control machinery from afar. Surely, nobody talked to Memo about healthcare, pensions, or union drives. His world is all too convenient for the American bosses who get "all the work without the worker," as Rivera put it.[17]

On AMT, Aaron Koblin asked people to draw a sheep facing to the left at a rate of two cents a pop. Forty days later, 7,599 supporters had contributed 12,000 drawings of sheep. Participants in *The Sheep Market* project were not made aware that their creative process was recorded and that Koblin planned to later sell these animated drawings at the price of $20 for a set of 20.[18] In this way, Koblin mimicked AMT's crowdworking system.

In 2010, Mechanical Turk workers from Columbus Ohio, Bristol Tennessee, Weston Massachusetts, Brooklyn New York, South Carolina, Toronto, Singapore, and Bangalore (India) responded to a task that the artist Jeff Crouse had posted on Mechanical Turk. Crouse asked them to talk about their hopes. With the help of an audio crowdsourcing website, he later edited their audio responses and created a podcast, which you can still access at Crowded.fm.

Hearing the voices of workers invalidates claims that all MTurk workers are poorly educated. When asked what it is like to toil on Mechanical Turk, one person responds, "it's like working for a mystery man."[19] Asked what their virtual bosses – the consignors – might think of them, one worker responds that these are "probably people who think we are suckers who are doing HITs for two cents, or three cents, or five cents." We encounter two young engineering students, one residing in India with plans to work for NASA one day, and an American, dead set on becoming a patent attorney. We also hear from Sarah Allen in Belfast (Northern Ireland) who wants to learn with children about gardening. There is also a single, unemployed mother of an eight-year-old child, a worker who has high hopes for a job as a hairstylist, and a student who wants to become a medical transcriptionist. Crouse's audio piece "Crowded" makes it hard to sustain stereotypes of Mechanical Turk as a place where "even the dimmest bulb can make a few dollars," as Jonathan Zittrain once put it.[20]

Like a cheetah in pursuit of a sickly gazelle

But Amazon's reputation is not built solely on its online labor market. In the context of a dispute with a group of publishers including the Hachette Book Group, Jeff Bezos had proposed: "Amazon should approach…publishers the way a cheetah would pursue a sickly gazelle."[21] In an exposé by *The New York Times*, the white-collar workers who toil for Amazon in Seattle were interviewed. One Amazon employee said "Nearly every person I worked with, I saw cry at their desk."[22] So far, there is no evidence that would suggest that Bezos would treat digital workers any differently than a predator pursuing its vulnerable prey.

If this sounds like a stretch, consider how Amazon is controlling work in its own warehouses. In Leipzig, Germany, a worker in an Amazon "fulfillment center" who was accused of having been inactive on two occasions was informed five minutes after his second digression that he was being fired. Following the logic of digital piecemeal work and surpassing the cruelty of Walmart, laborers are issued "inactivity protocols":

> Colleague…was inactive 07:27am to 07:36am (9 minutes). Worker… and worker…were seen standing in between shelves 05–06 and 05–07. Already on…. 2014…was seen inactive from 8:15am – 8:17am (2 minutes). Also on…2014…was inactive from 07:13 to 07:14 (1 minute).[23]

Such densification of work is possible because workers are carrying scanners that can be tracked and supervisors constantly monitor warehouse workmen.[24] Or consider the 2015 US Supreme Court ruling stating that Amazon.com workers don't need to be paid for the time they are waiting for mandatory security screenings when exiting the warehouses.[25]

With Amazon becoming one of the wealthiest and most powerful players in international labor markets, we should pay close attention to its harsh and predatory labor practices. While Mechanical Turk's active workforce is only a small part of the overall workforce, its business model stands in for an undesirable tendency; it provides a glimpse of the future of work.

AMT allows for a project to be broken down into thousands of bits, which are then assigned as individual tasks to so-called crowd-workers. Turkers log on to the website and pick tasks from long listings, referred to as Human Intelligence Tasks (HITs). Just like traditional piecework, the breaking down of tasks is nothing new; it has been a commonplace not only on the assembly line but also in the garment industry. Social theorist and legal scholar Jonathan Zittrain warned that given the anonymity of the "requesters," it would not be inconceivable that authoritarian regimes would use the site to identify faces in a crowd of protesters, for example.

On MTurk, subcontractors – the individuals, foundations, aca-demic researchers, or firms – are referred to as "requesters," and workers are described as "Turkers," "mTurks," or – tongue in cheek – as "Turkeys." *The New York Times* referred to Amazon's piecemeal workers as "data janitors." While often considered anonymous, it is apparently not impossible to reveal their personal information.[26] Turkers have also been compared to migrant workers because both groups are underpaid, work long hours, are not protected by labor laws, have few or no benefits, and are frequently treated poorly by their bosses.[27] It is not surprising that the turnaround among Turkers is roughly 70 percent every six months.

As subcontractors are not offering employment, I refer to the crowdsourcers as quasi-employers or consignors. Referring to them as employers would be inaccurate because they are not employing Turkers. Turkers function as independent contractors and are usually paid as freelancers, which also means that they are solely responsible for paying their own taxes. Amazon provides the labor platform on which quasi-employers request particular work to be executed by independent contractors. These quasi-employers, not the Turkers, are Amazon's clients; they are functioning as subcontractors in AMT's ecosystem.

Quasi-employers remain anonymous and only pay if they are fully satisfied with the results – even then, some crowdsourcers reject accurately executed work to avoid payment. Rejecting it, does not, however, stop these "black hats" and scammers from still using the work. This common practice of wage theft is explicitly (and shockingly) tolerated by Amazon. In AMT's conditions of use it states:

If a Requester is not reasonably satisfied with the Services, the Requester may reject the Services.... all ownership rights, including worldwide intellectual property rights, will vest with the Requester immediately upon your performance of the Service.[28]

Quasi-employers own the work immediately upon receipt, which means that they can do whatever they please with it. In a further twist, crowdsourcers don't even have to explain their rejection of already performed work to the data workers and, again, this a practice explicitly condoned by Jeff Bezos's company. It's a feature, not a bug. The MTurk system, by virtue of its very design, makes it arduous for Turkers to figure out how to contact quasi-employers and for those "requesters" it is equally difficult to contact workers.[29] That said, it is not surprising that the lack of communication between quasi-employers and workers is a principal problem in this ecosystem.

Below minimum wage

The crowdsourced micro-tasks mentioned above are paid at a rate between one cent and several dollars each. Tasks include the description or categorization of products, the filling in surveys, the filtering out of social media content that violates terms of service (pornography and so on), the tagging and labeling of images, and the transcription of audio and video recordings or receipts. One AMT worker, interviewed for Salon.com, describes his work as categorizing shoes based on a list of basic colors: red, blue, pink, purple, white, green, yellow, multicolored. "This is not exactly a brain-busting task; I'm doing it while talking to a friend on the phone."[30]

New workers on MTurk frequently earn between $2 and $3 an hour, a ruthless devaluation of their time and the smoking gun of exploitation of digital labor. It is also an unpopular statistic among seasoned Turkers who hope to change AMT's public reputation as being a below minimum wage workplace. Their hope is that quasi-employers will expect to pay at least minimum wage. For some qualified, middle-tier AMT workers with access to better-paid HITs, however, the hourly compensation is between $6 and $7. Some Turkers reported making even up to $100 for eight hours of work.

"Only when you harness all the tools available can you make a living wage, or [even] a good living," says Kristy Milland (also known by her Turker pseudonym *spamgirl*), a young mother and student at Ryerson University in Ontario, Canada. Milland reports that she made "double the poverty line" by turking full-time, which was enough to support her family and pay medical bills for two years after her husband lost his job.[31] Milland's resilience, however, entailed 17-hour days to make ends meet.

One study showed that about 18 percent of Turkers are treating AMT as a full-time job; workers stated that they are "sometimes or always" relying on Mechanical Turk to "make basic ends meet."[32] Another Turker reported:

> I spent a day crowdsourcing for Amazon's Mechanical Turk and all I have to show for eight hours in an online work marketplace is a measly $4.38.[33]

One Turker, Rochelle LaPlante, also reports that some workers seek out academic surveys because they gain a sense of accomplishment from contributing to research. "There is both financial and emotional payment, and some workers seek out one type of payment over another. Some say: 'It's okay if this study only pays $1/hour because I feel good about contributing to science,'" she notes.[34] LaPlante has been working online to help cover her family's expenses since 2007. She writes:

> You go to the candy store and you see a candy bar, and you think "Is that worth two surveys?"[35]

Lilly Irani, a former Google employee and professor of Communication at the University of California San Diego, provides two examples of how AMT is used by subcontractors.

> Since the early 2000s, Google has relied on data workers to fine tune and train its algorithms. The company constantly refines its search algorithms in a war for higher rankings with other search optimizers and spammers. How do Google engineers figure out if their new algorithm produces high-quality results? They have to rely on workers called "raters" – contractors often working from home – to judge the search result pages and rate them; workers can label resulting pages as "vital," "useful," "slightly relevant," or even "maybe spam." Google engineers then feed these worker-generated ratings back into their algorithm so the algorithm can learn to see more like the rating workers.[36]

Irani also points to Mitt Romney's startling comment about his diversity strategy, complete with ready-to-go "binders full of women." Twitter's algorithms could not be trained quickly enough to distinguish tweets referring to Romney's "binders full of women" and Office Depot's binders, on sale for 99 cents. To speed up the training of the algorithms, Twitter hired cadres of data workers to sort and classify tweets, Irani writes.[37]

Today's Turkers hail largely from the United States and India. One study found that 57 percent of AMT workers are based in the United States, 32 percent are based in India, and that the remaining workers are from countries ranging from Australia to the Ukraine.[38] The reported average age of the workers on Mechanical Turk is 31 and, in the United States, half of them have a college or other advanced degree. Almost a third of them are currently unemployed. However, toward the end of 2012, AMT stopped accepting non-US accounts. The reasons are unclear; it could have to do with foreign workers trying to scheme the system or with difficulties processing payments for people abroad.

Who are the Turkers? Lilly Irani describes the Turkers whom she has encountered online as "laid-off teachers, mobility-impaired professionals, military retirees, agoraphobic writers, undersupported college students, stay-at-home parents, and even Malaysian programmers-in-training."[39]

Kristy Milland, who joined AMT as a Turker in 2005, said there are three categories of AMT workers.[40] First, there are the well-educated and experienced workers. They are pursuing crowdwork because of some circumstance in their life or simply because they are bored, according to Milland. That's about 20 percent who are well-educated and are on AMT full-time. Instead of watching TV, they might turk. Financially, they are doing relatively well on MTurk. The second group is made up of people who cannot find a job right where they live. They are desperate; for them it's a choice between AMT and bankruptcy. And the third group is comprised of people who are disabled in some way; people who have physical or psychological illnesses or who are socially ostracized and cannot hold a regular job. This group also includes sex offenders or former convicts, Milland reports. Rochelle LaPlante adds that they noticed more transgender workers in 2014. According to LaPlante, they enjoy the platform because of the anonymity that exempts them from discrimination. Sixty percent of disabled people in the United States are unemployed. Online labor brokerages like AMT, for them, are enabling, but at the same time we should not forget that the digital economy is also creating disability in the suicide factories in Shenzhen where the health of workers is held in low regard.

For many Americans, "turking" is like a self-exploitative version of a crossword puzzle, which they do to "keep the mind sharp," "kill time," or "learn English," as Panos Ipeirotis explains.[41] In the US, it is largely women (many of whom say that they are doing it for the joy of it), while the majority of Indian workers are male and they are strictly toiling for the money. Turkers are paid in dollars and rupees.

Workers in other countries can only be paid with Amazon gift certificates.

Gauging the size of the online workforce of Internet labor companies is difficult, in part because so many workers join and abandon these platforms or only use them sporadically. Accordingly, the exact size of the AMT workforce is a known unknown. Amazon claims that it has 500,000 registered workers[42] but the authors of the 2011 paper "Amazon Mechanical Turk: Goldmine or Coal Mine" estimate that the number of active workers is between 15,059 and 42,912. And even within that group, it is 3,011 to 8,582 workers who perform 80 percent of all HITs.[43] Another paper suggests that there are about 10,000 active workers.[44] Today, the number might be even lower because international workers can no longer register for AMT. As Amazon does not release updated statistics, one cannot be sure about the size of the labor pool.

Workplace surveillance

Turkers also have to qualify to gain access to better-paying tasks. Looking for HITs takes time. Those minutes or hours are neither recorded nor compensated. One condition for access to tasks could be that Turkers had a high acceptance rate of prior work.

There are a number of approaches to decide algorithmically which workers are doing "good" work. A common approach to vetting workers is to include tests to which subcontractors know the answer but that look just like any other data processing task. Workers that answer correctly can be authorized for future work; subcontractors often assume those who get the wrong answer are either inadequately skilled or try to scheme the system. One concern is that some tests that qualify workers to perform certain tasks are unpaid.

Another approach, referred to as "majority rule," is to hire several workers to do the same information task; employers then count the workers who offer the most common result as correct while workers with outlier results might be denied pay or even blocked from future work.[45] If three out of four workers are doing a bad job, the one Turker who did a good job gets penalized.

Sitting in their homes or in cyber cafes, their every mouse click is monitored. To control the crowd, Amazon and quasi-employers use scare tactics. One of the students in my seminar *The Digital Work Notebook*, working on Mechanical Turk, noticed the following:

> *After transcribing roughly three dozen items from a low-quality photo of a receipt with extremely small print, I proceeded to submit my work. Above the green "Submit Receipt Data" button was a warning alerting*

me that if I submit receipts with "missing, invalid, or misleading infor-
mation" or "report images as hard to read when they can actually be
read," they will be "forced to block" my account. When I hit submit,
another warning popped up saying that if I submit the wrong informa-
tion my account may be suspended. I suddenly grew unreasonably
concerned about the potential for being penalized by this invisible
authority for making a mistake. I took extra time to go through and
double-check my work. While performing subsequent tasks, knowing
the potential consequences of making a mistake, I was far more atten-
tive; I began working harder.[46]

The anxiety relating to the threat of having your account temporarily
blocked or closed down altogether is worth noting when thinking
about this digital workplace. In the case of an account suspension,
Amazon does not inform workers what happened or if they can do
anything to fix the situation. It's a constant state of working in fear
of account suspension with no recourse.

In his submission for the "Digital Labor: Sweatshops, Picket Lines,
Barricades" conference at The New School in 2014, media scholar
Mark Andrejevic spoke about the "drone logic" of the "always-on
workplace," evoking the figure of the drone to consider the ways in
which monitoring, data mining, and predictive analytics become pervasive. Andrejevic labeled it "drone labor."

4) The Ecosystem of Compensated Digital Labor

What allows companies like Mechanical Turk to flourish? The practices that I discuss throughout this chapter wouldn't be possible
without the infrastructure of the Internet, initially funded by the
Department of Defense and developed in academia. This ecosystem
would not be possible without the human effort of computer engineers and the hardware – satellites, cables, Wi-Fi routers, and mobile
phones – that makes online communication possible in the first place.
Labor companies like Mechanical Turk, Uber, or UpWork did not
contribute a dime to this spadework.

This ecosystem would also collapse without the computational
labor by programmers, system designers, game developers, production managers, and designers. Labor scholar and activist Andrew
Ross commented on creative labor in books like *No-Collar: The*
Humane Workplace and Its Hidden Costs and *Nice Work If You Can*
Get It. Ross describes the casualization of the workplace, flattened
hierarchies between workers and management, project-based work,
flexible working hours, intense schedules, and an acute need for

re-skilling due to the obsolescence of technology. The work of the developer is also reflected in Ellen Ullman's *Close to the Machine*. Another account is from Erin Hoffman who, in 2004, anonymously blogged a sharp critique of labor practices at Electronic Arts (EA), the company that brought you the Sims and Madden sports. EA made its developers work one crunch time after the other, until three years later, Hoffman's fiancé, EA employee Leander Hasty, became the main plaintiff in a class action suit on behalf of software engineers at EA, resulting in a $14.9 million payout for uncompensated overtime. We cannot consider paid digital labor without considering the computational labor that is hidden behind the screen.

The "weightless economy" would sink to the bottom of the ocean were it not for the over one million Foxconn workers in Shenzhen and the miners of rare earth minerals in China and the Democratic Republic of Congo who work under devastating conditions mining coltan to facilitate the "digital lifestyle" of the overdeveloped world. But you don't have to go to China to find bleak prospects for a future of work; just consider the 650,000 people currently returning from prison each year.[47] Rarely acknowledged are also the networks of care that sustain contingent workers. Just for one moment, think about the families that are paying the price for just-in-time scheduling of work hours. Who is caring for their children when they face unpredictable work schedules, often decided only days or hours in advance? And let's not forget that government programs like the Food Stamp Act of 1964, introduced by President Lyndon B. Johnson, are essential in providing subsistence for crowdworkers and Walmart "associates" alike. In this way, personal networks of care, global supply chains, American taxpayers, academia, and the military sustain the digital economy.

Since the late 1970s, the productivity of American workers has steadily increased, while their real wages stagnated. Stanley Aronowitz, a sociologist at CUNY's Graduate Center, writes that "in the United States, twenty six million jobs were created between 1973 and 1986, the great majority of them both low-paid and low-skilled."[48] This trend is amplified in today's "sharing economy." A 2010 study by the American software company Intuit found that 80 percent of large American corporations planned to substantially increase their use of flexible workers in coming years, which means that a regular paycheck is increasingly unlikely to include legal protections or benefits. In 2015, between 31 and 40 percent of the American workforce worked as "free agents." From 1979 to 2013, the productivity of American workers rose 64 percent while their wages increased only by 8 percent.[49]

Ever larger parts of the economy are being reengineered to move away from the employment relationship and closer to freelancing and independent contract work. In this labor market, people are working short-term or just casual hours, which is a choice for some while others are forced into such "atypical work" by economic circumstance.

Growing numbers of workers no longer pursue a career path, a job for life, while young people have been increasingly asked to "pay their dues" by working for free as interns. "Temp" work has become the permanent way of life.

5) Ethical Crowdwork? MobileWorks and Samasource

Examples: *MobileWorks (LeadGenius), mClerk, Jana (formerly TxtEagle)*

There are several crowdsourcing companies attempting to create ethical business models. MobileWorks, for instance, promotes their crowdworkers based on performance and, importantly, the company pays minimum wages depending on the workers' country of residence. MobileWorks, mClerk, and Jana (formerly Txteagle), all focus on economically developing countries, but MobileWorks' approach to business is different. Its values are expressed through a belief in the individual worker; it does not think of its workforce in terms of replaceable assets. Instead, the company is developing relationships with its workers, even facilitating meetings in some cases. Workers can improve their computer skills and on occasion even gain direct employment within the company.

The company seeks to hire from disadvantaged and marginalized groups, from military veterans to refugees. MobileWorks functions based on the understanding that workers are not interchangeable. Unlike most other crowdwork companies, it pays by the hour. The idea is to root out poor-quality work by removing the incentive to complete assignments hastily. Lower-skilled tasks are often assigned to developing countries.

"When people are badly paid and it's relatively transactional, they show up, do the work and disappear. There's no incentive to do a good job," says Anand Kulkarni, chief executive of the upstart MobileWorks, whose LeadGenius crowdsourcing platform launched in 2010 and has "several hundred" full-time workers in 50 countries. Predictably, the minimum wage model based on country of residence causes tensions between international workers, whose compensation for the exact same work varies widely. In 2014, MobileWorks raised

$6 million on top of the more than million dollars in early-stage funding.[50]

A US-based crowdworker for MobileWorks can expect up to 40 hours of work per week, says Mr Kulkarni. "Pay is almost always above the minimum wage in the countries we are working in,"[51] he adds. At the end of the day, however, MobileWorks' distributed workforce is still contingent, lacking the social benefits traditionally associated with employment.

Founded in 2008, Samasource, a crowdsourcing firm that works in a similar way to AMT, is a not-for-profit that aims to pay fair wages that can sustain a family in the country of residence of the worker. The organization selects predominantly women and youths as workers, people who would not have much of a chance in the labor market otherwise. Samasource works on educating its more than 14,000 workers so that they can take on more challenging and better-paying tasks. Trained workers educate novices. While Samasource is interested in revenue, it does invest in workers in economically developing countries.

6) Content Farming

Examples: *Demand Media, Associated Media, SpunWrite*

Another variety of digital labor includes content farms that are about the maximization of advertising revenue for algorithmically optimized stories. Following the logic of the network, the topics for stories are calculated based on algorithms that determine what will receive the highest number of hits and best search engine placement. Their goal is to satisfy the logic of the algorithms that drive search engines rather than producing original journalistic content. Content mills are stressing search engine optimization goals over factual relevance. Content farms such as Associated Content and Demand Media threaten "traditional" sites with well-written and thoroughly researched journalism by producing a deluge of low-quality articles and videos that are merely passable. These sites offer "listicles" about topics such as weight loss or job hunting. Demand Media, just like the popular media site Buzzfeed, is data driven. But Buzzfeed's click-bait model, more often frivolous than rigorous, is set up as a honey trap for millennials. To be fair though, Buzzfeed is not a content farm, and occasionally, they are also breaking hard news, written by a very small number of professional journalists employed by the company.

The more than 7,000 independent contractors who are steadily working for Demand Media are commissioned to write articles based on computer-generated headlines. They are paid between $25 and $30 per story. Each story is copyedited and run through a plagiarism detector. Copy editors are paid $3.50 per story.[52]

Unsurprisingly, there are lots of such contaminating articles: over one million of them are circulating on the Internet already with the weekly addition of 20,000 new ones. Demand Media's YouTube videos are streamed over two millions times a day. In 2010, Google reported that the majority of the links it listed resulted from content farms. Consequently, a year later, Google announced that it would fine-tune its algorithms to better filter such low-quality sites.

7) Competitive Crowdsourcing

Examples: *99Designs, DesignCrowd, Threadless*

The practice of competitive crowdsourcing suggests that the crowd responds to a call for entries by providing fully executed submissions. Only one entry, however, will be "honored" with a prize while all others go home empty-handed. It's the logic of architecture competitions on steroids. Also in the design sector, Requests for Proposals (RFPs) are a common practice, quite similar to such competitions. On crowdSPRING, for example, firms can get coding and design projects done. They describe what they need and then receive a large number of completed works to pick from. Only one worker gets paid.

99designs functions in a similar manner: designers compete for a job that is offered through its website. One of the three headquarters of this Melbourne-native company is Berlin, Germany. Currently, the company has a pool of 200,000 registered designers. If you are a client who is looking for a logo, you might spend about $300. In return, you receive an average of 116 completely executed designs.[53] As a client, you can even specify that you'd like your job to be executed only by designers of a certain age group or country of residence. A company that specifically requests job applications only from those under the age of 40 would be in violation of the Age Discrimination in Employment Act (ADEA). However, the client, platform, and designers are merely linked through a contractual relationship rather than employment, and therefore liability under the ADEA is unlikely. While this behavior may or may not be illegal, it is certainly discriminatory. Only one of the 116 designers who entered the competition receives the payment of $180 while 115 designers worked for free. This means that $120 went to the intermediary, the company that connects workers with those who are looking for work. For designers, the high chance that their work will not be paid, of course, also lowers the quality and, specifically, the originality of the design. Designers are inclined to creatively "borrow" design elements if the likelihood of getting paid is minimal. In 2013, 99designs claimed that it had run 180,000 of these kinds of global competitions. Workers underbid each other to come out on top of these mini-competitions, a situation that capitalists in the nineteenth century could only have dreamed of. Not only do wages hit rock bottom but degrees in design, decades of experience, and reputation are potentially cut out of the equation; any talented high school student can compete with experienced designers. While today, the design agency business and institutional credentials are not yet fully invalidated, what it means to be a designer threatens to be changed by the alarming trend exemplified by 99designs. On the other hand, designers, artists, and artisans in developing countries are granted access to major clients through such competitions. These workers would never stand a chance in the nepotistic and elitist business world of the United States.

Competitive crowdsourcing services like 99designs are a bitter reality for design firms because somebody somewhere may always be willing to work for less. Sites like SpecWatch and No!SPEC watch competition-based design platforms and warn designers of possibly exploitative work. The Canadian Designers Guild even banned its members from contributing to such competition-based design sites.

Threadless is also based on the logic of the design competition. Individuals submit T-shirt designs which are then put to a vote on the site. If the design receives a sufficient number of votes, the T-shirt gets printed and the artist receives a $2,000 cash prize and a $500 Threadless gift certificate, which seems reasonably fair. The T-shirts are also made available for purchase in Threadless's Chicago retail store. In an online video, the creators of the company describe their goal as giving artists a real outlet to sell their work.[54] While it is accurate that artists and amateurs now have access to these production processes, Threadless, like 99designs, bolsters a waste of unpaid creative labor.

The overwhelming spectacle of informal competition

Examples: *InnoCentive, IdeaConnection, OpenIDEO, Walmart, My Starbucks Idea, Peugot, Kraft, BMW Customer Innovation Lab, Dell's IdeaStorm, Fiat Mio, LEGO Factory, Crowdtap, Clickadvisor*

Crowdsourcing research and development is a wonderful thing when you are a for-profit company at a time when there is a structural shortage in formal jobs and rising unemployment. Within the broader context of the global informal economy, American urbanist and historian Mike Davis called this an "overwhelming spectacle of informal competition."[55] For Davis, such competition led the emergence of an informal proletariat of at least one billion people who are cut off from formal economies.

For-profit firms are casting themselves as "open innovation companies," mobilizing the progressive associations and goodwill that is widely associated with altruistic projects like Wikipedia or FoldIt (open always sounds good, does it not?), while raking in revenue as a private enterprise. A good example is Massachusetts-based InnoCentive, a company that accepts research and development problems from "seeker organizations" – corporations, government, or nonprofits – and gets paid for putting out an open call for entries. The calls come from a wide range of domains including engineering, computer science, chemistry, life sciences, physical sciences, and business. Here is one such call found on InnoCentive's website. "Think you can find a way to prevent orange juice stored in see-through bottles from turning brown? There may be twenty thousand dollars in it for you."

The company's business model is based on the fact that international scientists are paying attention to this website and are willing to risk working for free. On the other hand, such sites do give underemployed or jobless scientists worldwide the opportunity to work on important scientific problems. Beyond that, there is the fact that the potential payout channeled through InnoCentive would be much larger than most university grants or corporate R&D funding.

The winner of such "challenges" wins a "prize," as they refer to the payment for the research, but similar to competitions in other fields, only the selected team gets paid for its labor while all the other scientists squandered their creative energy and time. Some argue that they gain in experience but at the end of the day, fiscally speaking, losing competitors are down-and-out. InnoCentive didn't have to commission dozens of groups of researchers to find solutions, it benefits from the willingness of participants to be used in this way. "Seeker organizations" save even further by not paying for office space and continuous salaries of researchers. InnoCentive has worked with more than 270,000 scientists, technicians, students, and engineers, most of them PhD-educated, predominantly from Russia, China, and India.[56]

The language of open "innovation challenges" muddies a sober understanding of the labor relationships and the impact on institutionally employed scientists. Who needs a high-priced scientist if you can get a cheap "solver" from Russia, Brazil, or India?

8) User-led Innovation

At this point, I am adding a reference to the work of MIT Professor Eric von Hippel who has researched unpaid user-led innovation for over a decade. This section belongs into this chapter because free, user-led innovation is closely aligned with the business model of companies like InnoCentive. In the conclusion of his book *Democratizing Innovation*, Hippel answered the question "How does innovation work?" by explaining that unpaid users/consumers are more likely to innovate than corporate R&D divisions.

In the process of what Hippel calls "free revealing," democratic access is given to consumers to work for free, to make their mark. In the past, it was exclusively researchers in corporate R&D divisions who worked on product innovation. The language of workplace democracy is age old but it should be reframed as genuine workplace democracy, which would also entail profit sharing. "What is mobilized from consumers for the process of production isn't just their creativity, ideas and labor power, but also their commitment and loyalty as consumers," von Hippel writes. "Citizen innovators" are becoming more deeply entrenched in brands. The process of the democratization of innovation should not be deceptively framed as the struggle of citizens who fight for access to innovation while also serving brands; it should be defined in terms of contributions to the innovation commons.

Vendors are exceedingly good at mass manufacturing and marketing products. In very many cases, however, product users – from serious mountain bikers and skateboarders, to university surgeons – are the ones who can show companies how to modify their products. People are adapting products to meet their own needs. They are not paid for their innovations, but their ideas are noticed and incorporated into improved products, which are then manufactured on a large scale. Von Hippel suggests identifying, acknowledging, and compensating such lead innovators.[57]

The list of companies that open up their R&D section to the public in order to draw in ideas and creativity is too long to include here. Walmart and Starbucks run forums for employees but also for the public with the stated goal of gathering ideas to make their businesses more environmentally sustainable. In this way, of course, the companies also use such outreach to improve the public image of their enterprise. R&D becomes part of corporate propaganda and the school of Design Thinking with terms like "user-centered design," which is supposed to involve all stakeholders. The new motto:

"Corporate R&D needs open engagement to progress." You might also think of consumer surveys that ask participants to join in order to "improve their experience" or the quality of "customer service."

At this point in the chapter, I will turn to in-game labor, the daily toil of the so-called gold farmers.

9) In-game Labor

Examples: *Goldfarming in MMORPGs like SIMS and World of Warcraft, or Camelot*

What is in-game labor? What is gold farming? The practice had its debut in the late 1990s in South Korean cyber cafés, but by 2005, barely a year after the release of the hugely popular World of Warcraft, more than 100,000 "gold farmers" were working 10–12 hours a day in "gaming workshops" not just in South Korea but also in China, India, and Mexico. Two years later, more than 1,000 such sweatshops existed in the city of Wuhan, central China, alone. Worldwide, the number of gold farmers is estimated to be roughly 400,000. "They toil in a fantasy world to pay rent in reality," as legal scholar Miriam Cherry put it.[58] Cory Doctorow:

> I understand that your "work" is just playing games, is that right?
> We work in the games, yes
> And so you organize people who play games.
> How are they workers?
> They sound like players to me.[59]

In the shadowy world of massively multiplayer online role-playing games (MMORPGs) like World of Warcraft, Everquest, Magic Land, or Lineage, the goal of virtual farmers is to slay dragons, kill monsters, and build up their own veritable treasure trove of magic weapons, armor, virtual gold coins, or animals. Farmers can then sell their virtual assets to players in the US, Japan, or Taiwan through PayPal and other sites in exchange for actual money. But gold farmers do not merely loot; they also go through "the grind," a time-consuming and tedious process of building up high-level avatars in the game, which are then purchased by players in the overdeveloped world. It's not just workers who are gold farming. There are also "bots," programmed to complete these same tasks. The Canadian author Cory Doctorow explains the value of high-level avatars.

> As fun as the game is, it's always more fun if you're one of the haves, with all the awesome armor and killer weapons, than if you're some

lowly noob have-not with a dagger, fighting your way up to your first sword.[60]

Companies like Sony and Zynga forbid gold farming in their games, but the legal situation is not always clear. Some leisure players from overdeveloped countries despise these low-wage Asian worker-players whom they understand as an undesirable minority in the game.[61]

In 2007, Julian Dibbell published an article in *The New York Times* that drew attention to the practice of gold farming in China.[62] In the same year, a middle school in China's Muslim Northwest assigned their students as unpaid interns to gold farms to acquire "practical computer skills."[63] Students worked full shifts and were so outraged that they organized a strike.

The play-workers make about 30¢ an hour. Their wages are very low but so is their cost of living. As one gold farm owner put it: *"They get paid dirt. But dirt is good where they live."*[64] Defenders of the practice pose that such game sweatshops do in fact offer jobs that are paid at a rate similar to that of an average factory job and that working there could create transferable digital skills. For the owners of game sweatshops, "farming" can be about serious real-world money. The economist Edward Castronova has estimated that the economy of Sony's game EverQuest and its virtual world, Norrath, has a per capita gross national product equivalent to that of Bulgaria.[65] In 2011, gold farming was estimated to have a billion dollar annual global market that led China to even force their prisoners to join this in-game labor force.[66]

Some gold farmers are also spending the few remaining hours after work playing the game that occupied them all day; it is no longer exclusively about externally imposed necessities; drudgery is turned into creative production and self-expression. Working for amusement, gaming, and scamming virtual worlds all hides labor in games, wrapped in the ideology of play.[67]

10) Online Labor Brokerages

Examples: *Upwork, Craiglist, OnForce, LiveWork, TopCoder, RentaCoder, Peopleperhour, Envato, Thumbtack, Fivver*

The labor brokerages oDesk and Elance merged in 2013 and now claim to have a pool of close to 8,000,000 registered workers. Now called Upwork, this service offers a "bulk-order tool" for hiring workers; it allows businesses to hire 50 workers at a time to complete larger jobs. Legal scholar Alek Felstiner has pointed out that these services go far beyond functioning simply as listing jobs; they are also framing and defining the work itself.[68] People no longer work on a platform; what they do is changed by the platform.

Quasi-employers that use Upwork are mainly headquartered in the US, Australia, the UK, and Canada, while workers mostly reside in Germany, the UK, India, Canada, the Philippines, and the US. They are an important segment of the overall market which spent $300 billion worldwide on "contingent workers" in 2012. But it also needs to be understood that Upwork – as well as Amazon and TaskRabbit – play up the number of their workers by stating how many people set up an account. These numbers do not reveal how many of these accounts are dormant or hardly used at all. On the upside, Upwork created a structure where the payment for a freelancer goes into an escrow account when the work starts, so that it can be effortlessly dispensed once the work is done. As freelancers are often paid much too late, this is a feature appreciated by workers.

Taking cues from Jeremy Bentham's panopticon, Upwork monitors the labor process by using the in-built camera in most laptops to take photos of individual workers at random intervals. The company calls this collection of workplace surveillance data, a "worker diary." This "diary" also contains arbitrarily recorded screenshots that Upwork takes of the worker's computer screens. The company justifies this invasive disciplining practice by arguing that they need to follow the progress of the work to see if it will be finished in time. Additional evaluation criteria used to further discipline workers include quality of the product, communicability, professionalism, punctuality, and honoring the budget. Upwork's workers are in full view at all times; it is an oppressive amount of social control.

The general trend on Upwork seems to be that employers that are located in the US get work done in developing countries where the rate of labor is cheaper. Most of the work in Upwork's virtual hiring hall requires computer programming skills or intricate knowledge of mobile phones. But there are also other types of work available. A professional translation company in New York might charge $1,500 for a given translation job, while a competent translator from Argentina, Brazil, Indonesia, Mexico, or the Philippines may offer a flat-rate of anywhere between $33 and just $22 on Upwork, according to an article in *The Economist*. Here, Upwork was described as a "talent exchange" that hires gigging "contingent workers." In 2012, prior to the oDesk/E-Lance merger, most of the $360 million spent on oDesk came from American employers, and the main recipients of this money were workers in India. The article claims that the people these companies "enroll seem to enjoy the experience, which is why the numbers signing up are growing fast."[69]

11) On-demand Labor

Examples: *TaskRabbit*, *Zaarly*, *Otetsudai*, *UberX*, *Lyft*, *SideCar*, *Kitchensurfing*, *Postmates*, *Favor*, Pro.com, *Homejoy*, *Handy*

The apps of labor companies like Uber, Lyft, or TaskRabbit connect customers around personal services like transportation. It's all so charming and convincing: you can sell the fruits from your garden to people in your neighborhood, you can camp out in a tree house in Redwood Forest, or stay in a mansion in Rome. In Oakland and Berkeley, you can even purchase and pick up a home-cooked meal from your neighbors.

Technology becomes the savior from the crisis in human connection and the flaccidity of post-crash recovery. Solo workers and lonely freelancers are now connecting while consuming. Just think of Lyft where the driver is obligated to fist bump you and, in fear of a bad evaluation at the end of the ride, she is willing to become your new best friend.

Terms used to describe this brave new apps-economy range from "sharing economy," "peer," to "collaborative peer economy," "crowd-based capitalism," "peer marketplaces," or, following Robert Reich, the 'share-the-scraps' economy." The most sustainable, honest definition, in the end was the "on-demand economy." Referring to the economy of Uber, TaskRabbit, or Mechanical Turk as a "peer economy" is like mistaking Napster for Spotify. It's like interpreting a technology used among peers with upstarts that profit from the interactions of clients. The term "sharing economy" is a misnomer; it is deceptive because these businesses are not about genuine sharing: they are dedicated to the renting out of assets such as rooms, labor, tools, and, importantly, time. We must be clear: renting is not the new sharing.

The Spanish researcher Mayo Fuster Morell points to practices that attempt to cover up the financialization of user data through the projection of a corporate image that is all about sharing, collaboration, and openness. Corporate projects are likened to Wikipedia, even if they do not benefit the public.[70] Fuster Morell calls it "wiki washing," and that's exactly what the extractive sharing economy incarnates.

Uber's marketing campaign is falsifying the facts. Uber's numbers have been compared to industry data provided by China. What they purport to be stands in stark contrast to the labor practices on the ground. They claim, for example, that an Uber driver in New York City is earning over $90,000 a year, which nobody was able to verify.[71] In 2015, one estimate of Uber driver pay in Boston, taking account of expenses in that city, comes out to $12.76/hour.[72] And in June of the same year, in a blog post, Uber's CEO Travis Kalanick, inserted himself into the ongoing discussions about regulation, stating: "All we ask of these cities is that they allow their citizens to start serving their neighbors."[73] If only these cities would let us profit.

People who are in dire need of extra income can become amateur chefs, painters, furniture assembly experts, personal assistants, or cabbies. These one-off gigs are mostly low paid. They do, however, help workers to bridge the time between two jobs. Frequently, these innovations are improvements that genuinely help consumers, but the workers are stripped of all the social standards of employment. One worker wrote: "If you want to 'Uber' as a moonlighting thing, it's great." But driving full-time, "basically you're in a service industry job making eight to ten dollars per hour and getting clobbered on the depreciation of your vehicle."[74]

Social philosopher Andre Gorz warns that "unemployment, poverty and absolute destitution are spreading."[75] He gives the example of the system introduced by Japanese car firms in the United Kingdom. In this system, Gorz writes, "the 'employees are not employed, but are required to be permanently 'on call.' They will then be employed when the company needs them, being paid at the agreed hourly rate for only the few hours or days they work. This marks a return, more or less to the day laborers of Dickensian times."[76]

In Germany, however, work-on-call contracts are illegal. Here, a minimum amount of hours, determined by the law, has to be guaranteed and if the company isn't able to put the person to work for that many hours, it still has to pay them as if it had.

I am using the term "platform capitalism," introduced by Sascha Lobo[77] and Martin Kenney, to bypass the fraudulent togetherness of terms like "peer," "sharing," and "economy." How can we talk about genuine sharing or innovation when a third party immediately monetizes your every interaction for the benefit of a small group of stockholders? Platforms are replacing firms, and subcontracting practices direct big payouts to small groups of people. Even occupations that previously could not be off-shored, the pet walkers or home cleaners, are becoming subsumed under platform capitalism.

With the glaring shift from employment to contingent work, more and more people are simply trying to get by and the new task masters – UberX, Postmates, Favor, Fiverr, and Mechanical Turk – are exalted as saviors. What if the engine of the "sharing economy" is not the instinct to share, but rather economic desperation? Just consider the 8–10 million Americans who are unemployed and the almost eight million who are working part-time because they cannot find full-time work, according to the Bureau of Labor Statistics.[78] They are piecing together a living wage by working with companies like Uber but only few make a good living in the Hunger Games.

Business gurus making connections between the "sharing economy" and Occupy, the Arab Spring, hippie ethos, or the solidarity economy lost their pull for anybody who has been paying attention. The posturing of the sharing economy as a social "movement of movements" misses the point that the owners of the digital real estate – the Amazons, CrowdFlowers, and 99designs – skim off profits while using the language of ecological sustainability, open access, and trust. It might be true that 80 percent of seats on the road are empty but Uber and Airbnb are also financializing your property, your car, and, importantly, your time.

In 2015, Uber boasted on its blog that they will "deliver hundreds of millions of rides, and plan to create one million jobs in the process." It remains unclear, how they could be creating that many *jobs* when they don't actually employ any of their workers. I also want to emphasize that Uber is a labor company, not simply a tech startup, which means that it is reliant on the availability of an abundance of cheap labor and a permissive regulatory environment.

The inevitable labor conflicts include the classification of workers as independent contractors. You can find a more in-depth discussion of this topic in the conclusion of this book. The category of independent contractor doesn't always match the reality of those workplaces. The Internal Revenue Service taxes workers as if they were entrepreneurs who operate a small business, which frequently does not reflect the realities on the ground. What happens when a TaskRabbit or Uber worker gets seriously hurt (or hurts others) while performing a task under the auspices of the company?[79]

While Uber, Lyft, and SideShare added passable insurance, there are still endless legal ambiguities. Early in 2015, Uber introduced price cuts across 48 cities, for example, but temporarily guaranteed that drivers would continue to earn their existing wages.[80] If Uber exerts more control over drivers, it is more likely they will be legally held to be those workers' employer, according to legal scholar Brishen Rogers and other legal scholars.[81] But if they don't exert more control over drivers, they may see declines in the quality of service, and perhaps even more accidents. Uber is walking a tightrope on this legal question. Legal scholar Tim Wu talks about the golden phase in the early days of all monopolies. During that time, monopolies are innovative and contribute to the public good. Later, they innovate far less and assert their power to suppress innovation by young incumbents. Such practice makes it nearly impossible for the competition to survive; once Uber's contenders are out of the way, the company can treat its workers whichever way it likes. And in the absence of a binding contract, drivers' occupations and work conditions are tenuous at best.

A different version of this labor practice exists on Etsy, where people can sell what they – for the most part – create in their home. Or, take Shapeways, which is a place where you can create and sell your digitally manufactured 3D creations.

The principle of all of these businesses is that they function as brokers of services through an app. Again, this has little to do with "peer-to-peer rental marketplaces" or networked peer production; this is about people who are looking for work and others who try to get things done. UberX, one of several parts of Uber, for example, connects passengers and drivers using the company's smartphone app. Drivers are regular people who repurpose their own car into a taxi to make some extra cash. Uber's slogan is "Everyone's private driver."

Uber is the hungry ghost of profit. It takes 20 percent from its drivers' incomes, which seems excessive considering what it is actually offering. The fact that it affords access to a new market does not make this less questionable. But it is also good to keep such practice in perspective: Apple, for example, is taking 30 percent on the App Store.

Uber is also working with "surge pricing" during times of peak demand. On Saturday nights, for example, rates may substantially increase. Many of the company's actions appear to be illegal. Uber claims that it can reduce costs because it is cutting out the middlemen, but let's not forget that it flatly installs itself as the globally consolidated taxi magnate in their place. And as a word of advice for disgruntled drivers, Uber CEO Travis Kalanick offered the insight that driverless cars will replace them all sooner rather than later anyway. Kalanick might be right about automation, but using this probability to keep down workers is reprehensible. And as Frank Pasquale has pointed out, Kalanick's job is not beyond automation. His own logical reasoning could also be translated into algorithms. "Automate the automators," as Pasquale put it.[82] Uber follows the logic of the exchanges in the stock market, cable companies, search engines, or social networks.

I'm referring to Uber drivers and TaskRabbits as solo workers. The term solo worker applies to much of digital work. While there are relationships between Turkers who may point each other to better-paying tasks, for instance, companies like TopCoder discourage workers from contacting each other. Regulators should step in and make sure that workers are able to connect; decent digital labor cannot be left to algorithms.

In some cases, these marketplaces allow amateurs to take on gigs that used to be performed by trained, experienced, full-time employees. And what used to be favors among friends now has a price tag: the pickup from the airport, hauling clothes to the laundry, or helping to paint the apartment. Shares are shared and sharing becomes shearing.

Mobilizing platforms for political lobbying

Venture capital – Google Ventures, Baidu, Goldman Sachs, Jeff Bezos, and so on – is clearly behind Uber. The company attracted $300 million in investment and its speculative value far exceeds $60 billion. It's the perfect commodification of the future, reminiscent of financial speculation bubbles like the tulip mania of 1637.[83]

In 2015, Airbnb spent over $8 million to lobby residents in San Francisco and thwart regulation. In 2014, in Washington DC alone, Uber spent over $300,000 on lobbying efforts to tame regulatory headwinds from local government.[84] Millions in venture capital behind Uber put them into a superior position to strike a regulatory sweet spot between the legislative protections that play out in their favor and the calls for corporate responsibilities that do not. Uber can influence regulation on a city level and might even be able to sway national labor laws. In 2015, for example, a Philadelphia court turned away taxi drivers and their dispatch companies who had truthfully claimed that Uber violated the state's rules.[85] Like Facebook and Google, Uber is working to turn the world into an environment where they will do well. In 2015, when New York City mayor Bill de Blasio discussed the possibility of limiting the number of Uber cars in the city because of overcrowding, the company added a feature to their app that would allow users to complain to the Mayor's Office. Confronted with the results of this campaign, de Blasio retracted his push for regulation for the time being.

There is a possibility that the regulatory templates established by Uber could be taken on or over by worker cooperatives that would benefit from established legal templates. An equally likely outcome of these regulatory struggles is that Uber emerges as a monopoly ruling the transportation industry worldwide; its will to innovate will be outmatched by its will to power. Along with exploding financial products and student loans, such labor platforms are among America's most toxic exports. Uber is becoming the noxious rose of the sharing economy; the Amazon of the streets. And who is picking up the slack for the care for those workers? It is networks of care – family, community, or government – that now have to provide what employers no longer offer.

TaskRabbit

Lean and mean micro-staffing companies like TaskRabbit are on the rise and that is hardly surprising. In the summer of 2014, thirty seven percent of the unemployed – 4.4 million people – had been out of work for longer than six months.[86]

In 2015, more than 54 million Americans worked as freelancers, part-timers, independent contract workers, or day laborers. Some 160,000 drivers are on the road for Uber, 50,000 for Lyft, Odesk claims some 10 million workers, CrowdFlower 5 million, and Crowdwork 8 million. Services like TaskRabbit sometimes functioned like a backup, which also follows the logic of the history of temp agencies, which became especially popular as a result of the recession in the 1970s. TaskRabbit was founded in 2008 and seven years later it has 33,000 workers in 19 cities. "Out of all the contractors, seventy percent have at least a bachelor's degree, twenty percent have master's degrees, and five percent have a PhD."[87]

The founder of TaskRabbit, Leah Busque, does not beat around the bush: she wants to revolutionize the world's labor force. The rapid growth of this company is completely consistent with an overall development in the temp industry, which added more jobs between 2010 and 2012 than any other industry in the US.[88] Sixty percent of the people working for TaskRabbit are women. A total of 10 percent of the workers are trying to make a full-time occupation out of TaskRabbit despite the fact that the company does not offer a family-supporting wage, health insurance, pension plan, sick leave, basic worker protections against discrimination, or the right to organize.

But let's step back for one minute. The idea at the heart of TaskRabbit is that neighbors would come to your rescue – they would do your daily errands. In 2014, the company, threatened by a decline in "task masters" who are looking for "task doers" changed its operating principles quite dramatically.

Let me start with the system that made the company so popular. In the past, if you needed someone to do any odd job, this would be the place for you. Bake madeleines, bring cupcakes to a friend, and sing her Happy Birthday, for $20 you would find somebody. Pick up a few boxes from my office and drive them across town tomorrow; four or five errand runners would compete for that within minutes. An episode of Gabe & Max, a poignant YouTube comedy sketch, shows two gay men during couple's therapy. When the exchange becomes too emotionally taxing, one of them calls in an on-call worker to take his place.

TaskRabbit workers will install your air conditioner, or assemble IKEA furniture, help you wrap your Christmas presents, or buy your dad a gift for Father's Day. You could even find somebody who would iron your dress shirt. "Planning a BBQ this weekend?" No problem, somebody will swing by and bring the heavy charcoal or the bags of ice that you might require.

Thus far, there was no dedicated market for such tasks. Second, TaskRabbit offers temporary office help, usually focused on positions that need little training or knowledge. Why hire a full-time assistant who will end up watching YouTube videos and chat with co-workers about restaurants on the job if you can get a TaskRabbit that is willing to come in for just two hours. TaskRabbit's transaction fee for this kind of thing is only between 22 and 26 percent of the workers' wages, which, compared to the 60 percent that traditional temp agencies traditionally pocketed, is not bad at all. They are in direct competition with temp agencies and can make the job of an office temp even more temporary.

People who wanted to get something done posted a description of the task to the TaskRabbit website along with the maximum amount that they were willing to pay. This was followed by a bidding process, with four or five workers competing for the job, often within minutes. Sometimes, workers tried to underbid each other while at other times, nobody would take the job at all. You would get a message from one of the workers stating that what you are asking and the amount you are willing to pay for it simply doesn't add up to minimum wage after TaskRabbit has taken out its 12–30 percent from the workers' income. When you are looking for somebody to work for you, you will find the reputation score for each individual worker. Just like on Upwork, workplace surveillance is ever present in the sense that workers are evaluated after each job. Just imagine somebody writing a report about you every four hours and then putting it online. On a worker's profile, you can see how many tasks they have completed and you can read the testimonials. Finally, you pick one of the workers and once the work is done, the money is simply deducted from your credit card.

The new TaskRabbit system requires every worker to have an iPhone or another smartphone. TaskRabbit is now much closer to the model of a regular temp agency. It offers work in the categories of delivery and moving help, furniture assembly, minor home repairs, organization, cleaning, heavy lifting, personal assistance, event staffing as well as planning. And importantly, workers can no longer select the tasks they would like to do, but after an initial screening of their preferences, they are automatically allotted to the requests that are coming in. Also the price is no longer determined by task, but each worker has an hourly rate, which is displayed when you make your selection. If you're looking for somebody to assemble your furniture, you will have to make that selection in your phone app, which then displays a list of workers from which you can choose. Workers are also supposed to wear a TaskRabbit T-shirt when they show up to work but who can control that? There does not seem to be a penalty for not wearing it. Workers, now called "Taskers," have to use the mobile app to show if they are available. Once the system offers the task to a worker, they only have 30 minutes to accept it, or it goes to another worker.

The language that is used to describe the workers has also changed from the old to the new version of TaskRabbit. Initially, we saw the neoliberal hijack of language that referred to employers as "senders" or "task posters," while workers were labeled as "TaskRabbits" or simply "rabbits." Now they are simply called "Taskers."

CrowdFlower, a company which claims to have the largest on demand workforce in the world, refers to their workers as "contributors." ShortTask talks of "solvers" and "seekers." It's important to deflate such ideological obfuscation aimed at avoiding accurate classification of workers by the Internal Revenue Service.

The services that TaskRabbit is offering used to be performed by friends and neighbors at no cost. They would have picked you up from the airport or helped you paint your house. They might have even cheered you on at the marathon. You could have knocked on their door and asked them for that special ingredient for the triple chocolate cake that you were trying to bake. In Brazil and India, maids traditionally performed much of the domestic work – at least for parts of the population.

With companies like TaskRabbit, we are witnessing a financialization of activities that used to be an expression of social capital, support for Robert Putnam's argument that post-World War II social capital among Americans collapsed. But then Putnam suggested that we should spend more time with our neighbors and that neighborhoods should be redesigned in ways that facilitate such connections, he did not anticipate that in urban centers workers have increasingly little time left considering their commute, housework, and childcare.

This monetization of private life is also reflected in services like "Shiva Sisters." This service will send two people to help you along through the grieving process and take care of the paperwork that needs to be done when somebody in your family passes away.

Now, there are personal dog walkers, potty trainers, and companies with elusive names like "rent a husband," "rent a dad," or "rent a friend." Paid services have entered the sphere of private life and set new emotional rules. Party planners and other service providers start to shape our emotional life. The love for your child may be expressed by paying $200 for a clown who appears at your kid's birthday party. Or, if you are uncomfortable in couples counseling, why not have a TaskRabbit take over mid-session.

Erin Hatton, a professor of sociology at SUNY Buffalo, describes the novel kind of work that is based on "renting workers" rather than "buying them" with the example of the temp agency Kelly Services that ran a series of ads in the human resources journal *The Office* in 1971, promoting the "Never–Never Girl," who the company claims:

> *Never costs you a dime for slack time. (When the workload drops, you drop her.) Never has a cold, slipped disc or loose tooth. (Not on your time anyway!) Never cost you for unemployment taxes and Social Security payments. (None of the paperwork, either!) Never cost you for fringe benefits.... Never fails to please.*[89]

These kinds of slogans suddenly seem much more honest than the TaskRabbit motto, which reads: "Do More. Live More. Be More." Hatton describes how traditional temp agencies throughout the 1960s avoided union opposition by framing temp work as "women's work" instead of "breadwinning" union jobs. They advertised thousands of images of young, white middle-class women performing a variety of short-term office jobs.[90]

Today, for TaskRabbit, the mere fact that the work relationship doesn't constitute employment means that the multiplicity of rights guaranteed for that very relationship do not apply. The confrontation with unions now is circumvented through a shift away from employment altogether. Similar to the branding efforts of Amazon Mechanical Turk, the temp agency Kelly Girl describes their workers already in 1958 as not wanting full-time work. "The typical Kelly Girl...is bored with strictly keeping house. Or maybe she just wants to take a job until she pays for a Davenport or a new fur coat."[91] The same rhetoric, obfuscating economic necessity, is used today.

Anne Raimondi, TaskRabbit's Chief Revenue Officer, stated that their workers are "choosing this because they don't want a full-time job. They want a lot of flexibility and diversity in their lives and control over their destiny."[92] But Raimondi's comment glosses over the lack of choice of some workers when joining TaskRabbit. The founder of the company, Leah Busque, acknowledged that the 13 million people who are actively looking for work in the United States make up their potential standing reserve of labor. Or take the company's spokesperson who stated that "These TaskRabbits aren't just willing to [perform this work], they're excited to."[93] The tens of millions of Americans who are struggling to survive don't have a choice to pay their bills. Their willingness to perform discount labor is no longer sufficient; they are also mandated to love what they do. DWYL. Workers for companies like TaskRabbit can make a decent living if they don't ever get sick, weak, or old. They have to be fountains of youth and resilience.

12) Online Assistance

One of the more curious recent developments in this broader area is that of online personal assistance, which is also referred to as "life crowdsourcing." Sometimes simply referred to as "life sourcing," workers take on the tedious office tasks of professionals who are pressed for time. The upstart Zirtual.com, for example, describes its service as a way to help people "find an apartment in a hot market" or "manage a busy calendar." According to the company's website, Zirtuals' workers are specialized in research, scheduling, and reservations.[94] The turnaround with independent contractors became too tiring for Zirtual, which decided to switch to an employee model with hourly rates starting at $11 an hour. Zirtual's CEO wrote that "At first people like the flexibility of being a contractor, but at the end of the day most people don't have the luxury to bring in half a paycheck."[95]

At The Internet as Playground and Factory conference, Jonathan Zittrain gave a rundown of distributed labor starting with LiveOps, an outsourcing agency that enabled the Red Cross to recruit in-home freelance agents (the company calls them "mompreneurs") that processed 17,000 phone calls in the days after Hurricane Katrina had struck the Gulf Coast in 2005. LiveOps is a distributed network of people who run a "cloud call center." What is of particular significance here is that these workers are at home as opposed to a call center and that they can be mobilized from one hour to the next because of that. This "homeshoring" approach was also used by the American airline JetBlue, whose home-based customer service has earned them high marks.

But virtual assistance is also used in more conventional commercial settings. In the US, anybody who ever tried to get a representative of his or her bank on the phone will have had some kind of experience with a call center in India or elsewhere. Or, you may have experienced call centers of a different kind when approaching a drive-through restaurant and noticing that the person with whom you connect when ordering your food is in fact located in a country far away. The person who will take your order might sit in a country thousands of kilometers away but then put in your purchase of French fries, burgers, and a coffee with the workers at the restaurant 30 feet down the road.

In fact, the person on the other end of your call was likely one of the 330,000 Indian call center workers in India or one of the 350,000 such workers in the Philippines. The systems that make all of this global interaction possible are deeply embedded with features of control. In her 2007 study of Indian call centers, Winfried Poster emphasizes that these centers are subcontracted by foreign-owned companies, a practice which aligns with traditional sweatshop economies. The subcontracting arrangement removes responsibility from companies like General Electric, Dell, and American Express who initiate this work. While these companies are not owned by American enterprises, they are completely accountable to those clients regarding production, labor conditions and work time.[96] They serve the conveniences of the northern consumer in multiple time zones, Poster presciently writes, which unhooks them from their local time zone and leads to a complete reversal of awake life, isolated from their families, their social circles, and the rest of society.... "The time of the global belongs, in a sense, to the powerful."[97]

The 2005 sci-fi documentary *John & Jane* by Ashim Ahluwalia sheds light on the lived reality of six call center agents that answer to American 1–800 numbers in the Dubai call center. They have American aliases – John and Jane – and they get coached in American culture and language, and even accent ("Canchoo do it? Donchoo like it?), to make clients on the other end of the phone line forget that they're not talking to an American. What this means for the identity of the worker is hard to imagine. "John" and "Jane" work 14-hour night shifts oscillating between their urban Indian reality and their virtual presence in the United States.

13) Conclusion

Much of what I offered throughout this chapter was critical of specific practices and crowdwork in particular. In 2014, the unethical crowdwork practices at Amazon Mechanical Turk became more center stage of the public discussion and a year later, similar critiques of on-demand labor and the discussions about the future of work became the topic of many events and articles. In this conclusion, I consider work rights and the role of technology in this shift of labor markets to the Internet. I comment on the myth of choice, flexibility, and autonomy that is so frequently mobilized to make the case for contingent work.

Worker rights

Every morning before you can pour the next cup of coffee, an app like Lyft or Sweetch muscles in on yet another industry, potentially making a traditional job obsolete faster than you can say, "Amazon. com." This is not the world of Henry Ford, for whom it wasn't only important to make production processes more effective; he at least understood his workers as consumers of the products they were making. Ford knew that even hecto-millionaires could only buy so much; they cannot spend enough of their wealth to have a truly significant impact on the economy.

A close associate of Henry Ford observed: "cars are the byproducts of his real business, which is the making of men."[98] Today's executives, especially in the digital labor surveillance complex, have short-term profits on their minds; the well being of "providers" or "contributors" – formerly known as "workers" – is a minor if any concern. You can, for example, sit in conferences about the "sharing economy" for days without ever hearing any mention of workers.

What do crowd workers do with their earnings? In 2014, Norwegian designer Daniel Jackson[99] set up a task on CrowdFlower asking 1,000 workers what they are doing with the money earned on that platform. The first group of responders talks about covering their existential needs, the bottom of Abraham Maslow's pyramid of needs: water, food, clothing, shelter, and physical safety.[100] They use the money to pay for gas, electricity, water, Internet access, baby formula, diapers, and milk. Others mention buying chocolate for a niece, for instance. For many workers, however, this is not extra spending money but essential income.

To further illustrate the disregard for workers, you can also follow the linguistic trapeze acts of a company like TaskRabbit, which literally likens its workers to perpetually energized animals. Like MTurk and other companies, they attempt to make workers forget that they are workers, while at the same time conveying a brutal truth, perhaps, when tacitly comparing them to animals.

On the other hand, you might know crowd workers who are doing just fine. Indeed, for the highly skilled, freelancing can be advantageous in the overdeveloped world, and even in the economically developing world; William Thies, Aishwarya Lakshmi Ratan, and James Davis of Microsoft Research have concluded, "Paid crowdsourcing has the potential to improve earnings and livelihoods in poor communities around the world. However, there is a long way to go before realizing this potential. To date, most workers on microtasking platforms come from relatively well-off backgrounds, and there has been limited impact on low-income individuals.... While there are many challenges to overcome, the rewards are great. We believe that a new focus on low-income workers is critically important to unlock the potential scale and impact of paid crowdsourcing platforms.[101]

Indeed, other models exist: the crowdsourcing company MobileWorks pays the minimum wage specified by a worker's country of residence, for instance. While such a model has its own difficulties, MobileWorks shows that the crowdsourcing industry would not go to rack and ruin if adherence to minimum wage standards were introduced. The search for other ethical crowd work upstarts is on!

While there are definitely advantages to being an "independent," it also signals the loss of legal protections with regards to minimum wage, workplace harassment, paid overtime, employer-financed health insurance, and the eight-hour workday. Organized labor had fought for the eight-hour workday for at least 100 years. Under the New Deal, these rights were explicitly reserved only for employees, not for all citizens. In poorer countries, increased reliance on crowdsourcing companies headquartered in Silicon Valley also reinforces colonial relationships that exploit cheap labor without building up infrastructures that would allow the workers to improve their situation systemically, for the long haul.

What we need today are employee-like rights for all. One way of reaching this objective would be to loosen the definition of employment to include the realities of twenty-first-century labor.

Blame the Internet or Web technologies?

The lives of digital laborers, whether they be on Upwork or CrowdFlower, follow the real-time demands and pulsating rhythms of the network. In the discussion about the future of work, critics are frequently branded as Luddites. The good guys in this story are Amazon, Uber, and progress; on the other side are the Luddites afraid of technology. And indeed, online labor brokerages, The Internet of Things, user-led innovation, or on-demand labor can be beneficial but they also introduce new vulnerabilities for workers. Digitization allows for new business models, novel chains of value extraction, and forms of division of labor – some of which are obstructing its emancipatory and humanizing potential.

The Internet, computers, and crowdsourcing technology are not neutral; they have embedded values. On-demand labor, crowdsourcing, or content farming are not the ultimate predators of labor; the Internet does not have to be a job-killing infrastructure.

However, the Internet has become a highly efficient enabler of unethical work arrangements. Technologies in a genuine "sharing economy" – platform cooperatives and public interest startups – can be operated with embedded values that support the commonwealth. Beyond technology, other factors that impact the role of the labor platforms discussed in this chapter include a lack of regulation, the decline of labor unions, the society-wide reorganization of work, and publicly traded stockholder companies, which are driven by growth imperatives and the fiduciary duty to maximize profits.

Since 2001, the number of people participating in the United States job market has drastically decreased. The suggestion of technology somehow inevitably being linked to the destruction of jobs is put to question when studying developments in Germany, the Netherlands, Norway, Sweden, or Denmark, where the number of participants in the job market has increased over that same period despite the fact that these countries also invested in technology.[102] Clearly, the introduction of technology does not have to lead to job losses; it is the social vision behind technologies that colors its use.

Briefly consider the vision of scientific management of Frederick W. Taylor who, in 1911, proposed a total regime of control over the increasingly de-individualized, de-skilled factory worker who was now asked to move her body following a dehumanizing micro-choreography. Only a few years later, also Vladimir Ilyich Lenin was infected by the Taylor-bug. Putting a Communist spin on Taylor's ideas, Lenin dreamed of Soviet factories where "a million hammers striking at the same moment would set the entire world vibrating."[103] Taylor's idea also coincided with the dawn of "self-help" literature, namely Samuel Smiles' book *Self-Help* ("heaven helps those who help themselves"), which seemed to suggest that it was not, most of all, the brutalizing workplaces of industrial capitalism that needed fixing but instead the workers themselves. Add a bit of chemically induced ideological euphoria, as Bifo would put it, and you get the ideal capitalist worker.

But even in this case, Taylor's contemporary Frank Gilbreth presented a different vision of the use of technology. Gilbreth had hoped to put his time and motion studies into the service of the well being of workers instead of owners. Instead of blaming technologies for destroying traditional jobs, we should instead ask what the United States government can do to stop ethically unsavory (and possibly illegal) labor practices that leave workers without social benefits. And we should ask what new ownership structures could do for workers. In chapter 7, I argue that we should apply the lessons of very old contingent work to better online markets. Instead of spreading wealth and democratic decision-making, the extractive sharing economy funnels money and control toward the top. Instead, I propose that labor platforms should be owned by the people who are doing the work to facilitate a way of life that is more endowed with social and ethical values.

The Zugzwang and the myth of choice

> No one is forced to take a job he doesn't like. No one gets tricked into a job he didn't sign up for.[104]

Throughout this chapter, I explained how platform owners use the language of choice, autonomy, and flexibility to sell the reorganization of work. Technology is presented as an integral component of the good life; it's all about choice and freedom. I am reminded of an advertisement for one of the first laptops, the Commodore 64. The ad, launched in 1982, featured a man in his fifties sitting bare-chested next to a pool with his Commodore, a cocktail and two young women in bikinis. Another ad of this period features a couple lounging in beach chairs, working on their laptops while enjoying the sunset. Today, the reality of flexible, mobile computing looks different. Check out the commuters on their laptops at 6 a.m. in an airport cafe.

I began this chapter with the story of Ryan Bingham, whose job it is to induce a feeling of liberation in the people he fires, the liberation from the heavy backpack of the old life of employment. Bingham invites them to enter a world of flexibility, autonomy, and choice; they too can fulfill their dreams and become entrepreneurial, flexible workers. Surely, for some, this will be true. In reality, for one of the former employees confronting Bingham, this meant that he was no longer able to pay for his daughter's asthma medication. In his book *The Myth of Choice*, Kent Greenfield sums up the limits of the suggestion of choice in the market:

> So we are faced with a tension. On the one hand, our political and legal rhetoric applauds and deifies choice, autonomy, and personal responsibility. On the other hand, there are profound questions about when choice is real, and about the reality of pervasive constraints on our choices. Once we take into account the influences of biology,

*culture, authority, and economics, the scope of our choices is much
narrower than we have long assumed.*[105]

The spokeswoman of the crowdsourcing system CrowdFlower:
"Crowd contributors are free to work whenever, wherever, however
they wish, for whoever they wish, for as long or as short a time as
they wish."[106] They are "contributors," not workers.

Even the think tank D64, a political group convened by the Social
Democratic Party of Germany, presented a steadfastly euphoric take
on what they called the "historically new emancipatory potentials"
of digital labor, which can "bring the worker a positive vision of
freedom."[107] They write:

> *For the first time, people work where they want, how they want, and
> in a way that suits them....It frees them from the bonds of space
> and time and therefore delivers extraordinary possibilities for dignified
> and good work.*[108]

We are told that millennials want to take their clock back; they
prefer to work at night, following their inner clock. Workers, sta-
tioned in a cafe, their living room, or a co-working space, can freely
follow their interests and they even get to travel. There are, of course,
significant advantages to not working in an office as nobody controls
what you're doing as long as the project gets done on time. In reality,
however, this contingent work setup often leads to loneliness, fake
flexibility, a lack of consistent opportunities to work, and longer
work hours. What is marketed as flexibility and autonomy, at least
for the most vulnerable workers, is in fact much closer to what Mike
Davis calls "forced entrepreneurialism."[109]

On a Mechanical Turk coffee mug it reads: "Why work if you can
turk?" suggesting that crowdwork for Amazon does not even feel like
work. And who would do it if it'd feel like exploitation? Net critic
and consultant Clay Shirky suggested that much and the CEO of
Amazon Mechanical Turk posed that workers can vote with their feet
if they don't approve of their pay; they have a choice.

But for some workers toiling in the platform economy is about
"Zugzwang." "Zugzwang" in chess, means that no matter what the
players' next move will be – and a move she has to make – there are
not any good options. Here is how a crowdworker on Mechanical
Turk describes "free choice:"

> *I don't know about where you live, but around here even McDonald's
> and Walmart are NOT hiring. I have a degree in accounting and cannot
> find a real job, so to keep myself off of the street I work 60 hours or
> more a week here on MTurk just to make $150–$200. That is far below*

*minimum wage, but it makes the difference between making my rent
and living in a tent.*[110]

At first, it appears as if contingent workers have unlimited flexibility
when it comes to the days and even hours of the day that they wish
to work. But in reality, they need to be continuously glued to their
computer screens to be able to catch and respond to higher paying
tasks. On the other hand, they could use scripts to parse out those
tasks or they could pass up such opportunities altogether without
losing the ability to continue to work on AMT. Systemically, working
for Amazon is hardly a choice. You might ask how a rich country
like the United States can tolerate the very real cruelty in the hustler
economy, its wage heft and pay of $2 or $3 an hour. Demands to
shut down Mechanical Turk are understandably rejected by many
Turkers but it is not only them who are hurt by Mechanical Turk, it
is workers all across the economy who feel the impact of this template
of work.

Toward decent digital work

Which questions about the future of digital work are getting asked?
Which ones are never posed? What would decent digital labor and
positive platforms look like? In 2013, in San Antonio, Texas, a group
of American computer scientists from universities including Stanford,
Carnegie Mellon, New York University, and Harvard, presented a
paper with the title "The Future of Crowd Work." It started with a
striking question: "Can we foresee a future crowd workplace in
which we would want our children to participate?"

Imagining a positive future for paid crowdsourcing, Aniket Kittur
and his co-authors ask how crowdwork could become sustainable,
valuable, and pride-worthy. The authors suggest that "while not all
jobs are amenable to being sent down a wire, there are portions of
almost any job that can be performed by the crowd." It's a market
with tremendous career opportunities for improving productivity,
social mobility, and the global economy, they write, then quoting
one CEO whose company uses Amazon Mechanical Turk: "We estimate saving 50% [on AMT] over other outsourcing methods."[111]
Crowdwork "has the potential to support a flexible workforce and
mitigate challenges such as shortages of experts in specific areas (e.g.,
IT work) or geographical locations."

But Kittur and his co-authors also see the negative tendencies such
as the fact that most crowdsourcing is a cul de sac for the careers of

workers. Crowdwork, they admit, may "replace some forms of skilled labor with unskilled labor as tasks are decomposed into smaller and smaller pieces." They write:

> We foresee a serious risk that crowd work will fall into an intellectual framing focused on low-cost results and exploitative labor. With diminished visibility and communication channels vis-à-vis traditional workplaces, workers may be treated as exchangeable and untrustworthy, having low or static skill sets, and strong motivations to shirk. Workers may become equally cynical, having fewer bonds, enforceable contracts, and power than with traditional workplaces.

Far from being merely an intellectual framing, exploitation and the lack of deep solidarity are, as I demonstrated, a reality for much of digital work. The paper by Kittur and his colleagues suggests "*Such concerns may grow ever sharper unless this trajectory is somehow altered.*"

Kittur's San Antonio paper proposes interventions in areas like workflow, task assignment, hierarchy, synchronous collaboration, quality control, better interaction with "requesters," job design, reputation management, pay, and worker motivation. What this does not address is the more fundamental question of ownership and democratic governance. Like some of the literature in sociology and anthropology, the authors propose the fine-tuning of the crowdsourcing ecosystem with the goal of a well-functioning, efficient, and harmonious system as if such fine-tuning is a predominantly technical concern and not a problem inherent in extractive platform capitalism. Beyond this study, there is much ethnographic research that is dedicated to the ecosystem of MTurk. Research questions include: What motivates MTurkers to pick up a task? What are the motivations, hierarchies, and power dynamics in this socio-technical system? How can we better support the future of crowdsourcing? Which individuals and institutions are involved? How do crowdworkers communicate and collaborate?[112] How can spaceship crowdsourcing be optimized?

Kittur and his colleagues ask:

> What new services, systems or features are needed for a future of crowd work that the reader would be proud to see his or her children take on as their livelihood? Is this a desirable path for the next generation?[113]

Tying in neatly with the Silicon Valley ideology of changing the world one app at a time, they propose that "better services, systems, and features are apparently the new markers for the future of crowd-work." The "Future of Work" paper notably ignores the cruel realities of capitalism; it mistakes social problems for design challenges. Perfect design features will not stop platform capitalists from exploiting the overabundance of vulnerable workers. While the paper does also discuss some worker-centric questions like the issue of professional satisfaction and long-term commitment to employers, its answers are firmly techno-centric. The shortcomings of paid crowd-work cannot be rectified through new tools and technical systems alone. The future of work is not solely determined by ever more intelligent techno-organizational changes, it is about a democracy that ought to regulate such work, a democratic society that does not tolerate exploitation, and that encourages cooperation.

In American discourse, "decent, good work" usually connotes work that is executed to the satisfaction of the employer. As you'll see from what follows, the European understanding differs quite a bit. For the German service worker union ver.di, good work is about job security, protection against arbitrary behavior, good pay, a pleasant working atmosphere, a weekly work time of 30–40 hours (depending on life situation), harmony between work and life, at least partial flexibility in terms of the location and time of the work, challenging tasks, acknowledgement and appreciation, chances for future development, possibilities to contribute and be heard, and the protection of bodily and psychological health.[114] It's a call for the humanization of digital work.

On the municipal level, Seattle allowed Uber drivers to unionize, but on the federal level, policy makers increasingly legitimize the political elite that solely draws on the competencies of external experts leaving citizens, workers, and consumers with a feeling of shared powerlessness. The whistleblowers of labor, the tweeting Uber drivers, the Cassandras of twenty-first century work, need to be protected from employers and this protection needs to be anchored in law. Policymakers need to support efforts to harness the risks of mobile, digital, and self-employed work. The right to point out significant violations of legal statutes needs to be cemented in legal structures. Good digital work needs to improve possibilities for legal recourse and class action suits. The punishment of employers who violate labor law is essential. Companies like Mechanical Turk need to make the quality of the work front and center and acknowledge the qualifications of their workers.

Beyond the darkness of digital labor lies its promise. The gains from these new forms of organizing economic activity should not only be left to platform capitalists. Decent digital work leads to a better life for everybody along the supply chains and the digital laborers. The future of crowdwork must not simply be about a sea-change in Human Resources Divisions; it is not merely about an optimization of crowdwork. It is about a society that fosters more visibility and dignity for digital workers. Instead of relying on intelligent algorithms, we need to address the plumbing of the system to create fair digital workplaces.

2

Playbor and Other Unpaid Pursuits

Poem: 'Visions of Labour'
Lawrence Joseph
I will have writings written all over it
in human words: wrote Blake. A running
form, Pound's Blake: shouting, whirling
his arms, his eyes rolling, whirling like flaming
cartwheels. Put it this way, in this language:
a blow in the small of the back from a rifle butt,
the crack of a blackjack on a skull, face
beaten to a pulp, punched in the nose
with a fist, glasses flying off, 'fuckin' Wobblie
wop, hit him again for me,' rifle barrel slammed
against the knees, so much blood in the eyes,
rain, and the night, and the shooting pain
all up and down the spine, can't see. Put it
this way: in the sense of smell is an acrid
odour of scorched metal, in the sense of sound,
the roaring of blow torches. Put it in this
language: labour's value is abstract value,
abstracted into space in which a milling machine
cutter cuts through the hand, the end of her thumb
nearly cut off, metal shavings driven in, rapidly
infected. Put it at this point, the point at which
capital is most inhumane, unsentimental,
out of control: the quantity of human labour in
the digital manufacture of a product is progressing
toward the economic value of zero, the maintenance
and monitoring of new cybernetic processes
occupied by fungible, commodified labour
in a form of indentured servitude. Static model,

dynamic model, alternate contract environments,
enterprise size and labour market functions,
equilibrium characterisation, elasticity of response
to productivity shocks: the question in this Third
Industrial Revolution is who owns and controls
the data. That's what we're looking at, labour cheap,
replaceable, self-replicating, marginal, contracted out
into smaller and smaller units. Them? Hordes
of them, of depleted economic, social value,
who don't count, in any situation, in anyone's eyes,
and won't count, ever, no matter what happens,
the truth that, sooner than later, they will simply be
eliminated. In Hanover Square, a freezing dawn,
from inside bronze doors the watchman sips
bourbon and black coffee in a paper cup, sees
a drunk or drugged hedge fund boy step over
a passed-out body. A logic of exploitation.
A logic of submission. The word alienation. Eyes
being fixed on mediated screens, in semiotic
labour flow: how many generations between
these States' age of slavery and ours? Makers,
we, of perfectly contemplated machines.
(This poem first appeared in the *London Review of Books*:
www.lrb.co.uk)

Every day, one billion people in advanced economies have between two billion and six billion spare hours among them, writes legal scholar Yochai Benkler.[1] He offers these numbers to demonstrate the huge potential to better humanity through free labor in the information commons, what he labels as commons-based peer production. But it will not come as a surprise that with each search, status update, and tag, the potential to work cooperatively can also be captured by capital. Clay Shirky's thesis of cognitive surplus postulates that economic changes have freed up many hours in a day and that each generation has found different ways of investing this free time.[2] For newly industrialized London, he writes, the solution was gin, while in the United States of the 1980s, people stuck to sitcoms. Today, Shirky suggests, it is the Internet. For him, this generation's cognitive surplus is no longer completely wasted. Now, people can make and share things; just think about the millions of hours that went into editing Wikipedia; 35,000 editors worked on the English version alone. Or consider the hours spent on extractive social networking services every day; we are moved into the working position: "Sisyphus might have ultimately been convinced to pay a monthly fee for the pleasure of pushing that rock up the hill," as Scott Rettberg remarked.[3]

Italian media theorist Franco 'Bifo' Berardi expresses a sense of possibility and danger by pointing to the significant expansion in average labor time through the 1980s and 1990s. He adds that a major effect of technological and organizational transformation of the productive process in the last two decades of the twentieth century opens completely new perspectives for self-realization and new energies for the valorization of capital.[4] The economist Yann Moulier Boutang invites us to think of Google as a beekeeper while the cultural critic and curator Suely Rolnik describes data labor as surrender to a procurer or a pimp.

Internet culture fostered the sharing of data and "value creation takes place outside [of the] direct productive processes [of society]," as Italian theorist and activist Tiziana Terranova noted in 2000.[5] Referring to Mario Tronti, who wrote about the concept of the "social factory," she describes outernets of production that reach much further than digital labor. And indeed, we are caught in these nets daily: from the self-checkout in the grocery or hardware store, the check-in at the airport, to the pesky self-assembly of furniture.

Many of the practices that I introduce in this chapter overlap with traditional economies of unpaid work, especially less visible forms of domestic labor that were traditionally considered women's labor, including housework and various forms of caregiving.

Overview

1) Data labor
2) The development of an ecosystem of digital work
3) The performance of self
   • Data coupling
   • Intellectual property
   • Geospatial labor
   • Terms of service
4) Free labor is not the problem
   • Crisis mapping
5) Hybrid public/private business models
   • Tagging and curation
6) Hope labor
   • The Huffington Post
   • Interns
   • Reviewers
   • CAPTCHAs
7) Gamification

8)   Fan labor
9)   Universal Basic Income

This chapter contributes to a typology of forms of unremunerated digital work: the data labor, performance of self on social networking services, hope labor, the "laborization" of games, fan labor, unpaid internships, the Internet of Things, and the cognitive exertion that fuels Google's reCAPTCHAs, and virtual volunteering. The chapter explores the tension between self-realization, the public spiritedness of networked peer production, and the valorization and extraction of this labor through capital.

1) Data Labor

We only see and value work that conforms to our mental models of what work is. How we think about and conceptualize work has real consequences for what is seen and valued as work.[6]

Only few people would think that working for Amazon Mechanical Turk or Uber does not constitute labor. Far fewer observers, however, are willing to categorize day-to-day participation on social media as labor. But that is also changing; ethnographers and computer scientists like Andrew Crabtree realize that they have to revise what constitutes work; it can no longer solely reflect the traditional workplace, they have to consider actions and interactions, wherever they occur.[7]

Once I came across a story about Isaac Newton, the inventor of the electrostatic generator, in which he allegedly used visitors to his residence to generate electricity. Each guest when opening his garden door had to push hard to open the gate and would thus generate a bit of electricity for the Newton residence.

Today's social media platforms are similarly extractive in nature, leading the Brazilian cultural critic Suely Rolnik to suggest that we are surrendering voluntarily to a pimp, becoming the very creators and constructors of the world fabricated by and for a new-style capitalism.[8] Indeed, data labor, while predominantly enjoyed, is turning us into extras of platform capitalism, taking hold of our vitality, desire, eroticism, and time.

Self-mining sits skin deep; our online identity, so eagerly performed, has a curious afterlife in faraway data centers where subjectivities and data are turned into monetary value. Without being recognized as labor, our location, expressions, and time spent on the network can be turned into economic value. With the instruments of commercial surveillance out of sight, our data remain out of our reach. The tracking and monetization of users is frequently justified with the significant operating costs of platform operators. It is unclear, however, what exactly is recorded, how its value is measured, to whom it is sold, and for what purpose. How exactly this is done and what precisely is extracted is a trade secret, inaccessible even to those who follow the technology sector closely.

However, some of the details of the mechanics of data collection are widely known. It is no secret that a Google search on my personal computer will lead to different results than a search for the same terms on someone else's laptop, for instance. In the *Filter Bubble: What the Internet Is Hiding from You*, tech entrepreneur and author Eli Pariser describes how Google's algorithms determine the advertisements that the company deems to be most agreeable to individual users based on their search history. We are becoming Google's agent, fine-tuning their product, making it more relevant to us and by extension more profitable for them.

Digital labor is like a meeting with free pizza and soda but the Stasi is listening in.

While our participation is also about genuine, valuable connection to friends and colleagues; for the emotionally needy, participation can lead to the temporary gratification through "likes," regrams, and comments. "Most users quickly appreciate that there is no free ride in digital networks," writes Ulises Mejias, "we pay for free" services every time there is an ad on a page.... However, most of us are happy to be such products, given what we perceive to receive in return. Participation in digital networks is not coercive in a straightforward manner.[9]

There are also benefits of an online writing practice. Blogging, as much as writing book reviews promotes a writing practice. Lawrence Lessig points out that "with a practice of writing comes a certain important integrity. A culture filled with bloggers thinks differently about politics or public affairs, if only because more have been forced through the discipline of showing in writing why A leads to B."[10]

But despite these benefits, the social costs of convenience and ease of use are sneaking up on us, if only over the long haul – not unlike smoking or eating vast amounts of white bread. The data-mined crowd is producing a set of behavioral data without their explicit knowledge.[11] Big data help to predict consumptive behavior; Walmart, for instance, already knows that after the next hurricane, strawberry pop-tarts will be in high demand.[12] Facebook, in a similar way, uses collected data to extract insights into behavioral patterns, likes, and moods. The connection between our various bits of information could eventually influence our credit score, which might then cause the algorithms of dating sites to behave differently.

Already in the early 2000s, the artist Burak Arikan playfully called attention to the financialization of online activities. His project Meta-Markets[13] is a virtual stock market for the trading of social media assets. Participants submit the login details for their profiles on social media platforms and the site then translates these "assets" (i.e., photos, posts) into stocks that can be traded in "Burak," the in-market currency.

Life today is reduced to work and a timeline on Facebook. In pursuit of micro-celebrity – our 15 Megabytes of fame – we comment, share, tag, link, chat, forward, read, subscribe, re-post, and "favorite" to keep the digital stream in motion. (Some of these activities should have never been turned into verbs.) In turn, our commitment is prodding others to join. While being stripped of ever more of their disposable time, most cognitive workers never take issue with their unpaid toil. As the meme goes: If the service is free, you are the product.

Yann Moulier Boutang wonders if performing searches and toiling in the capturing apparatus of the knowledge factory, does not turn us into worker bees for Google, which depends on our pollination. Millions of people are clicking and feeding data to Google – "the true paradigm of people working for the firm."[14] When will the pollination become intolerable? "How can the bees be freed from the beekeeper?," Boutang asks. Or, will Google eventually eat itself, in a scenario proposed by some artists?[15]

It is not surprising that social media "users" are sighing with exhaustion. Millennials started leaving Facebook some time ago when their parents came on board; despite the Messenger App, a growing number of fake profiles, and a supposedly new "weird Facebook" (complete with meme pages), they can't be bothered to tune in. They are fed up with all the anxiety, mild depression, and interpassive boredom; the imperative of being moved by what moved others and the filtering of their day-to-day life for the suitable and institutionally appropriate states of mind that can find resonances in the real-time stream.

2) The Development of an Ecosystem of Digital Work

At the Internet as Playground and Factory conference[16] in 2009, I pointed out that online, play has become important in terms of work, and that Internet users – to use the dreaded term – appoint themselves as unpaid workers who take on the maintenance of their own identity.

Historically, platform capitalism intensified in the run up to the financial collapse of 2008, hallmarked by imaginative ways of motivating and manufacturing online communities. Google collects data that are in reach of its algorithmic tentacles to then sell them to their clients, which are ad agencies.

The ecosystem of data labor kicked off with ARPANET in 1969. Originally, the network was made for time-sharing, not communication; its purpose was to broaden access to extremely bulky and expensive computers. Mail was a tiny, peripheral feature that would allow programmers to communicate with each other to fix bugs, and yet, completely unexpectedly, it spread like "plankton on the Internet."[17] A network sponsored by the military and academia had become the tool for human chatter.[18]

Email quickly took up most of the bandwidth on the Internet. In 1981, an ARPANET completion report concluded that "the largest single surprise of ARPANET has been the popularity and success of network mail."[19] Access to people was the most sought-after affordance of the Internet from its inception.

But data labor is also predicated on access to hardware; the first PC was shipped in the early 1980s. One of the first experiments with the monetization of online sociality was Lucasfilm's Habitat, an online role-playing game where players could get married, play games, go on adventures, found religions, wage wars, and protest against them.[20] The makers of Habitat, Chip Morningstar and F. Randall Farmer faced criticisms about the trivial nature of communication in the game, but as it turned out, players were willing to pay for virtual togetherness, no matter how trivial the content really was. The biggest surprise was that users were willing to pay for these trivial exchanges.

Access to hardware was not the only precondition for the ecosystem of data labor. Another essential step was the creation of one unified communication interface that would cut through the chaos of communication on the Internet (e.g., FTP, Telnet, or Gopher). These were (and partially are) protocols that allow Internet users to communicate with one another. The World Wide Web, created by Tim Berners-Lee in 1989/1990 was that interface, and Mosaic became the first user-friendly browser. Without the accessibility of PCs, affordable Internet connections, a decent browser, and the united interface of the World Wide Web, digital labor would not have been as instrumental for platform capitalism.

3) The Performance of Self

Rob Hornig, writer and editor of the online magazine *The New Inquiry*, wrote:

> *Constructing our identity and duplicating our social networks in online platforms has become a kind of capitalist production, effacing the old boundaries between "work" and "life" that structured the idea of leisure time.*[21]

The pressure is on; simply being professionally competent is no longer sufficient. One's private life ought to become "normcore," just like the fashion trend that boosts unpretentious and average-looking clothing. Our presentation of self has to demonstrate just the right mix of servility and rebellion, strategically tailored to fit not only the expectations of the job market, but also those of friends and thousands of other viewers.

Daily activities like emails, status updates, and tweets – the performance of the "publicizable personality," as Alice Marwick put it – are not widely enough acknowledged as labor. "Achieved microcelebrity," she writes, "is a self-presentation strategy that includes creating a persona, sharing personal information about oneself, constructing intimate connections to create the illusion of friendship or closeness, acknowledging an audience and identifying them as fans, and strategically revealing information to increase or maintain this audience."[22] "Authenticity" then becomes key to attracting a large number of fans/followers.

Appropriate emotions lubricate these social milieus; public identity has to come across as dynamically upbeat, emotionally balanced, confident, verbally richly expressive, internationalized, attractive, and aggressively ambitious. In his book *24/7: Late Capitalism and the Ends of Sleep*, Jonathan Crary discusses how all facets of individual experience are "continuous and compatible with the requirements of accelerated 24/7 consumerism." Everything "becomes culturally figured as software or content detachable from the self, [it becomes] something that might be circulated electronically," he writes.[23] Relationships and professional linkages are put on public display while noonday demons are too often kept in the closet. On Instagram and Vine, snapshots make it look like we only set foot into the most picturesque landscapes on this planet and family life is portrayed as either non-existent or as a state of endless harmony. Who can afford to make themselves vulnerable in this regime of lateral surveillance where friends and bosses intermingle? This can lead to a kind of unfailing niceness that is always in control, spelling out nothing but bored perfection.

The artist Julien Deswaef created the software project "[loveMachine]," which pushes the social media affirmation game to its logical conclusion: Once linked to your Facebook account, it simply clicks all "like" buttons that are available on the timeline.[24]

In *The Managed Heart* and *The Commercialization of Intimate Life*, renown sociologist Arlie Hochschild describes how emotions are becoming important economic resources, core skills in the labor market.[25,26] Emotional labor, for Hochschild, is the attempt to call up, amplify, and alter emotions in order to adapt to societal and professional norms, leading to institutional success. Traditionally associated with nurses, secretaries, and restaurant workers, I expand the term emotional labor to also include the management of emotions so that they are consistent with the unspoken imperatives of platforms.

> *Why, generally speaking, do people feel gay at parties, sad at funerals, happy at weddings? This question leads us to examine, not conventions of outward comportment, but conventions of feelings.*[27]

Jonathan Crary, again, comments succinctly:

> *Now there are numerous pressures for individuals to reimagine and reconfigure themselves as being of the same consistency and values as the dematerialized commodities and social connections in which they are immersed so extensively. Reification has processed to the point where the individual has to invent a self-understanding that optimizes or facilitates their participation in digital milieus and speeds.*

The "situations" for expression have changed. The experimentation with identity on the Internet that was thriving in the early 1990s is long gone. Today, the all-time, best-selling cartoon of The New Yorker: "On the Internet, nobody knows you're a dog," published in 1993, looks like an artifact from your grandparents' photo album. Now, rather than experimentation, identity forking gets the upper hand. Under the auspices of Facebook, we express ourselves differently than in the presence of close friends at the kitchen table.

Data coupling

The biggest threat of surveillance capitalism lies in the connection between our various data sets. Beyond the hold of data labor on our performance of self, citizens also lend their medical information to research databases that have significant commercial potential. Now, data labor is also about "clinical labor," with Apple's Health applications[28] and devices like Fitbit. Now you can even buy Band-Aids embedded with circuitry that can analyze and communicate your blood pressure and glucose levels. Such data can now join the flow of connected information that also includes data from your subway card, credit card, Amazon account, Google search history, and location. This changes not only the future of consumption but also that of dating and most other areas of life. Daniel Solove, a leading expert in information privacy law, wrote:

> Combine all of the information available about people on the Internet – some of it true, some of it false, with our insatiable curiosity and desire to glean information about others, and some troubling implications emerge. Increasingly, information fragments about people on the Internet are used to make judgments about them.[29]

In his novel *Super Sad True Love Story*, the American novelist Gary Shteyngart evoked a near-future dating scene that pushes data labor to its logical conclusion. The mobile device of the future, which Shteyngart calls the äppärät, not only measures one's heart rate and conveys it to a prospective dating partner who may reciprocate such bio-transparency, it also cross-links such bio data with an analysis of the person's social media output that is translated into a "personality score." There is a count for "male hotness," and overall "fuckability," as Shteyngart puts it. The äppärät also reveals political leanings, medical conditions, parental ailments, a five-year income average, as well as outstanding liabilities.

> *"You look at a girl. The EmotePad picks up any change in your blood pressure. That tells her how much you want to do her."*
> *"Here, let me see your profile."*
> *Vishnu slid some other functions, and my profile shimmered on my warm pebbly screen.*
> *LENNY ABRAMOV ZIP code 10002, New York, New York.... Consumer profile: heterosexual, nonathletic, nonautomotive, nonreligious, non-Bipartisan. Sexual preferences: low-functioning Asian/ Korean and White/Irish American with Low Net Worth family background; child-abuse indicator: on; low-self-esteem indicator: on. Last purchases: bound, printed, nonstreaming media artifact, 35 northern euros; bound, printed,...[30]*

Shteyngart doesn't only paint a plausible picture of the near-future of dating, he also understands data labor, and the intricate linkage between our health data and other information on centralized private servers. Already today, the potential is jaw-dropping for targeted drug advertisement or forcibly adjusted health insurance policies based on your data. If you have "perfect data," why would you not share them with your health insurance provider; they might lower your premium. The implications for those who do not step forward – the losers of the biometrics data game – will be severe.

Intellectual property

While platform owners from Facebook to Google and Instagram all claim ownership of our so-called "user-submitted content," their business model does not depend on selling your photos or intellect to the highest bidders. On a practical level, the ownership of submitted content matters because owners need to be able to remove material that violates their terms of service such as pornography. An entire subset of workers, distributed all over the world, filters "dick pics" and beheadings on Facebook.[31] But ultimately, Facebook does not care about your post outlining an exegesis of Trotsky. Understood in this way, intellectual property is not at the heart of the discussion about data labor because platform owners do not depend on directly selling your knowledge labor or creative designs; they rather monetize your linked data and interstitial, personalized advertisements. While Instagram has used photographs to advertise its service, this is hardly their core business model. The density of connectivity and information created by millions of users on social networking services keeps them with the service; network power is great, subtly producing economic value.

My comment about intellectual property only focuses on the fact that all too often, commentators pretend that extractive platforms care about the intellectual value of content shared on those platforms, but they do not. In aggregate it does care about the attention that your piece will garner; it contributes to the lure of the platform. Facebook has become a cultural center where resident workers are the engineers of their own entertainment. They are using Facebook for "free" while consuming a culture of their own making.[32]

You may also remember that Linden Labs, the company behind the virtual world SecondLife (SL), handed over the intellectual property rights of the resident's virtual creations in SL to the users, which sounded good, but this act of corporate goodwill was of little real consequence as residents could not seamlessly migrate their creative expressions out of this enclosure. And then in 2013 Linden Labs changed its terms of service so that it could use resident-generated content in whichever way it pleases.

Author and professor of Latin American Studies George Yúdice notes that "profits are made by holding property rights; those who do not hold these rights...are relegated to working for hire as content and service providers."[33]

> *The more Google knows about us, the better it can sell that information to people who want to target ads at us. The hegemony of networks is insidiously evident in examples such as this one in which participation is presented as a fait accompli, in the absence of options and alternatives, and as an almost naturalized form of commodification in which a social act (send email to students to colleagues) is transformed into a revenue-generating opportunity for a corporation almost invisibly.*[34]

I agree with Yúdice and in chapter 7 I will make the argument for the importance of collective (platform) ownership.

Geospatial labor

Data labor is not only about your social liaisons, it includes your movement. Your mobile devices – the iPhone, RFID-enabled passport, "smart watch," Nabaztag, Fitbit, or Jawbone – may connect to a local wireless network and emit data, reporting on your whereabouts. I refer to it as geospatial labor.

In 2013, Edward Snowden, a former system administrator for the Central Intelligence Agency and infrastructure analyst for NSA contractor Booz Allen Hamilton, provided evidence for the overwhelmingly pervasive and indiscriminate mass surveillance conducted by the US government via the Internet. Snowden posed that "Arguing that you don't care about the right to privacy because you have nothing to hide is no different than saying you don't care about free speech because you have nothing to say."[35] The larger objective of this surveillance became clear when CIA chief technology officer Guss Hunt stated that "it is nearly within their grasp to compute on all human-generated information" and that "fundamentally [the CIA is aiming] to collect everything and hang on to it forever."[36]

One would have had to lead a Kaspar Hauser-esque existence not to be affected by this. One rarely discussed group of profiteers is the telcos who are selling customer data – including your real-time movement – to government agencies. Already in 2009, the American telecommunications company Sprint had created a website allowing law enforcement to track the location data of its wireless customers for only $30 a month. It was able to offer this service at such a discount because it had eight million requests in that year alone.[37] Did law enforcement have warrants for all these eight million requests?

The military has been using GPS tracking devices for many years in submarines and on airplanes. It started with sailors who needed to be pinpointed to allow for rescue missions. In the civilian market, the tracking of pets and livestock is the most common application thus far. All of these technologies are ultimately framed as pervasive or ubiquitous computing, location-based media, or simply locative media, urban computing, or ambient informatics. The "Internet of Things" is an assembly of a bundle of distinct technologies – sensors, code, etc. – at the intersection of the Internet and the built environment.

An ad by IBM shows a globe, covered with glittery dust, with each particle being made up of sensors, all connected to the Internet, communicating with one another. With The Internet of Things, even your cat, dog, car, fridge, and washing machine can now join the grand data swap.

One of the technologies that facilitates the data rendezvous of geospatial labor is Radio Frequency Identification (RFID). Walmart could not do without it because all its products are tagged with RFID so they can be scanned from a distance.[38] That is possible because computers can recognize RFID-carrying objects and people.

Companies like Petsmobility.com and RFIDpet.com allow customers to introduce invisible fences so that fewer cats and dogs end up in shelters.[39] DigitalAngel.com takes that logic to seniors with Alzheimer's disease.[40] You can track your child on the playground or your teenager after school. "It's 10 pm. Do you know where your children are?" For the right price, you can track your teen and even monitor how fast they drive. RetailNext uses data from the smart phones of consumers to identify returning customers and analyze the time between visits. Companies are also tracking the movement of shoppers in their stores, and even some coffee stores are measuring the signals between smartphones of passersby and Wi-Fi antennas to determine how many of them are actually entering their stores. In one country, the satellite car-navigation company TomTom faced bankruptcy and decided to sell the driving data of its customers to the police.[41] The EZPass, MasterCard's PayPass, FastTrack, TxTag, and other systems automatically collect tolls on highways or bridges.[42] Movement generates data that are then harvested and translated into profits: geospatial labor.

Terms of service

Contract law, the terms of service to which we have to agree when starting to use a platform, often do not offer meaningful protection for the user. In her book *Boilerplate: The Fine Print, Vanishing Rights, and the Rule of Law*, legal scholar Margaret Jane Radin argues that we underestimate the risks of clicking "I agree."

> *Is a firm justified in concluding that by clicking "I agree" the recipient actually is consenting to be bound to its terms?*
>
> *Those who click are almost certainly not thinking about, or intending to consent to unread – or, even if read, not understood – terms that may deprive them of important legal rights that they might not know they have and probably don't consciously think they will ever need. Heuristic biases, which apparently are powerful and not readily escapable, tend to make us underestimate risks to ourselves and fail to consider situations that may result in future harm.*[43]

The Terms of Use of online intermediaries are marked by a take-it-or-leave-it attitude, which means that when you click that "agree" button, you really do submit yourself in the most vulnerable sense of the word. Some companies even allow unilateral amendments – allowing them to change the agreement at any time without the user's consent. In 2012, for instance, Instagram controversially changed its terms of use to say: "you agree that a business or other entity may pay us to display your username, likeness, photos (along with any associated metadata), and/or actions you take, in connection with paid or sponsored content or promotions, without any compensation to you."[44]

4) Free Labor is not the Problem

> *Free labor is only problematic under conditions of precarity and non-reciprocal value capture…under conditions of social solidarity, the freely given participation in common value projects is a highly emancipatory activity.*[45]

> *Work isn't only a side of exploitation, domination, and antagonism, but also where we might find the power to create alternatives on the basis of subordinated knowledges, resistant subjectivities, and emergent models of organization.*[46]

In chapter 7, I will discuss the information commons and platform cooperativism to show that digital labor can indeed be redeeming, that work online, paid or uncompensated, can also be fair and beneficial. Like Yochai Benkler, I am optimistic about commons-based peer production and platform co-ops as realistic pathways to a culture that is more democratic, co-determined, and fair. At the same time, we also need to acknowledge that, right now, captured and exploited digital labor is the norm rather than an aberration.[47]

If the German photographer August Sander were alive today, he would have to include digital work in his series *People of the 20th Century*. And the French philosopher of the Enlightenment Denis Diderot would have to add volumes to his *Encyclopédie*.

Free labor itself is not a problem outside of extractive platform capitalism; it can in fact be a site of resistant subjectivities and emerging forms of solidarity. My own proposal of cooperative ownership models on the Internet, formulated in chapter 7, adds to this vision of the Internet as a commons, theorized by Michel Bauwens (*P2P Foundation*), David Bollier (*Viral Spiral*), Yochai Benkler (*Wealth of Networks*), and many others.

Various platforms and projects support citizen or governmental initiatives that aim to orchestrate and channel everything from civic crowd funding to information crowdsourcing, sharing among peers, democratic decision making, and data access. Projects include FixMyStreet, SeeClickFix, Lendoo.com, Kiva, and tools coming out of Civic Hall[48] in NYC and the Center for Civic Media at MIT, to name but a few.[49]

In 2015, artist Golan Levin and developer David Newbury called on creative volunteers to contribute a drawing to their Moon Arts Project.[50] Golan Levin prompted prospective participants by stating: "your doodle will be etched on a sapphire disc, sent to the (real!) Moon, and potentially traced by a rover into the Moon's soil – where it will remain for millennia!" To be sure, such virtual volunteering has a much longer history.

As early as in 2000, Distributed Proofreaders started to provide error markup support for e-text publications by Project Gutenberg (PG), which transfers public domain books into digital format. Distributed Proofreaders, while not directly associated with Project Gutenberg, is assisting PG with the creation of proofread versions of scanned books. Books are scanned, analyzed with Optical Character Recognition, and then converted into text characters. To date, Distributed Proofreaders has helped to publish over 28,000 books.[51]

Volunteer crowd work, however, has also been put to controversial use. An infamous example is the Blueservo/Texas Virtual Border Watch. In 2008, a company called BlueServo introduced real-time crowdsourced surveillance of the Texan border with Mexico supported by a $2 million grant from Republican Governor Rick Perry. "Virtual deputies" monitored CCTV cameras, installed all along the border region and anonymously reported sightings of undocumented immigrants to the United States Border Patrol. Two years after its inception, participation in the site dwindled and the site was shut down.[52]

Crisis Mapping (Ushahidi), Co-Research (FoldIt!, eBird)

The mapping project Ushahidi (Swahili for "testimony" or "witness") was designed by a not-for-profit company in Kenya. Ushahidi is a free and open source crisis mapping software tool that uses the organizational logic of crowdsourcing for social activism.

To make aid efforts easier, Ushahidi allows large crowds of participants to contribute eyewitness accounts of conflicts such as the 2014 attack on the Westgate Mall in Nairobi, Kenya, or the 2010 earthquake in Haiti, and then visualize them on a Google map. Local observers can report election fraud or text-in verified reports of violence. Ushahidi analyzes these reports and once it has two verified accounts of the same incident, it adds them to the map.

Crowdmap, another platform built by the Ushahidi team, allows users to set up their own instances of Ushahidi. The global Occupy movement was one of the deployments of Crowdmap.[53]

While not primarily based on crisis management, Open Street Maps[54] is also a collaborative mapping project. The ambitious goal of this "co-researching project" is to create a free map of the world that can be edited.

Open Street Maps makes free geo-data available, which then allow the creation of maps that can be used for navigation. Sometimes local contributors organize mapping parties as part of which data about pubs, schools, or hospitals in a specific area are collected and then collectively entered into the Open Street Map Database.[55]

Other examples of such co-researching/citizen science initiatives include GalaxyZoo, EyeWire, Linux, Wikipedia, Science Commons, NASA's Clickworkers, Challenge.org, and GuttenPlag. Discussing all of the examples is beyond the scope of this chapter.

FoldIt! is one such crowdsourcing initiative. It started with the work of the biochemist David Baker who also founded Rosetta@home, an adaptation of a distributed computing software created at the University of California Berkeley in 2002. The goal of Rosetta was to solve challenges in the understanding of protein folds. Initially, the public was able to contribute by lending the computing power of personal computers to the project. Participants install a small piece of software, which put the unused computing power of a PC to work for a given project. But to Baker's surprise, people wrote to scientists proposing solutions to structure of proteins that they had found on their own. This led Baker to collaborate with programmers to develop FoldIt!, an online puzzle video game about protein folding. Developed at the University of Washington Center for Game Science, the objective of the game is to fold the structure of selective proteins using various tools provided within the game. Later, researchers analyze the highest scoring solutions to determine if these structural configurations could be applied to actual existing proteins. Such folding solutions by the more than 57,000 players could help scientists to design new proteins to fight HIV, cancer, and Alzheimer's disease, outperforming also algorithmically generated solutions.

eBird. Another project that makes inspiring use of unpaid volunteer labor is eBird. It is a collaborative endeavor between the Lab of Ornithology at Cornell University and the National Audubon Society, which furthers ornithological research by incorporating the observations of birdwatchers worldwide who document the presence of particular species at their location. One objective of the crowdsourcing and citizen science project is to make the submitted data useable for bird enthusiasts all over the world. As of July 2013, over 100,000 unique users have contributed more than 100,000,000 observations of more than 10,240 different species of birds.[56] Another significant citizen science project that originated at Cornell is YardMap,[57] which "collects data by asking individuals across the country to literally draw maps of their backyards, parks, farms, favorite birding locations, schools, and gardens."

5) Hybrid Public/Private Business Models

Tagging and Curation: Flickr Commons and The Library of Babel Reddit

The Library of Babel Reddit is a hybrid, commercial but "public-leaning" project. It is extractive in the sense that Reddit is a commercial platform. Unlike FoldIt or eBird, it's a quirky literary experiment inspired by The Library of Babel by J. L. Borges. It is an experiment with letters, a museum of the written word where anyone can post random strings of letters, copied and pasted from around the Internet, written as if it was a diary.[58] "In essence, it is the futile attempt to recreate the Library in its infinity. A place where all text is possible."[59] Spelling errors are welcome.

Flickr, an image-hosting service owned by Yahoo, had 87 million subscribed members in 2013. In 2014, its revenue reached an estimated $4.618 billion.[60] Only four years prior to that, Flickr started the Flickr Commons in collaboration with several museums and archives including the Smithsonian and the Library of Congress. Yahoo hosts largely unseen images that are under a "no known restrictions" license. Flickr Commons solves two problems: it hosts the images and makes them available to the public online, but most importantly, it makes them findable because in the absence of descriptive metadata, images online cannot be easily discovered by image searches. The data labor – the tagging or curation – that volunteers are performing is essential for the success of the project as it brings these images into online circulation.

Yet the Flickr Commons is a hybrid project, a collaboration between various public institutions and Yahoo's online media-sharing site. The project simultaneously generates an aura of corporate goodwill and the perception of performing a selfless public service. Contributions by institutions like the Smithsonian attract more visitors to the site.

Other benefits for Flickr include profits from its print service that permits users to order large prints of photographs that are protected by a Creative Commons license (CC). In November 2014, Flickr offered wall-sized prints of CC-licensed photographs for sale with all profits going to Yahoo. While the CC licenses of these photographs explicitly permitted commercial use, photographers did not get paid and a controversy ensued.

6) Hope Labor

In 2013, communication scholars Kathleen Kuehn and Thomas F. Corrigan coined the term "hope labor" to describe "un- or under-compensated work carried out in the present, often for experience or exposure, in the hope that future employment opportunities may follow."[61] It's hard to write about hope labor without thinking about the work of journalists and especially bloggers who are frequently asked to write without getting paid because they would benefit from the exposure.

In 2013, the writer Nathan Thayer was approached by *The Atlantic* to repurpose a piece that he had previously published. After Thayer enquired about being paid, the magazine responded:

> *Thanks for responding. Maybe by the end of the week? 1,200 words? We unfortunately can't pay you for it, but we do reach 13 million readers a month. I understand if that's not a workable arrangement for you, I just wanted to see if you were interested. Thanks so much again for your time. A great piece!*

Thayer then published this conversation, and when asked by *New York* magazine about writing for exposure, Thayer replied: "I don't need the exposure. What I need is to pay my fucking rent. Exposure doesn't feed my fucking children. Fuck that!" he continued, adding that he can't even afford to get online. "I actually stick my fucking computer out the window to use the neighbor's Internet connection. I simply can't make a fucking living."[62]

The Huffington Post

In 2005, Arianna Huffington founded *The Huffington Post*, a news aggregator and blog. The co-founders of the site for left-leaning commentary included Kenneth Lerer, Andrew Breitbart, and the founder of Buzzfeed, Jonah Peretti. As a platform, HuffPo was envisioned as an umbrella under which existing content, such as blog posts, was aggregated. To increase the social capital of the site, Huffington started to invite celebrities like Oprah and then-senator Barack Obama to write for the site. The bloggers and guest writers didn't receive any financial remuneration for their work but all was good in the land of HuffPo until early 2011.

Unexpectedly, Huffington and her investors turned around and sold the company to AOL for $315 million. Huffingon Post is not an exception. When Yahoo acquired Tumblr for over $1 billion, that speculative value was also predicated on the free work of those who write on that platform. Blogger Alex Blagg tweeted "congrats to us all on Yahoo buying our blogs! So will the 1.1. bil be divided up by the followers or 'likes'? Will Tumblr direct deposit us?"

On HuffPo, not only was the sale to AOL an obvious affront to the writers who had not seen a dime for their labor, but also Huffington herself came across as utterly blasé in her response to the outrage of the bloggers. "Go ahead, go on strike," she quipped.

And that is exactly what they did. In February 2011, Visual Arts Source, which had frequently cross-posted material on the site, announced a boycott, and a month later, the strike and call to boycott was joined and endorsed by the National Writers Union and the Newspaper Guild. Just a month after that, the labor rights advocate Jonathan Tassini filed a class action suit asking for $105 million in back wages for the thousands of uncompensated writers. The strike and boycott remained inconsequential and the class action suit was lost as the writers had never been promised any pay. The prominent conservative blogger Andrew Sullivan posed that "Hey, it's a model and it's working. And no one is forced to write for free. If you can make a fortune off people's vanity and desire to express themselves, why not?"[63] If writing for exposure is the expected norm, how are writers supposed to make a living? For Arianna Huffington and her co-founders, to take home a fortune from the labor of the bloggers turned out to be legal, but it was unethical to monetize their support. In April 2016, Huffington joined the board of Uber, now honing her business skills in the transportution sector.

Interns

Hope labor reigns supreme also when it comes to unpaid internships. Internships can be advantageous to both the student and the hosting company. For students, off-campus work/study programs are invaluable but in too many cases they have been shown to be classist and exploitative. The work of the intern, shifted more and more to the Internet, is in many ways speculative; it is hope labor, supposedly a down payment on a job.

But there has been some pushback. In April 2014, Condé Nast settled a lawsuit over unpaid interns, which created a significant backlash for unpaid internships. In June 2013, former *W Magazine* intern Lauren Ballinger and former *New Yorker* intern Matthew Leib filed a lawsuit in federal court in New York arguing that they were paid below minimum wages when working for Condé Nast. The presiding judge ruled that the unpaid interns were indeed employees. While the case was still in progress, Condé Nast decided to discontinue its unpaid intern program.[64]

The number of students attending four-year college courses in the United States equals about 9.5 million and as many as 75 percent of them undertake at least one internship before they graduate.[65] According to one study, 77 percent of unpaid interns are women.[66] And at least in this context, the grass isn't always greener on the European side either. In Germany, for instance, 400,000 unpaid or underpaid academic student assistants work in universities all across the country. They live in hopes of a better tomorrow and if that doesn't come to pass, they are already accustomed to a culture of self-denigration.

New York University sociologist Ross Perlin astutely points to the fact that corporate America enjoys a $2 billion annual subsidy from internships alone. These internships, largely unpaid or underpaid, are often framed as "paying your dues." Unpaid internships can be found not only in the context of for-profit institutions, but also in museums and architecture firms. The question quickly arises: who can possibly afford to work without being paid? Self-exploitation becomes a privilege of the affluent upper middle class with parents subsidizing such free labor. The opportunity to work as an intern, then, is denied to those who cannot afford to work for free over longer stretches of time.

Some universities follow the controversial practice of asking students to pay for the course credits earned through unpaid internships. But in 2014, Columbia University and its partner institutions stopped requiring learners to pay thousands of dollars for the privilege of taking an unpaid internship.[67]

According to Perlin, unpaid internships are about structural discrimination, decreased diversity in terms of class and race, and a lowering of the dignity of the work itself. To describe internships as work that is voluntarily arranged deemphasizes the fact that systemically, there is very little choice about committing to such arrangements.

Online and off, unpaid internships are desired and abhorred. So-called "virtual interns" are physically not present in the office: they are instructed via Skype, SMS, or email. Frequently working in the IT sector, journalism, marketing, or design, they are meant to gain work experience while translating documents, writing articles, or moderating online discussion groups. Virtual internships, while increasingly common, are frequently criticized for not offering the kind of supervision that internships are meant to provide.

Reviewers

And then there are the reviewers on Amazon.com, Yelp, and many other sites. The Amazon review section started with books in 1994 and soon thereafter, a former acquisition librarian from Pennsylvania named Harriet Klausner would become one of its most prolific contributors. Klausner reads two books a day and in the Amazon reviewer community she has a stellar reputation. By December 2015, she had written more than 31014 reviews, which if they were priced at $5 per write-up would add up to more than $155,000. But still, not being paid didn't stop Klausner from thinking of her writing practice as a career. "I watched my book reviewing career begin to take shape," she wrote. And her motivation? "I take immense pleasure in informing other readers about newcomers or unknown authors who have written superb novels...."[68]

In Amazon's old rating system she had gained some notoriety; she was their top reviewer. *The Washington Post* profiled her and she even has her very own Appreciation Society. The praise, perhaps hope labor, the free time, and peer acknowledgement might make it easier to understand why Klausner is so fervently at it, but what motivates reviewer #3467? What do the reviewers in the lower ranks get out of it? What motivates them?

CAPTCHA/reCAPTCHA

Even if you are not already familiar with the term, chances are that you recently used a CAPTCHA to overcome a digital roadblock. CAPTCHAS are designed as hurdles that prompt us to prove that we are indeed human, not hostile spam bots. We are able to decipher text appearing in an image or in sections from books that Google scanners and their optical text recognition systems cannot make sense of. In order to gain access to a particular website, we are performing small acts of labor, contributing to this privately-owned digitization project. In 2004, when the Google Books project (books.google.com) launched, the company argued that it would help to move out-of-print books or those that are already in the public domain into widespread circulation online. Following the logic of Fuster's "wikiwashing,"[69] Google's project gained legitimizing power from its proximity to the Access to Knowledge movement, suggesting that helping Google to digitize the world's knowledge would make it available to all. Today, more than a decade later, Google has indeed scanned over 25 million books[70] but how many freely downloadable public-domain books do you regularly come across on Google Books?

What will stop Google from selling an expensive license for complete access to all digitized books to the highest paying academic institution, let's say Harvard University? In this scenario, less affluent universities would only be granted access to a small portion of all digitized knowledge. Google's exclusive access to the sum of all of human knowledge leaves it wide open to the possibility of mission creep.

Google's reCAPTCHA project describes its objective concisely:

> *Every time our CAPTCHAs are solved, that human effort helps digitize text, annotate images, and build machine learning datasets. This in turn helps preserve books, improve maps, and solve hard AI problems. reCAPTCHA digitizes books by turning words that cannot be read by computers into CAPTCHAs for people to solve. Word by word, a book is digitized and preserved online for people to find and read.*[71]

Luis von Ahn, the Guatemala-born American founder of CAPTCHA and reCAPTCHA, now a professor at Carnegie Mellon University, was directly inspired by spam (porn) companies that were hiring people to fill in captchas, paying them $2.50 an hour.[72] In this way, these companies managed to sneak in through the digital fence, getting access to websites, which they would then curse with their product. The BBC later reported about so-called "CAPTCHA sweat-shops" where workers decode 12 captchas a minute, all day long.[73]

Ahn's latest project, DuoLingo,[74] is taking the unpaid crowd fleecing logic of reCAPTCHAS to crowdsourced language translation. To quote from Federici's Wages for Housework campaign; "They say it is love. We say it is unwaged work."[75]

7) Gamification

Techniques for gamification have been used in the context of physical exercise, employee productivity, and even lifelong learning. In 2015, the government of China gamified obedience to the state by creating a social media tool called Sesame Credit, which gives people a high score for "good citizenship."[76] Silicon Valley's boardrooms were swarming with slideshows evoking the American culture of "fun at work" and people's desire for achievement, competition, and status. Platforms offered so-called leader boards, and the possibility to earn virtual goods or currency, experience points, special badges, or levels. With gamification, the act of labor is hidden behind layers of play. Play-workers are becoming part of a game-inspired choreography of labor. According to legal scholar Miriam Cherry, workers might find that playing a game provides them with a welcome break from tedious repetitive work. Even the most boring jobs, she writes, can fly by if we are with friends and have a "fun attitude" toward an assigned task. Similarly, people might simply believe that they are playing a game when in fact they are really working.[77] The video game designer and researcher Ian Bogost has suggested that the term gamification is nothing but a marketing fad. For Bogost, gamification is "exploitationware."[78]

Gamification is now also taught in business schools. There, it is described as the use of game elements and game design techniques in non-game contexts such as marketing, employee productivity, or customer engagement. Gamification is where Human Resources meets Candy Crush, Farm Heroes, or 8 Ball Pool; how can work be made just as addictive as games? They can't get no satisfaction; they will have to click again. Already Business School students aim to tap deeper into the desires and addictions of the worker to make them work harder and longer.

Gamification has been popular for corporate loyalty programs, such as Foursquare's check-ins at Starbucks or Wholefoods, and more and more enterprises have announced that they will introduce gamification in corporate training and game-based learning.

Crowdsourcing has been gamified in the aforementioned Foldit, aimed at manipulating proteins into more efficient structures. But one of the best examples for the double-edged sword of gamification is the ESP game, which started with a serious problem in computing: generally, computers were able to interpret what is depicted in an image. Luis von Ahn created the ESP game to put people in the position to help out. He called this "human computation." The game became wildly popular, even addictive. Not restrained by embarrassment or guilt, Ahn stated in the 'about' section of the ESP Game that the project "encourage[s] people to work for free by taking advantage of their desire to be entertained."[79]

How did it work? Once logged into the ESP game, two randomly paired players who could not communicate with one another were simultaneously shown the same picture and asked to label it. Each listed a number of words that described the image within a given time limit and was then rewarded with points for a match. The matched term was an accurate description of the image and could be used for more accurate image search technology.

The ESP game lived on, licensed by Google in the form of the Google Image Labeler, from 2006 to 2011. The game was a way for Google to ensure that its keywords were more accurately matched to images. While the unpaid players enjoyed the game, they also unwittingly improved the quality of Google's image search product, thereby benefiting themselves and the company.

In her book *Reality Is Broken Here: Why Games Make Us Better and How They Can Change The World*, the game designer Jane McGonigal advocates the use of games to collaboratively solve real-world problems. She uses the game Chore Wars as an example. Here, players are asked to "recruit a party of adventurers from your household or office, and log your chores to claim experience points for them."[80] Following that same logic, McGonigal suggests that games could transform people's lives, or at least that they could make them *feel* as if they are doing something worthwhile. Commenting on this feel-good aspect of gamification, New School journalism professor Heather Chaplin remarks:

> Why not just shoot them up with drugs so they don't notice how miserable they are? You could argue that peasants in the Middle Ages were happy imagining that the more their lives sucked here on earth, the faster they would make it into heaven. I think they would've been better off with enough to eat and some healthcare.[81]

So far, techniques of gamification have been put more in the service of platform owners than those of regular citizens, consumers, and

players. What would a democratically ruled and player-owned gamification platform look like?

8) Fan Labor

Fan labor refers to the activities of various kinds of devotees, remix-
ing, adapting, or creating mashups of films like *Star Wars*, TV series
such as *Survivor*, games, music, video clips, novels, and more. Fan
fiction, for example, further develops features of the original plot of
commercially produced film and television by expanding the narrative, even adding characters or introducing different settings.

Franchises seek to integrate their most devoted consumers and fans
on their platforms by allowing them to create their own content while
the franchise still retains the copyright of the generated material.
Through their creative labor, fans not only add to the narrative of
the franchise, they also create free promotional material that keeps
it alive. Motivated by mutual respect and acknowledgment instead
of monetary compensation, fans show off their skills and knowledge,
and celebrate their own creativity.

In the PBS Frontline documentary *Generation Like*, Douglas
Rushkoff introduces the New York teen Ceili Lynch who is a fan of
the *Hunger Games*.[82] Rushkoff interviewed Ceili who tweeted so
frequently about these movies that she was eventually identified as
one of the top fans on the official *Hunger Games* website.[83] Much of
her fan labor is about "liking" and reposting new posts about the
Hunger Games; she is spending an excessive amount of time on it.
For Rushkoff, when kids like something online, it becomes part of
the identity that they broadcast to the world, the way bedroom
posters defined him when he was a teen. According to Rushkoff, for
kids today "you are what you like."

While the content that Ceili produced contributes to the continued
success of the *Hunger Games* franchise, her labor also becomes a
license to reclaim her agency. Everything she encounters – from texts,
to images, and mp3 files – can be reconfigured. Kenneth Goldsmith
describes this approach as follows:

> Words very well might not only be written to be read but rather to be
> shared, moved, and manipulated, sometimes by humans, more often
> by machines, providing us with an extraordinary opportunity to recon-
> sider what writing is and to define new roles for the writer.[84]

Fan production both challenges and celebrates franchised content.

Chinese Harry Potter fans, for example, wrote a book that imag-
ines what it would be like if Harry Potter were a student in a Chinese

classroom. On the /r/harrypotter subreddit, long discussions are dedicated to Harry Potter (189,000 subscribers) and the MyLittlePony franchise on /r/mylittlepony (65,000 subscribers). Fandom was also used for activism in the case of The Harry Potter Alliance, where this group of Harry Potter fans used the hashtag #MyHungerGames and #StrikeFastFood to call on Americans to tell their stories about income inequality and the Fight for $15. Activists picture themselves with the three-finger-salute from the *Hunger Games*.

On YouTube, tens of millions of fans watched Ghyslain Raza (aka The Star Wars Kid) swinging his golf ball retriever, imitating Darth Maul's lightsaber. Frequently, there are legal tensions between creative fans and copyright holders. The more enlightened members of the latter group understand these creations as significant contributions to the promotion of their brand.

In the context of games, the German media theorist Julian Kücklich developed the term "playbor," in the paper "Precarious Playbour: Modders and the Digital Games Industry," published in the open access journal *Fibreculture* and brought to larger public attention at *The Internet as Playground and Factory* conference in 2009. There, Kücklich suggested the term "playbor" especially in the context of the production of digital games where "the relationship between work and play is changing, leading as it were, to a hybrid form of playbor."[85] In particular, Kücklich referred to computer game modifications of the 1980s, which gathered steam in the 1990s, when computer game players became involved in modifications of the game. Game modders fix bugs, add content, or create entirely new games; the social factory is cloaked by an ideology of play.[86] A more recent example of game modding involves Everquest 2's content creation model, whereby users are given access to creation tools and then have the chance to get them featured in-game – without getting paid.

In the previous chapter I reflected on the myth of choice, autonomy, and flexibility. In this chapter, I am asking what motivates workers all across the digital labor landscape; I am elaborating on the ways in which workers are called upon to do what they love. Productive labor, in that scenario, is no longer understood as work. Unsurprisingly, YouTube hires countless consultants to better understand how to trigger the participation of the crowd. They wonder how they can get unpaid producers to create value. But equally, on the not-for-profit site, Wikipedia is asking how they can draw in more female editors, for instance.[87]

You might still remember the AOL chat room moderators in the late 1990s who were lured into working for free by the promise of a job. Or, think about the days when you could still talk to an actual Apple representative online. The process with which companies like Apple handed over their customer service to unpaid consumers has been thoroughly naturalized. The next level of social experimentation is signaled by the psychological experiments that Facebook, OkCupid, and Google conducted with their users. Facebook, for instance, surreptitiously showed thousands of its users a selection of more positive updates written by their friends, speculating that such filtering of the newsfeed might motivate them to post more.[88]

Companies like AOL, Verizon, Apple, or Facebook, all too often make it look as if they are merely helping people to do the work that they are keen to do already. It's about whitewashing the fence for the twenty-first century, which is reminiscent of one of the most widely known stories about motivation in American literature: Mark Twain's *Adventures of Tom Sawyer*.[89] But the popularity of social networking services is also related to American commuter culture. Large parts of the population from coast-to-coast, from Massachusetts to Florida, are living in one-family houses nestled in suburbia, which is marked by low population density and, frequently, racial segregation. While there has been some successful reversal of urban sprawl in cities like Portland, Seattle, Los Angeles, and New York over the past 20 years, the suburbs can still be locals of social isolation for young people. Parents drive children to far-away play dates, school activities, and hangouts. A manufactured culture of fear and overprotectiveness means that parents keep their children away from public spaces.[90]

In this environment, social networking can help to reestablish and maintain relationships with friends and acquaintances. Facebook, a platform defined by peer, state, and commercial surveillance, satisfies the gluttonous curiosity about the lives of others while also being a tool for organization, coordination, self-expression, and sharing with distant colleagues and friends. Data labor becomes a temporary and by all means partial remedy for problems that are in part related to failures in urban planning.

In *The Great Good Place*, the sociologist Ray Oldenburg illustrates the exiling of youth from public life. Teenagers have few places that offer them affordable entertainment. Youth has "no place to go, nothing to do." The only options in such isolating conditions, Oldenburg suggests, is to graduate from the "kindergarten of consumerism – the televised children's commercial" to the "university of suburban materialism, the shopping mall."[91]

What are other motivations for data labor? In Germany, the government considered paying Wikipedia editors, but it is not clear if someone who works for several days on an article and considers her contribution intellectually valuable would not in fact understand such compensation as a put-down. In some scenarios, compensation does not lead to better performance. In fact, Wikipedians frequently describe their work as enjoyable. After all, they are working on something that is of direct use to them and the public. They believe in their work. Benkler writes "for any given culture, there will be some acts that a person would prefer to perform not for money, but for social standing, recognition, and probably, ultimately, instrumental value obtainable only if that person has performed the action through a social, rather than a market, transaction."[92]

Much work is exempted from monetary exchange: parents don't expect their children to pay them for help with homework or for driving them to swimming lessons. Frequently, there is no monetary reward for working in a soup kitchen, classifying a star system on the website GalaxyZoo, or lecturing as a volunteer docent in a museum. Historically, too, labor has been predominantly performed outside of the confines of salaried jobs. In the case of contemporary India, it is still only 7 percent of all work that is compensated through a regular wage.[93]

Yochai Benkler offers the example of being invited to dinner at a friend's house. The friend is likely to make an effort to be a good host: to provide delicious food, a few jokes, and scintillating conversation. If, at the end of the evening, you leave a check for $50 on the table, Benkler suggests, chances are that you would not be invited back. Monetary rewards can be discouraging; friendship cannot be easily turned into a market transaction.

Benkler refers to a major study by the British autodidact and pioneering social researcher Richard Titmuss who, in the early 1970s, compared the blood supply systems in the United States and the UK.[94] The American system was largely commercial at the time – a combination of private for-profit and not-for-profit actors – but the British system, organized through the National Health Service, relied entirely on volunteers. Titmuss pointed out that the quality of the blood in the British system was much higher, by which he meant that there was less blood waste, fewer blood shortages in hospitals, and a smaller likelihood to contract hepatitis from transfusions. Blood donors described that they enjoyed helping others and that they felt a sense of moral obligation or responsibility. The study showed that the British blood procurement system was more ethical and efficient; Titmuss pointed out that in the US system, the rich exploited the desperately poor by buying their blood.

If we are putting Wikipedia to the "Titmuss test," it is likely that payments would probably lower the quality of the articles and overall participation. There is a tension; on the one hand, Jaron Lanier's suggestion of micro-payments for every small creative contribution to the

Internet is not only impractical but also undesirable; not every act of labor should be subsumed under the logic of the market. But at the same time, we should not think of peer producers as Samaritans who magically float in the upper echelon of Maslow's pyramid of needs.

In the German Wikipedia, writers that contribute particularly thoughtful articles are rewarded with the label "Exzellenter Artikel." For some Wikipedians at least, acknowledgement from peers may seem to matter more than pay. Wikipedia editors described that they write articles because they may feel bored or undervalued in their day jobs. Volunteering for Wikipedia allows editors to create value outside of the control of the dominant corporate players. Peer production for this encyclopedia is production for need and use; it is not directly marketed for financial gain later.

But the wealth of networks does not only benefit Wikipedia, it also boosts extractive platforms. Free labor per se is not the main culprit; it is crowd fleecing, and the imperative of productivity in the context of extractive platform capitalism that should be questioned and restricted. It is time to talk about the structural manipulation of platform capitalism: all the wasted speculative labor, the hope labor, and the draining performance of identity on Facebook. Sometimes, the carrot is just the stick by other means, as Bob Black quipped. The Precarious Workers Brigade[95] and the CarrotWorkers' Collective[96] carried large papier-mâché carrots as part of a demonstration in central London. They described the carrot as "a classic symbol of empty promises posed as incentives." Their banner read "Take your carrot and shove it!"[97]

Instead of talking about how professionally useful these platforms are, let's act on our ambiguity and denaturalize the 24/7 capture mills of the web. Thinking about the realities of work and our various motivations, a sharp grasp of the carrots that are held in front of us is important when trying to cool down our positivity for, and loosen our identification with, these regimes of work. Platform owners feed us the hungry ghosts of respect and peer acknowledgment. Therefore, to escape this cycle of dependency, we have to organize new structures of work and learn to respect our education, our time, our convictions, our experiences, ourselves.

9) Universal Basic Income

Workers, paid or uncompensated, are faced with growing levels of economic insecurity and uncertainty about their future. In 2013, more than 45 million Americans were living at or below the poverty line.[98] There is no way that the practices that I have described in this chapter can thrive if half of the population cannot sustain itself. You cannot even be taken advantage of through Google if your basic living needs are not met; Maslow's Hierarchy of Needs gets that right. How are they supposed to plan their lives and think ahead when the ground is constantly shifting? Why do people have to trade a human lifestyle for social security?

In the face of the rapid disappearance of long-term jobs, the French social theorist André Gorz extrapolates that "the right to sufficient, regular income will no longer have to depend on a permanent occupation or a steady job."[99]

In this chapter I showed how leisure and labor have become indistinguishable, which complicates how we think about what constitutes work. Traditional women's labor, including housework, surrogacy, and various forms of caregiving have often not been considered work. How could all of this care work and also so much creative labor be acknowledged? The actual problem, for Gorz, isn't a shortage of work but the failure to distribute the wealth, which is now produced by capital employing fewer and fewer people. In the United States, 1 percent of the population owns 36.7 percent of the country's wealth.[100] Acknowledging the realities of globalization, the lack of acknowledgment and pay for care work and creative activities as well as technological unemployment,[101] Universal Basic Income is one answer that would cover the bare necessities of all people.

One version of the concept of Universal Basic Income (UBI) is for the government to cut checks roughly equivalent to unemployment benefits, every month, unconditionally, without regard to financial needs or employment status, to each individual citizen: just for being alive. Experiments with basic income have been conducted in the Netherlands, Canada, Namibia, Switzerland, and the United States. In 2015, Finland announced that it is considering the introduction of a National Basic Income of €800 per month, which is too low.[102] In 2013, Swiss groups had reached 126,000 signatures in support of basic income. The delivery of these signatures to the government triggered a nationwide popular referendum on the topic of basic income at the level of roughly $2,800 a month. Two groups continue to lobby very actively in the French and German parts of Switzerland.

The roots of UBI can be traced back to the seventeenth and eighteenth centuries, Thomas Paine's proposal of compensation for all, and later, Richard Nixon, George McGovern, Milton Friedman, and many others. Basic Income appeals to different people for various

reasons. Libertarians and conservatives see it as an end of "bureau-
cratic government waste," the Kafkaesque arrangements for the
approval of needs-based social benefits, and the termination of all
federal welfare programs. Much of the money that is earmarked for
welfare programs ends up covering administrative and distributive
costs rather than going directly to those who need it. Citizen groups
worldwide are fighting for it, together with a long list of
supporters including the Italian philosopher Antonio Negri, the
French social theorist André Gorz, the American philosopher Michael
Hardt, the British economist Guy Standing, City University of New
York professor and labor organizer Stanley Aronowitz, and the
American Women's Studies professor Kathi Weeks. Even venture
capitalists like Netscape-founder Marc Andreessen and Union Square
ventures-VC Albert Wenger do not outright reject the idea.[103]

The proposal of Universal Basic Income has a long history in the
United States. In 1962, Milton Friedman proposed a needs-based,
"negative income," also based on a monthly payment plan. Seven
years later, Richard Nixon suggested a "family assistance program"
but that never came to pass. The US presidential candidate George
McGovern called for the Demogrant, a program that was similar
to Nixon's plan. The labor historian Jefferson Cowie describes
McGovern's program as follows:

> [McGovern] promised $1,000 to every single person in the United
> States – men, women, and children from the filthy rich to the destitute
> poor. A family of four, for instance, would receive $4,000 (over $20,000
> in 2009 dollars), and there would be no welfare; their tax obligation
> would begin at any dollar earned beyond $4,000. Plans to redistribute
> money to the poor through various "negative tax" schemes were eve-
> rywhere on the political landscape of the early seventies – from Nixon's
> Family Assistance Plan, to congressional Democrats who had been
> advocating $3,000 to $4,000 grants to the poor, to more radical redis-
> tributive plans of the National Welfare Rights Organization (which
> wanted to guarantee every family $6,500 per year). McGovern's "give-
> away" was going to be available to all citizens (quietly recouped from
> the stable and affluent through taxation) and was, in reality, little dif-
> ferent than Milton Friedman's negative income tax that had been a pet
> project of the conservative movement.[104]

In Alaska, the state government uses part of its profits from the
sale of oil to pay all Alaskans $878 once a year. Some Native American
tribes who operate casinos, specifically the Cherokee, use the profits
from these operations to disperse payments of several thousand
dollars twice a year. Would it really be so unthinkable to take the

Alaskan model and apply it to California, with all its budgetary troubles? Couldn't technology companies agree to pay just a small percentage of their profits into a fund that will then be used to support people living in that state?

The Cherokee and Alaska examples are not the only ones. There are experiments with Universal Basic Income not only in countries like Canada, Switzerland, and Finland but also in India and Namibia. Skeptics argue that basic income would serve as a disincentive for people to even look for paid work. One study in rural Manitoba (Canada), however, found that there was only a slight reduction of the effort to work: 1 percent for men, 3 percent for their wives, and 5 percent for unmarried women. The only people that worked considerably less were new mothers, who decided to spend more time with their infants, and teenagers who had to take care of family members. Basic income does not discourage people to work but it "enables them to refuse work and reject 'inhumane' working conditions."[105] The refusal of work, for Kathi Weeks, "is a matter of securing not only better work, but also the time and money necessary to have a life outside work."[106]

For those who never came across this proposal, it may sound far-fetched but a large number of studies suggest that it is feasible. Unsurprisingly, however, there are also many opponents who ridicule the proposal as a willy-nilly allocation of undeserved wages, a pie in the sky, and a big fat disincentive to look for a job. Select politicians strategically point to the burden that "freeloaders" or scroungers would pose.

The details of a plan of Universal Basic Income matter a great deal. The idea of basic guaranteed income is by no means a panacea for all problems related to platform capitalism; it only makes sense if it truly serves the most vulnerable members of society: especially women, the recently incarcerated, and black Americans.

High-tech venture capitalists and libertarians imagine something drastically different than the far left of the political spectrum. Basic income that is unconditional and paid at sustenance level is a social justice demand. Anything below that, such as the Finnish plan, will still put workers into the position of having to scramble for additional income; it would merely become a subsidy for large corporations like Walmart or Amazon.

An additional, crucial consideration is that basic income if only implemented in the overdeveloped world, would have the potential to instigate more migrations from poorer regions of the world. But Universal Basic Income, if implemented globally, could put an end to crowd fleecing.

André Gorz calls for a multi-active life in which professional work and unpaid activities supplement and complement each other; it's a shift from a work society to a culture society. For Gorz, the vision "is to shift the center of gravity of everyone's lives so that, from now on, business and work for economic ends have only a subordinate place."[107]

3

Vocabulary

The ability to draw a dotted line around the concept of digital labor matters if we want to change discussions about the political economy of the Internet. How can we reshape what we are unable to articulate?

Right at the outset, we need to acknowledge that this has been a cross-disciplinary conversation. Since 2007, discussions of digital labor have joined the perspectives of artists, social scientists, workers, labor advocates, cooperativists, owners, investors, legal scholars, data scientists, policymakers, designers, developers, journalists, civic technologists, and labor historians. In order to productively talk about digital work, all involved have to overcome disciplinary narcissism and political differences and start looking for a common language. Artists should not be kept safely separate on "artists' panels" and debates about methodologies, despite their importance, overshadow too much of the discussion about real life problems. Debates are often too isolated, focusing solely on practices in the so-called "sharing economy" (Uber), social media (Facebook), or the crowdsourcing sector (Amazon Mechanical Turk) when in fact, all of these forms are deeply intertwined.

Differences between compensated and unpaid work, as well as extractive and democratically governed practices, have to be acknowledged. While it is important to insist that "digital labor" is not somehow mysteriously different from traditional forms of labor (domestic, industrial, otherwise), there are also discontinuities that I outline in the next chapter.

It is crucial to clarify that emerging forms of digital labor play an important role in the economy, but they do not take over its entirety, with all other forms and practices vanishing into the night. Currents of techno-utopianism and postindustrial hyperbole fuel platform capitalism; we are not living the postindustrial dream. Germany, for instance, has maintained a strong manufacturing sector and worldwide, over four billion people do not even have Internet access at all.

This discussion becomes easier when we clarify the use of terms like work and labor. In this chapter I am using them interchangeably; let me explain why. I also reveal the tension between two main tendencies. On one hand, I describe digital labor as the shiny sharp tip of a gigantic neoliberal spear made up of deregulation, union busting, rising unemployment, and contingent work.

Just consider the vision of conservative economist Tyler Cowen that I mentioned in the introduction. In his book *Average is Over*, Cowen prophesied that soon there will be a super class, a "hyper meritocracy" of 10–15 percent of earners who will make over $1 million per year, enjoying fantastically interesting lives, while the rest will make $10,000–15,000 annually, "tranquilized by free Internet and canned beans."[1] What happens if we take Cowen's vision of the future of work seriously? We find that many emerging digital labor practices are in fact adding up to that future, dominated by even more hostile work realities. Reflecting on Cowen leads to a different understanding of supporters of the on-demand economy who characterize emerging sites of digital labor as beneficial for lower income groups.[2]

At the same time, however, I also recognize generative digital work that genuinely benefits the commonwealth. To that end, in chapter 7, I lay out the possibilities associated with what I call platform cooperativism.

For the past decade, attempts to define digital labor have heavily emphasized specific practices. The Austrian-born, British scholar Christian Fuchs, for example, uses Facebook to offer a Marxist interpretation of digital labor, which for him is a descriptor of the entire landscape of digital work. The legal scholar Miriam C. Cherry defines "virtual work" as "work [that is] taking place at the intersection of the Internet, crowdsourcing arrangements, and virtual worlds." For French economist Yann Moulier Boutang, cognitive labor is the new labor. Along similar lines, for Paolo Virno, such labor should be thought of as the casual expenditure of cognitive surplus. But inferring such definition from specific cases or trends, be that data labor on Facebook or crowd work on Amazon Mechanical Turk, does not capture the breadth and diversity of different modes of digital work.

For this reason, in chapters 1 and 2, I have started to work toward a typology of digital work. I distinguished compensated and unpaid forms to discuss internal/external crowd work, work facilitated through labor brokerages, and in-game labor, for instance. I explained how even crowdsourcing is comprised of a multiplicity of practices – from micro-tasking, and software testing, to commercial content moderation, mobile crowd work, and content farming. Specifically with regard to uncompensated digital work, I introduced data labor/playbor, volunteer crowd work, fan labor, the performance of self, and more.

In this chapter, apart from the suggestion of a more inclusive discussion, I oppose the myth of "immaterial labor," noting that conversations about digital labor should start with considerations about the all but "immaterial" practices all along its global supply chains.

Finally, in this chapter I also propose a continuation of the language of labor. Some scholars have argued that given the increasing blur between leisure and labor, the word labor may be no longer adequate. I resist the idea that somehow all processes have become labor, that life in its global totality is suddenly financialized.

Overview

1) The myth of immateriality
2) Work vs. labor
3) In defense of non-labor
4) Against a surrender of the language of labor

1) The Myth of Immateriality

Apart from the distinction between paid and unpaid work online, the definitional umbrella of the term also needs to be wide enough to make room for supply chains and networks of care – by which I mean families and friends that are necessary to survive the "flexible" digital labor regimes and make them sustainable.

Thinking about digital labor means contemplating global patterns of connection and accumulation that facilitate and promote such production. This means that all related processes need to be included in this definition; everything from the assembly of iPhones, the Xbox, cables, wireless installations, Foxconn's factories in the Longhua Science and Technology Park in Shenzhen (China) that brings us Apple, HP, Dell, and Sony products, and the mining of rare earth minerals in the Democratic Republic of Congo, Nigeria, and China's Nancheng County, without which many of our laptops and mobile devices would not work.

Labor scholar Andrew Ross reports that in 2010, at China's largest private manufacturer, Foxconn, 18 of the over one million workers, mostly recruited from the Chinese hinterland, could no longer cope with the oppressive working conditions at Foxconn and committed suicide. One worker wrote: "To die is the only way to testify we ever lived."[3] In response, Foxconn installed yellow mesh netting around dormitory buildings, increased wages by 30 percent, and now makes new hires sign a no-suicide agreement. How can Shenzhen be absent from discussions about supposedly clean "immaterial labor"?

Media scholar Ayhan Antes wrote that, "Immaterial labor isn't just immaterial, digital labor isn't just digital, and software doesn't exist (as Kittler argues) without hardware."[4] I am therefore uncomfortable with Maurizio Lazzarato's concept of immaterial labor, which the Italian theorist penned in 1997. He framed it as "a series of activities that are not normally recognized as 'work' – in other words, the kind of activity involved in defining and fixing cultural and artistic standards, fashions, taste, and consumer norms..."[5] Lazzarato writes:

> *You must express yourself, speak, communicate, co-operate...but the communicative relationship is completely predetermined in both content and form. It is, more precisely, made a function of, and instrument in the service of, the technical system, which requires coded information to circulate at a particular velocity.*[6]

For the system of "immaterial labor" to function, users can't just sit there, they are hounded by the expectation of participation. "Be active subjects!" is the command for the digital age.

Lazzarato's term refers to the fact that the products of this "immaterial labor" are not material. Importantly, he wants us to think about traders instead of truck drivers; Lazzarato's definition deemphasizes that this immaterial labor is based on – and could not exist without – the very material, warm bodies of workers and the sweated labor imprinted in the hardware that we are using, no matter how immaterial data labor purports to be.

Digital labor is a child of the low-wage crisis. It needs to be discussed at the fold of intensified forms of exploitation online and older economies of unpaid and invisible work, especially in the home. Here I am thinking about Silvia Federici, Selma James, and Mariarosa Dalla Costa's "wages for housework" campaign and, in the 1980s, cultural theorist Donna Haraway discussing ways in which emerging communication technologies allowed for "home work" to be disseminated throughout society.

Digital labor is everything but "immaterial;" it is a sector of the economy, a set of human activities that is predicated on global supply

chains of sweated material labor; it is about human activities that
have economic value and that are often performed through a range
of devices in real time, on a truly novel and unprecedented scale, on
highly monopolized platforms.

2) Work vs. Labor

In a discussion about a definition of digital labor, the semantic and
conceptual distinction between digital labor and digital work can
become an obstacle; a discursive sinkhole even. Therefore, clarity of
use matters. The terms labor and work have very specific meanings
in the writing of political theorist Hannah Arendt, cultural historian
and political theorist Raymond Williams, cultural critic Lewis Hyde,
and scholars like Kathi Weeks, and John D. Budd, which I will introduce below.

In his book *Key Words*, Raymond Williams reminds us that the term
"work" stems from the modern English form of the noun "weorc" and
the verb "wycran." Work is a most general word for doing something,
which is now mostly used to refer to regular paid employment. But
Williams points out that we are also speaking of working in the garden,
for example. Labor, on the other hand, has a strong medieval connota-
tion of pain and toil. Work was meant more as a general activity, but
soon, a laborer was also referred to as a worker. He also discusses the
specialization of one sense of working to the working class. "*The
specialization of work to paid employment is a result of the development of our job. But experience of every kind of work has capitalist
productive relations*," he writes.[7] "*Work is still essentially important,
and in much every day use means only labor or a job.*" Running along
the base of terms has been the short word "job," Raymond Williams
acknowledges. While it is not impossible to differentiate the terms in
historical context, there is much overlap in usage.

For American scholar Lewis Hyde, work directly refers to what we
do by the hour. Work "*begins and ends at a specific time and, if possible, we do it for money. Welding car bodies on an assembly line is
work;...computing taxes, walking the rounds in a psychiatric ward,
picking asparagus – these are work.*"[8] Hyde also distinguishes work
from labor. "*Writing a poem, raising a child, developing a new cal-
culus, resolving a neurosis, invention in all forms*," he states, "*these
are labors.*"[9] Hyde also reminds us of "mourning labor" and "the
labor of gratitude."[10]

For Hyde, crowd work, gold farming, on demand labor – all of
these categories that I introduced in chapter 2 – should be understood

as work. Data labor, fan labor, and playbor, should all be interpreted as labor in Hyde's book. Written in 1979, Hyde did not consider emotional labor, a term introduced by Arlie Hochschild in her study *The Managed Heart*, as paid work.

Now, take Hannah Arendt's distinction between work and labor. For Arendt, labor was the never-ending activity that is necessary to sustain life, to reproduce biological life – think of activities such as obtaining food, water, and shelter – nothing beyond that. For Arendt, nothing that would be left behind for the future can be associated with labor. For her, the creation of an object world, is left to work. She also introduces a third, and somewhat privileged, category, that of action, which refers to political activity.

Waged labor, the way I am using it here, refers to what Hyde would call work, while some of the practices described in chapter 2 would correspond to his definition of labor. Correspondingly, Arendt's distinction would not match up with my use of the terms "work" and "labor."

Beyond the distinction between the terms "labor" and "work," there is also the rejection of work altogether. Marx's concept of *living labor* could be considered the jumping off point for critiques of labor that lead to the development of more ideal ways of working, which are worthy of our support. Kathi Weeks, in her book *The Problem with Work*, hesitates to go down that route as such framing still conceptualizes the future in terms of an overemphasis on work and labor.[11] Weeks asks how we can escape the inflated emphasis of work and conceptualize a life beyond work. In this book, however, I use the terms work and labor interchangeably because the distinction is not central to my project.

3) The Fence Around the Produser Factory

Today, it becomes much harder to say: "I know labor when I see it." Labor time is no longer bound to the factory or office; the edges of work and "labor time" have melted away. Attitudes toward labor and leisure have fundamentally changed in accord with the needs of production. For Andrew Ross, *"The entire fabric of our everyday lives, rather than merely our workplace toil, becomes the raw material for capital accumulation."*[12]

For Paolo Virno, twenty-first-century labor includes all human activities. There are no activities, including our thoughts, dreams, and imaginations, which distinguish themselves as non-labor and the value of this labor becomes immeasurable. Free time is no longer solely dedicated to consumption or passivity; the distinction between free time and labor time becomes less meaningful. We are producing for a wage at work only to continue work off the clock at home or on the go. What used to be considered free time is also time for the production of subjectivities, big (and small) data, and cultural practices. Our abilities to communicate and interact with others are captured, sorted, analyzed, and ultimately sold. We are creating peculiar twin-identities online; we are performing ourselves just as we are becoming public relations agents for various brands.

In the face of such a broad understanding of digital labor, from supply chains to unpaid and compensated work online, is there anything that would be outside of digital labor? I'm arguing for an outside, for the possibility of non-labor. I will do so by introducing scholars for whom an outside of labor (digital or not) no longer exists and I will then show the limits of their arguments.

This discussion needs to start with Karl Marx's labor theory of value, and concepts such as "labor time" and "productive labor power." Following Marx's understanding of what constitutes productive labor, the workday ends when the workers are leaving the factory for what Germans refer to as their "Feierabend" ("home time," reserved for celebration) for which there is no fitting English translation.

For Marx, the labor process requires the presence of workers who change something other than themselves, in which their labor power – whatever they produced during the workday – can be measured. Or, in Marx's own words "labor power is the aggregate of those mental and physical capabilities existing in a human being, which he exercises whenever he produces a use value of any description."[13]

How much labor time does it take to pay for what it costs to employ a worker? From the perspective of the owner of the factory, everything in excess of that cost constitutes surplus value. From the viewpoint of the worker, surplus value is what he or she produces after his or her requirements are met, which goes beyond socially necessary labor time.

For Marx, virtuosos such as vocalists do not fall into the realm of productive labor. Marx's oft-repeated reference is that of the piano maker who, for Marx, could be safely considered a productive worker, whereas the pianist cannot. The pianist exchanges his labor for payment, but he doesn't directly contribute to the economy, following Marx's analysis.[14]

But today, the boundaries of productive labor have vastly expanded. Just consider Jonathan Crary's understanding of time in his book *24/7: Late Capitalism and the Ends of Sleep*. Here Crary suggests that sleep is no longer reserved as explicitly useless time of passivity. Now, even our REM sleep cycles can be pushed into the working position. Devices such as the "smart watch" or the Fitbit make every minute of the day accountable, measurable, and geared for higher efficiency.

Debates about "free labor" are frequently informed by the Italian school of Marxist thought called Operaismo, or Workerism, which distinguished itself from reform-minded Communist Party politics by rejecting the framing of the worker in terms of exploitation. Their theoretical work was heavily linked to workplace organizing and culminated in the so-called wildcat strikes in Turin during the "Hot Autumn" of 1969. Especially in the period following World War II, the Workerists involved themselves closely with labor struggles, aiming to envision "the formation of a multi-class precariat that was somehow linked by shared concerns about the insecurity of all aspects of their lives."[15]

Following one workerist theorist, Mario Tronti, laborers are not only exploited during work hours, they are also fodder for around-the-clock value extraction. Throughout the 1970s, Mario Tronti championed the concept of "the social factory." The sociality of production becomes the medium for private appropriation. Social relations, for Tronti, are inseparable from the relation of production; the relation of production is identified ever more with the social relation of the factory.[16]

In 1964, Tronti introduced the concept of the factory society or "factory without walls," also widening what we can understand as labor.[17] In short, Tronti describes how capital not only manufactures, produces in the factory proper but also expands its value capture beyond the bounds of that facility to include all of society, and all sociality, thereby making the factory vanish. "*When the whole of society is reduced to the factory*," Tronti notes, "*the factory as such appears to disappear*."[18]

In the late 1970s, the political economist Dallas Smythe argued that audiences should be considered as the principal commodity produced by advertising and broadcast media. The audience is sold as a commodity to advertisers, and therefore Smythe called it the audience commodity. "You audience members contribute your unpaid work time and in exchange you receive...explicit advertisements."[19]

Sut Jhally, founder of the Media Education Foundation, built on the concept of the audience commodity and proposed that in order to understand commercial media, especially television, we need to rethink the idea that this is all about putting messages or meaning into people (think of one of those advertisement jingles that you can't get out of your head). Instead, we should understand these media as extracting value from the audience. Watching television at home, according to Jhally, is organized around the logic of the industrial factory.[20] Both Christian Fuchs and I have linked this to user labor on YouTube, Flickr, or Facebook.[21]

As an audience, commodity Internet users also submit material; they participate. The people formerly known as the audience of broadcast media did not contribute in that way. They did not upload videos, write status updates, blog posts, or tweets. And in that sense, Fuchs proposes, we should rather talk of a "produser commodity."[22] Combining Tronti, Jhaly, and Fuchs, I label it the "produser factory," where social participation goes hand-in-hand with value extraction.

For Hardt and Negri, the "social worker" is the worker in the absolutely diffuse social factory.[23] All dimensions of the everyday life of the "social worker" are included in the concept of the proletariat and class struggle. The concept cuts across waged and unwaged labor – from the student to the self-employed, domestic workers, and also the unemployed, thereby opening up avenues for interconnected struggle for workers who were pushed to the tipping point of anxiety. And these interconnected struggles can be formed around emerging digital and traditional analog forms of work. Hardt and Negri also referred to this kind of worker as a "diffuse worker" – someone who doesn't have an assigned workplace but parts in various settings throughout society, applying themselves fully, with all their communicative and expressive force. And all that simply to get by. One segment of the workforce might choose this self-directed work lifestyle while another is forced into it. Having "free time" between jobs doesn't mean that you can take a vacation on a golden sandy beach given that many can barely come up with the rent. As Antonio Negri put it: "Social labor power is now extended throughout the entire span of production".

This fully resonates with what I call data labor and it also applies to other forms of unpaid work. When we are "giving off" data, we are essentially drafted to the ranks of Hardt's "social workers" and there is very little we can do about it. Net critic Andrew Keen refers to the gargantuan databanks that ingest our data as "siren servers." Globally, precarious "social workers" are essential to today's economy; they are good news for employers and a difficult reality for unions.

In 2012, the French economist Yann Moulier Boutang described the current moment as the "cognitive phase" of capitalism, again offering a totalizing account of the landscape of digital work. Cognitive labor is the new labor. It is not an aspect of the economy, it is "cognitive capitalism." Boutang characterizes this "cognitive capitalism" in terms of innovation, peer-to-peer file sharing, and the open source movement, largely not paying attention to moments of exploitation that I am highlighting in chapters 1 and 4. Instead, Boutang focuses on the lyrical image of all of us being worker bees, pollinating the fields of Google. What matters is "cognitive attention, time, and affective attention."[24] The lines of capital are reaching into our daily lives, expropriating our feelings, language, thoughts, and social relationships. Some of these small acts of labor used to be performed by paid employees.

Starting in 1940, McDonald's fast food restaurants pioneered self-service, shifting part of the work formerly executed by waiters to paying customers. Recent signs on trash cans at Burger King gamify the process of garbage disposal: "Toss it in. Drop it in. Just get your trash in here some way." Customers are asked to lend a helping hand when buying frozen yogurt for their children and their Google searches help that company to thrive. Shopping centers propel us to use self-checkout stations and also gas stations and banks have cleverly picked up on the outsourcing of such small acts of labor to us. Creatively, we are even asked to self-assemble our furniture; who would have thought. The tall chimneys of the social factory disperse their dark fumes.

In 2000, the Italian scholar Tiziana Terranova wrote one of the earliest critical essays about labor and the Internet "Free Labor: Producing Culture for the Digital Economy." In "Free Labor" Terranova describes the free labor of "net slaves," as she put it, as the source of economic value in the digital economy. Is there any corner of life that avoids subsumption by capital?

Focusing on the modification of software packages, updates of websites, and unpaid labor of moderators in AOL chat rooms, Terranova asks how we conceive of labor that is voluntarily given, unwaged, enjoyed, and exploitative at the same time. Terranova discusses what she calls the "outernets" of production – the network of social, cultural, and economic relationships that crisscrosses and exceeds the Internet.

Being entangled in these "outernets" also means that automated data exchanges are taking place involving electronic toll-collection systems, cell phones, or Wi-Fi-enabled devices. Sensors seek contact with the built environment; which is often referred to as the Internet of Things, as explained in chapter 2.

Coming back to Marx, the Italian philosopher Paolo Virno proposed that the importance of the Marxist notion of "labor time" decreases as a rule while Marx's concept of "general intellect" becomes increasingly significant. Virno argues that productive labor as a whole has adopted the particular characteristics of the artistic performing activity. For Virno, labor should be thought of as the casual expenditure of cognitive surplus, the act of being a speaker, and a performative prop within a communication system. Whoever produces surplus value in post-Fordism behaves, seen from a structuralist standpoint, like a pianist, a dancer, etc.[25]

Today, we would describe "general intellect" as a kind of know-how, let's say the ability to start up your computer and use software, and to communicate online. It is our expertise and ability to think, shape, and modify culture, and it is exactly that which is put to work 24/7. More broadly, it includes the ability to cooperate, which Marx argued would be a core factor of production in the future, much more so than the direct labor of the workers.

Marx's virtuoso is now also performing productive labor which, as described by Virno, sits uncomfortably with the current understanding of what constitutes labor. Our personal abilities, our "general intellect" is linked to value chains. Today, considered in the context of emerging forms of digital labor that are described in chapters 1 and 2, labor power extracts value also from virtuosity, collaboration, and even cooperation – in short, from the social production of value.

I do not agree with Virno's broad claim about total capture because worldwide, there are wide-reaching zones of non-work.

This rhetoric is invariably fueled by discussions about the postindustrial society. The myth of the postindustrial society emerged concomitantly to the process of labor struggles and corporate mobilizations, with theorists like Fritz Machlup, Zbigniew Brzezinski, Jacques Ellul, Alain Touraine, Ithiel de Sola Pool, and Marshall McLuhan who envisioned the shift from a manufacturing society to a society where knowledge is key. In 1973, the American sociologist Daniel Bell published *The Coming of the Postindustrial Society* in which he observed that:

> Post-industrial society is organized around knowledge, for the purpose of social control and the directing of innovation and change; and that this in turn gives rise to new social relationships and new structures...[26]

His widely read book prophesied a rapid transition from an industrial economy where most of the labor force is producing goods to a postindustrial society with a greater number of people working in the service sector. The transition period would last between 30 and 50 years. For Bell, this society was narrowly equated with the example given, the United States of America, where universities would become central nodes of society and technical work, and all kinds of knowledge work would supersede manual labor. Capitalism wouldn't just take care of business, but would also satisfy the needs of citizens, from healthcare to education. This didn't come to pass, and although corporate leaders and policymakers in the United States believe that the future of capitalism lies in the commodification of information, countries such as India and most countries in South America and Africa still need to be pushed far beyond the current stage to reach anything resembling a postindustrial age. Considering geopolitical regions without technological saturation, the four billion people who are not connected to the Internet – there are still expansive zones of non-work, time not captured by capital. Mark Zuckerberg dreams of Facebook access for all but so far, there is still a fence around the produser factory.

4) Against a Surrender of the Language of Labor

One can't just speak of labor anymore. One has to speak about all these other kinds of larger concepts, which would be praxis. So if by praxis we mean the transformation of the world and the transformation of the self at the same time, then maybe one is performing praxis in different ways when one labors, when one plays, when one gives to others...[27]

McKenzie Wark later contextualized his remark by explaining that "praxis," in Greek, refers to the process through which concepts become practices; Gramsci framed Marxism as "the philosophy of praxis." I do not, however, want to let go of the language of labor as a descriptor of contemporary sites of work.

Following Paolo Virno's suggestion that all of life is put to work, it would seem logical to surrender the language of labor. After all, labor has become a relic of the past, a weak descriptor for these emerging forms. However, by letting go of the language of labor we are losing its association with the history of organized labor and related struggles and movements. Not talking of labor is likely to depoliticize the discussion by disconnecting it from traditional labor practices and the accomplishments, sacrifices, and lessons of organized labor. They fought against conditions like the ones illuminated by Upton Sinclair in *The Jungle*. The book called attention to the horrid working conditions of largely immigrant workers in the meatpacking plants in Chicago.

Even if your first association with labor and unions may not be all that positive, it is ill-advised to throw the once mighty past of unions overboard. Do not forget the accomplishments of unions; these are the people who brought us the eight-hour workday, a federally mandated wage floor, employer-supported health insurance plans – these things didn't just fall out of the sky. May Day demonstrations demanded the 8-hour workday as early as 1886: "*May we all benefit from the legacy of the fallen, petrified, pressed, minted for profit.*"[28]

These changes happened through protests like the one in 1911, when more than 100,000 people joined a march down Broadway in New York City to protest the death of the 146 young, mostly immigrant women who had died in the fire at the Triangle Shirtwaist Company in Washington Square.

Even the 1972 Auto Workers strike in Lordstown, Ohio might not ring a bell for everybody. The Lordstown strike was important because it was not about higher compensation, but about an opposition to the way automation technologies were transforming the industry, and therefore the very lives of the workers. The presidential nominee of the Democratic Party, George McGovern, greeted the workers by declaring that "we don't want workers to be treated like robots or machines."[29]

When we cease to speak of labor, we lose the connection to people like the young labor feminist Karen Silkwood who lost her life in the process of delivering secrets about health and safety violations at Kerr-McGee plutonium plant in 1974. You might remember the film Silkwood where Meryl Streep portrayed this brave activist.

Again, when we cease to speak of labor, we are losing the connection to the Lawrence, Massachusetts, textile strike in 1912, where thousands of female workers bussed their malnourished children to New York City before they started a militant strike with the support of the International Workers of the World. They were less concerned about imagining some idealized future; what mattered to them were the actual work conditions there and then. "The final aim is revolution but in the meantime, let's find a bed to sleep in."

What would be lost when we give up on terms like labor and work? We would lose the legacy of the Triangle Shirtwaist Factory, Karen Silkwood, the strikes in Lordstown, Lawrence, and the Haymarket riots. This isn't about a romantic attachment to the past; it is about the language of labor and living within it; the cardinal lesson being that in confrontation with the power of the employing class, individual solutions are not working.

4

Crowd Fleecing

Exploitation is not new; there are immediate associations: with that term: from Lewis Hine's photographs of child labor,[1] to the adjunct faculty and unpaid intern, to the hectic solitude and self-exploitation of the gig worker in the "sharing economy." For art aficionados, Mierle Laderman Ukeles'[2] work about the invisible maintenance work in the sanitation sector and museums may come to mind. But apart from the awkward lunacy of employment put on stage by The Office, what is rarely considered are today's more hidden practices like online crowdsourcing, for instance. Or, what about the expropriation of data labor: the monetization of public display of moods and connections? Should that be considered exploitation or is that something else altogether?

Chapter Overview and Omissions

This chapter is not a contribution to the more technical discussion of exploitation among Marxist economists. Instead, it is about perceptions of exploitation given the global division of labor and the new kinds of labor and non-labor in the over-developed world. In addition to bringing together the perspectives from scholars such as Byung-Chul Han, Christian Fuchs, Mike Davis, Adam Arvidsson, Geert Lovink, Michel Bauwens, Mark Andrejevic, Brian Holmes, Nicholas Carr, and Alan Wertheimer, in this chapter I introduce the concept of "crowd fleecing" to describe a discontinuity between traditional forms of exploitation and contemporary forms such as crowd work.

In the first part of this chapter, I offer a short history of platform capitalism to show that the Internet was once cooperative and distributive, to remind us that it was once different, and to ask how we got to the deeply centralized, corporate, and extractive Internet of now.

With "crowd fleecing" I am suggesting that the real-time exploitation of millions of workers and netizens by a small number of companies online is a novel and urgent issue that any democracy must take seriously. The chapter is structured as follows:

1) Is this still exploitation?
2) The living museum of human exploitation
3) Crowd fleecing
4) Historical context
5) Sleep as a site of crisis

1) Is This Still Exploitation?

The Marxist concept of exploitation doesn't easily sit with many practices of digital work. Exploitation in the context of the Internet is hard to tackle, it is a complex topic that requires a degree of specificity about asymmetrical relationships of power, tools, platforms, and activities. Since 2010, curiously, the discussion about exploitation of digital labor has focused almost exclusively on unpaid data labor as if the millions of underpaid crowd and gig workers do not exist.

About data labor, Dutch media critic Geert Lovink writes that in "search for the social online – it seems a brave but ultimately unproductive project to look for the remains of nineteenth-century European social theory. This is what makes the 'precarious labor' debate about Marx and exploitation on Facebook so tricky."[3] Lovink puts his ear to the ground of current research trends and spots a growing tiredness of the "exploitation" thesis of social media in favor of a more comprehensive analysis of the "like economy."[4] The exhaustion that Lovink perceives could be attributed to the fact that the exploitation of digital work, not unlike traditional labor, is simultaneously a site of contradiction, utility, and pleasure.

What, for instance, do we do with the fact that some workers express that they don't feel taken advantage of? Perhaps it's not so surprising that there is so little buy-in for the e-word with workers on Mechanical Turk, for instance. In response to one of my live tweeted lectures, the central forum for Mechanical Turk workers responded: "MTurkers are doing just fine...No one is exploited, we choose to Turk."[5] Often this quickly defaults to accusations of false consciousness, which I will not assert. But not having gone through the daily grind that is Mechanical Turk for many years, do I even have a right to call out the apparent crowd fleecing? Alan Wertheimer, Fellow of the School of Social Sciences at the Institute for Advanced Study at Princeton University, responds to that question stating: "society is justified to prevent exploitative transactions because they are inconsistent with important social values. This means also that even if a transaction is consensual, it could still be advised to prevent it from continuing."[6] Wertheimer proposes that typically, we "don't understand the wrong of exploitation as a wrong against society or its norms. It is a wrong against the exploitee." If that is the case, it would seem that society would have no basis for prohibiting this exploitation because the worker was prepared to allow it to happen. The worker can refuse or accept. But an exploitative transaction is wrong and should be prohibited by society even if the worker willingly entered into the transaction, Wertheimer writes. Importantly, Wertheimer states, exploitation has harmful effects not only on the exploitee but also on others, not just the workers, and it is justified to prohibit such work on behalf of the worker. "Only by showing respect can we allow people to improve their situation by transacting with others in a way that is consistent with their own values."[7]

To acknowledge and work through such ambiguities is important and I still hold on to the term of exploitation and the thinking through that very lens. One way of tackling the subject would be to introduce different levels of exploitation. A clear understanding of unacceptable levels of exploitation, for instance, would make it easier to talk about necessary regulation.

Which practices should be characterized as being exploitative and which ones are merely coercive? Message monitoring and email checking – practices that have become fundamental requirements of professional life – surely eat into the free time of workers. Mobile and out-of-office work become part of the workday?[8]

This discussion is situated against the backdrop of labor markets rapidly shifting to the Internet, and global regimes of production marked by anonymity, temporality, and fractalized labor. It's hard to claim that all workers on a given platform are equally exploited, for instance. First, we'd need to concede that some workers might work no more than 3 hours a month while others commit a full 40-hour workweek, or more.

The Paris-based art critic and activist Brian Holmes makes a clear distinction when it comes to the exploitation of social media (what

I call data labor) by expressing that while it does try to control you and you do create value, it doesn't exploit you the way a boss does. Holmes states that something is different here because you do something with social media, something of your own. We are exploited and controlled – yes, but we are also overflowing sources of potentially autonomous productive energy, he writes. For him, not acknowledging this contradiction leaves that potential unexplored.[9] The generative potential of the use of extractive platforms can, for one, be understood through the lens of the spontaneous mobilization of tens of thousands of people in Madrid, Hong Kong, or the revolutionary upheavals in North African countries.[10] Our productive forces unleashed on corporate platforms can indeed be generative but for me, this ambiguity does not erase the reality of exploitation. Data labor is never exclusively exploited or entirely free from that burden.

Is the concept of exploitation really so passé when considering the various forms of digital work? As I will explain below, for the lowest-paid crowd workers – and many other "digital laborers" – exploitation is undoubtedly alive and well.

The discussion about the exploitation of data labor, specifically, hinges on the question whether or not the net value that is generated by the activities of users on social service platforms should in fact count as value or if it is simply negligible. Those who repudiate the existence of exploitation in this context, argue that the value that is created is solely speculative, based on stock market evaluations. Therefore talking about exploitation in the absence of substantial economic value creation would simply be misguided.

For Italian media scholar Adam Arvidsson, for instance, the value of companies like Facebook is determined by the exchanges that are taking place on the site. Arvidsson would not directly link this, however, to the value that is actually generated by each individual user but to suggest that they contribute more broadly to the brand of a given intermediary. The hefty social costs for users are strangely justified by the cost of operations including marketing, technical infrastructure, staff salaries, shareholder payouts, and investment in research and development.

American writer Nicholas Carr describes a sharecropping system in which the "sharecropped" are generally happy, because the interest lies in self-expression and socializing, not in making money. And, besides, like Arvidsson, he states that "the economic value of each of the individual contributions is trivial."[11] But Carr acknowledges that the massive scale of the Web makes such business still lucrative. He describes something that sounds like happy exploitation:

The sharecroppers operate happily in an attention economy while their overseers operate happily in a cash economy... It strikes me that this dynamic, which I don't think we've ever seen before, at least not on this scale, is the most interesting, and unsettling, economic phenomenon the Internet has produced.[12]

For Berlin-based media researcher Julian Kücklich

The one-size-fits-all concept of exploitation we have inherited from the Marxist tradition was probably never particularly useful to begin with, but when we talk about forms of living where labor and leisure are so deeply intertwined it is in danger of losing its meaning altogether.[13]

Michel Bauwens, not unlike Carr, Arvidsson, and Holmes, notes along similar lines that Facebook users are not workers because they are not producing commodities for a wage, and that Facebook is not selling these commodities on the market to create surplus value.[14] Facebook enabled a pooling of sharing and collaboration around the platform, and by enabling, framing, and "controlling" that activity, they created a pool of attention, Bauwens writes.

The arguments about negligible value of individual contributions warrant a cursory look at the actual numbers. In the first quarter of 2014, Facebook's "revenue from advertising totaled $2.27bn."[15] In the United States and Canada, the average revenue per user for that year reached $5.85,[16] which would speak to Nicholas Carr's point. On the other hand, Facebook has far over a billion users worldwide. The discussion becomes clearer when we are looking at the average Google user who generated a value of $233 annually for the company in 2014.[17] It would be difficult to argue that such value per user is negligible. My understanding of contributions to social networking services in terms of expropriation and exploitation includes both the fact that the user contributes to the brand while simultaneously generating actual economic value.

2) The Living Museum of Human Exploitation

There is nothing in the catalogue of Victorian misery, as narrated by Dickens, Zola, or Gorky, that does not exist somewhere in a Third World city today.[18]

I dedicate this award to all the people who have endured slavery, and the 21 million people who still suffer slavery today. – Steve McQueen at the Oscar's Award Ceremony for his film *12 Years A Slave*[19]

The exploitation of digital labor can never be considered in isolation from the history of racism, and colonialism, and what Mike Davis calls the living museum of human exploitation. The human misery worldwide, and our complicity in it, has to be posed first. Estimates of the number of people trapped in modern-day slavery range from 20 to 30 million globally and the price for a slave in 2009 was as low as $90.[20] Think of the enslaved miners in the Democratic Republic of Congo who extract the minerals that are necessary for our laptops and mobile phones to function. Similarly repugnant are the working conditions at the Taiwanese company Foxconn, which produces the Xbox and Apple products, including the iPhone, at its production halls in Shenzhen, China.

Mike Davis demonstrated that it was the overdeveloped world's "late Victorian imperialism" (1870–1900) and the brutal tectonics of neoliberal globalization since 1978 that put the people of Asia and Africa into such precarious positions in the first place. And this "global informal working class," overlapping but not identical with the slum populations, is about one billion strong, making it the fastest-growing and most unprecedented social class on earth.[21] We might just think of the impoverished area of Chennai in Madras, South India, where, for eight years between 1987 and 1995, a slum of drought refugees and day laborers was known as Kidney Nagar, because journalists estimated that at least 500 people, or one person in each family, had sold a kidney to raise money to support their children.[22] Davis writes:

> the forcible incorporation into the world market of the great subsistence peasantries of Asia and Africa entailed the famine deaths of millions and the uprooting of tens of millions more from traditional tenures. The end result (in Latin America as well) was rural "semi-proletarianization," the creation of a huge global class of immiserated semi-peasants and farm laborers lacking existential security of subsistence.[23]

Any discussion of exploitation in the digital realm must acknowledge global economic codependency, the super-exploitation and colonization on which digital lifestyles in the overdeveloped world are built. However, this does not mean that lesser forms of exploitation, of crowd work or on-demand labor should be trivialized and dismissed as Internet centrism. To complicate the discussion, the various tiers of exploitation are also overlapping. Digital labor has reached even sub-Saharan Africa where thousands now use the platform Jana, formerly known as Txteagle, on their cell phones.[24]

3) Crowd Fleecing

The concept of crowd fleecing can help to provide a framework for the economic exploitation and mistreatment of unprecedented numbers of globally distributed, mostly anonymous, invisible, solo workers, all synced and available to a small number of platform owners in real time. Crowd fleecing is a result of the reorganization of work that is marked by temporal uncertainty, supplanting the model of employment that was associated with social protections for workers. Laborers, working under conditions of wage theft, deregulation, an increased densification of work, and unprecedented workplace surveillance, are folded into the algorithms of platform owners; they disappear behind the heavy curtain of the Internet, where they are called upon to give everything and ask for nothing. We are facing an epidemic of invisible labor, where workers are getting drained of mental and emotional resources, only leaving detritus for friends and family. Living is no longer about life, time has become a key instrument of oppression, and sleep falls victim to privatization. Who can imagine a different life under these circumstances? Crowd fleecing is a blind spot in the discussion about contemporary work; it signals an intensification of exploitation with the lion's share of the wealth of networks being re-routed into the pockets of a handful of platform owners.

With crowd fleecing, it is possible to contract a single worker anonymously for two or three minutes, paying her one or two cents or even nothing at all, and fire her right after a given task is done. And work in the twenty-first century has its accomplices: the five-hour power shot, Ritalin, Modafinil, and Adderall, all make it easier to forget and feel strong and invincible; they assist in converting every minute of life into work. In the face of all this, Google's Larry Page might want to rethink his statement that "If you really think about the things that you need to make yourself happy: housing, security, opportunity for your kids. It's not hard to provide those things."[25]

But an analysis of crowd fleecing cannot stop with those workers. It must also include the super-exploitation along its global supply chains and its digital infrastructure; it ranges from the workers in Shenzhen to the people in rural Oregon who are suddenly surrounded by a growing number of corporate data centers.[26]

Historically, exploitation is the material welfare of one class that is dependent upon the material deprivation of another. For Marx, the share of output that was appropriated by the capitalist best represented the rate of exploitation. Work is not paid for at its value. Workers cannot control the product of their labor; they are excluded from productive resources. But to what extent does this definition apply to contemporary sites of digital work where owners exploit the vulnerabilities of workers?

American media scholar Mark Andrejevic, writing about YouTube, states that exploitation is based on an estrangement from the means of production and lack of complete control over productive activity. For Andrejevic, the exchanges that we are entering into, however freely, are dictated by the structure of ownership of the network service. Andrejevic concentrates on the ability of users to create, view, and share the videos that they have submitted, while also being suspects to data provision/data labor. The data is then translated with the help of analytics-based forms, resulting in "external influence." YouTube is used to induce the desires for commercial products.

For London-based Austrian communication scholar Christian Fuchs, the exploitation of digital labor (by which he, like Andrejevic, refers to data labor), involves three elements: coercion, alienation, and appropriation. Users are ideologically coerced to use commercial platforms in order to be able to engage in the sharing, creation, and maintenance of social relations, without which their lives would be less meaningful, according to Fuchs. And alienation, for Fuchs, suggests that companies – and not users – own the platforms on which they are active every day. In chapter 7, I show how this alienation can be eliminated when workers and users become owners. For Fuchs, appropriation means that users spend time on corporate Internet platforms that are funded by targeted advertising schemes. This time spent on uncompensated digital labor creates value. Digital labor therefore creates social relations, profile data, user-generated content, and transaction data (browsing behavior). Internet corporations offer this data commodity for sale to advertising clients, which are able to target specific user groups.[27]

While I agree with Fuchs' statement about appropriation and alienation, I am hesitant when it comes to his discussion of coercion and meaningfulness. Are Facebook or YouTube users really duped into submission or is it the network effect that drives them into the gravitational pull of these services? Data workers have agency; they have at least a basic degree of awareness of the processes of value generation on these sites. They may not know what exactly Facebook does with their data, they may not be sure what exactly is collected, for what purposes, and to whom it is sold, but they do have a sense that expropriation is taking place.

Convenience, pleasure, and usefulness of platforms cover up the social cost and intensification of exploitation. In the Google economy, Graham Murdock writes, a more general incorporation of gift relations into the economy of commodities signifies an intensification of exploitation.[28] McKenzie Wark suggests that "We get all the culture and they get all the revenue."

Nicholas Carr, evading the term exploitation, examines "capture." He writes: "one of the fundamental economic characteristics of Web 2.0 is the distribution of production into the hands of the many and the concentration of the economic rewards into the hands of the few."[29]

Communication scholar Lilly Irani suggests that rather than thinking about exploitation along the lines of ownership, surplus, and gender, we should use the alternative framework of responsibility and responsiveness. Irani is an expert on Amazon Mechanical Turk where workers are frequently left without response to requests about missing payments and other problems. Irani wants us to understand exploitation as a "failed sort of relation that has to be judged by time and situation, rather than by who has the capital or the breasts."[30]

Users may even express consent about their own exploitation. On the mailing list of The Institute for Distributed Creativity, as part of a 9-month long discussion leading up to the Internet as Playground and Factory conference, Howard Rheingold started an exchange on the topic of exploitation.

> We ought to look at the way profit motives have made available useful public goods. May Yahoo and Google live long and prosper as long as I can view and publish via Flickr and YouTube – this means that I have blurred the line between recreation and my labor, I have to testify that even after reflection I don't mind it at all. It's pleasurable, in fact. And I'm equally delighted that Google gives away search to attract attention, some of which Google sells to advertisers. How many times a day were YOU exploited by searching for something without paying a charge for the service? Informed consent seems to be crucial – I choose to be exploited, if exploitation is how you want to see my uploading and tagging my photographs and videos.[31]

Alan Wertheimer asks why we would assume that exploitation must always be nonconsensual. Wertheimer recounts the oft-held view that exploitation must be harmful, when in fact it can be mutually advantageous.[32] Wertheimer expects that most people who are exploited know that they are exploited, and do not falsely believe that the exploitation is fair. He also makes the important distinction between the choice made from a relatively satisfactory status quo, and the choice made from an unsatisfactory status quo. He distinguishes between the decision to join the Army when "one has few decent civilian career opportunities, and the decision to join when one has good alternative job prospects."[33] The struggle for Universal Basic Income enters into this as well; it'd be an entirely different situation if the bare necessities of underpaid crowd workers would be taken care of.

Participation doesn't preclude awareness of exploitation. Consider this scenario. A single mother of four might be aware that she is entering into exploitative relationships when she takes on three part-time jobs to pay the bills. In the late nineteenth century, Karl Marx introduced the labor theory of value, in which he described exploitation as a forced extraction of labor. But the Marxist understanding of exploitation does not suggest that these workers are being forced to work for a particular employer, as was the case with slavery and feudalism, but that general background conditions systemically compel exploited labor. Exploitation is frequently, to an extent, consensual, but freedom, choice, and liberty have little or nothing to do with it. This mother may be able to choose between McDonald's and Walmart but systemically there is no choice; she has to work such low-paying gigs.

4) Historical Context

How is exploitation today different from what E. P. Thompson describes in *The Making of the English Working-Class?* What constitutes current day exploitation? Are there discontinuities from classic understandings of exploitation? How appropriate is an acrimonious insistence that everything about exploitation is continuous?

At conferences over the past few years, I have repeatedly encountered the position that digital labor has absolutely no impact on the nature of exploitation. Digital labor, the argument goes, is a straight continuation of traditional forms of exploitation.

While I am drawing a straight line from traditional sweatshop economies to the production lines and social factories of anxiety and depression on the Internet, I am also proposing that there are discontinuities, which have to do with the combination of scale, the real-time aspect, and corporate concentration. To understand these discontinuities requires an understanding of the emergence of platform culture: the massification and the concentration of online sociality.

So, welcome to the early 1990s when the Internet had just taken a terrible turn for the worse. Private enterprises had started to monetize the public infrastructure of what used to be The National Science Foundation Network, NSFNET. Up until 1994, magazines like *Time* and *BusinessWeek* had portrayed the net as nothing but a medium for piracy and pornography.[34] What they missed in their analysis was that already since the 1980s, Internet service providers

like the content-monitoring Prodigy, America Online, and the notori-
ously pricey CompuServe, pushed a layer between their clients and
the Internet. Not only did they compel their customers to click
through interfaces crowded with advertisements and newswires, they
also – hilariously – insinuated that they were offering a different
Internet. "You've got mail." In fact, of course, we all know that they
were only selling the exact same water in different bottles.

To understand exploitation on the Internet, we need to discern the
move toward *platform capitalism* in that same decade. Now in the
hands of telecommunication corporations like AOL, CompuServe,
and Prodigy, the net was faced with the slow death of creativity, and
social experimentation. At least, a particular kid of creativity was
pushed to the margins. Early homepage culture, with its unique visual
taste of an overcrowded teenage bedroom, complete with blinking
visual elements, dragons, and broken links, gave way to a culture of
convenience brought about by templates, and the "free hosting"
services of fledgling Internet service providers like Geocities and
Tripod. A bit later, this wild indy-creativity of early web design was
taken over by the uninspiring cookie-cutter templates of LiveJournal
and later Blogger, which were, at least visually, a terrible bore. Do-It-
Yourself homepage culture, with all of its fresh imperfections of the
hand-coded web, was in decline.

For Geert Lovink, hegemonic Californian cyberculture had turned
the Internet into a medium without qualities.[35] Rampant commercialization seemed to lead to a loss of delightful mass creativity. The
quirkiness and political unruliness of the noncommercial playgrounds
of the Internet, however, with all their experiments with communication, wasn't entirely lost. Now, such free-flowing creativity was
tucked away from the Open Web in enclosures like deviantART,
Flickr, and later 4Chan. From here on out, everyone curious about
this kind of DIY creativity had to set up an account and summon
their insurrectionist friends to visit them on the well-groomed lawns
of walled gardens. Access to creativity was cut off in the process of
these privatization drives.

Already by 1996, commercial sites took up almost 70 percent of
the entire Internet with user-submitted content hastening that process.
People began to devote longer and longer hours to online activity,
which was increasingly concentrated on those commercial platforms.
Unsurprisingly, Newt Gingrich – whose avatar had been seen flying
through the virtual world Second Life early on – embraced the upward
spiral of the Internet, stating that the net "could empower elites, help
to build new businesses, and reevaluate traditional forms of
governance."[36]

Crowd fleecing is predicated by a *massification* of the Internet, which, by 2005, could no longer be denied. In that same year, Tim O'Reilly coined the umbrella term Web 2.0 to refer to a set of existing tools, technologies, and practices. Web 2.0 lent a patina of novelty to technologies like RSS, CSS, and Java. Now, with most of the technological obstacles to participation out of the way, it only took seconds from launching a browser to engaging with others, at least in the overdeveloped world. The amateur was the golden child of the Web 2.0 ideology that displayed a distaste for the "dictatorship of expertise" and would give preferential treatment to phenomena like "user-generated content," "the free service," "participatory culture," and "crowdsourcing." Ted Nelson's slogan "You can and must understand computers now!" had been turned into "Data to the corporations!" All of this discourse was embedded in the myth of the liberated user who finally had a voice, supposedly defying hierarchical culture industries. The Web 2.0 ideology limited the imagination of the future of the Web; it made it harder to envision a future that grows out of the genuine needs and desires of its users. While market exchanges are necessary to society, the market frenzy that ensued elevated them to complete dominance.

Web 2.0, to be fair, was incredibly successful as an ideology, a meme, and a marketing ploy with global effects. Already by 2004, the industry claimed that there were some 100 million weblogs. One didn't have to be a skeptic of numerical reasoning to understand that the claim that everybody on this planet was blogging was based on shaky statistics. Clearly, some of these projections were blind to the digital divide, and overlooked the fact that many weblogs were set up but then never used again. But still, we need to acknowledge that more than a decade after its emergence, blogging had roped millions into a daily writing practice; it made them walk through their lives with the eyes of a participant, somebody who could potentially participate or insert her own perspective.[37]

Divergent from a historic understanding of exploitation, under platform capitalism, work doesn't stop when you step outside of the factory or the cubical; work is now occupying all waking hours. Further complicating traditional notions of exploitation, Internet users also became producers of texts, photographs, tags, and videos: a set of activities which offered their own intrinsic rewards.

In 2005, the number of Internet users had reached one billion, which was not only a qualitative shift but also a change in the demographics of users; the net was no longer an exclusively Anglo-American network.[38] While millions started to spend time on the Japanese social networking site Mixi, the Chinese Mop.com, and the South Korean

Cyworld, tens of millions of Indians logged on for the first time as well. This was also the time for the rise of social networking that quickly catered to niche interests as specific as forestry. Today, the Internet is an easily accessible medium for billions of people. On the technical side, faster broadband connection, cheaper hardware, the massification of online sociality, and oligarchical rule of a handful of companies, set the stage for the Internet as a facilitator of the reorganization of work and crowd fleecing.

5) Sleep as a Site of Crisis

Human beings are not efficiently designed for a capitalist system of production.[39]

Thinking about crowd fleecing also means thinking about the privatization of sleep. Time has indeed become a key instrument of oppression. In *The Fatigue Society*, South Korean/German philosopher Byung-Chul Han describes this paradigm shift. A lack of alterity, Han writes, leads to a society where negativity is sidelined and an excess of positivity dominates. Depression, exhaustion, attention deficits, and burnout are not caused by negativity but by an excess of positivity, which can bypass all immunological defenses. The friendly fascism of flexibility and choice leads to complete exhaustion.

I'm thinking about the faces of my fellow New Yorkers in the subway. Selling their lifetime in exchange for survival, they look bone-tired and worn out, many of them trying to get in a few minutes of sleep in the subway on their way to work. Sometimes, there are tender and awkward moments of intimacy, when the head of one sleeper sinks onto the shoulder of her neighbor.

But today, even REM cycles can be made more efficient. Activity-tracking apps like FitBit, popular with HR departments, have become an expression of the zeitgeist. With censors shrunk to the size of ants, smartphones becoming ubiquitous, and social norms bending in the direction of uninhibited sharing on Facebook and Twitter, the Quantified Self is enjoying its moment of fame.

Once considered the only human act of profound uselessness and intrinsic passivity, sleep now collides with the demands of a non-stop 24/7 universe, Jonathan Crary writes.[40] No longer natural, sleep has become a site of crisis. Now, sleep has to be optimized, perfected, made most efficient; the hope is that "our greatest selves" can be unleashed if only we start crunching the numbers and share them with the rest of humanity. Now, self-help doesn't have to stop when we close our eyes. The stipulation goes that adding sleep data to your "personal prospectus" can lead to lower health insurance premiums, and higher competitiveness in the marketplace. You can see the job interviews starting with "Let me show you this stunning visualization of my personal productivity records and sleep cycles of the past four years." This really is a twist of the lesser known Situationist slogan "Remember, you are sleeping for the boss." Sleep becomes work on the brain that has to sort and delete information to ready us for the workday. Jonathan Crary writes:

> Of course people will continue to sleep, but it is now as an experience cut loose from notions of necessity or nature. Instead it will become a managed function, variable according to existing economic and institutional imperatives, a function that can only be justified instrumentally.[41]

Crary writes that the worldwide infrastructure for 24-hour non-stop work and consumption has been in place for at least a decade and a half, the missing ingredient being a human subject shaped to coincide with it more intensively. He describes how modernity has made steady inroads against sleep – the average North American adult now sleeps approximately six and a half hours a night, an erosion from eight hours a generation ago, and – hard as it is to believe – down from ten hours in the early twentieth century.[42] Crary concludes: "as the most private, most enclosed, most vulnerable state common to all, sleep is crucially dependent on society for it to be sustained."

Crowd fleecing signals the end of vacations. Few people in the United States still have the privilege of thinking about hobbies or returning from a real vacation with an attractive, competitive skin tone. Now, there are even *New York Times* articles instructing readers how to take a vacation, because they no longer know how to. More and more people lack the imagination of what to do with free time.

Time spent online means that we have less room in our lives to spend with friends – sitting together in the park or playing volleyball. Sometimes it seems like there is also less room for love, attention, and caring. Adorno complained about monetized leisure such as camping and tourism, which were both entangled with the profit motive, but today, even these activities have become a luxury.[43] Adorno rejected questions about his hobby as they suggested that he had a structured, definable, marketable hobby – "organized freedom" as he called it. For Adorno, if you didn't have a hobby, you would be ridiculed by society. Today, the opposite appears to be true; more and more leisure time is spent online, and hobbies and vacations, at least in the United States, are for the oligarchs.

Crowd fleecing is not solely about the data labor associated with the "worried well" or the super-exploitation of the poorest people on this planet. It is about the millions of underpaid digital workers: the crowd workers and Uber drivers, and TaskRabbits. Each form of digital work carries a different degree of violence, its own level of expropriation and cruelty; and it opens up new avenues for solidarity.

Part II

Part II.

5

Legal Gray Zones

The protective shield of the employment relationship has been cracked; US labor law, rather than watching out for twenty-first-century workers, is stuck in the nineteenth century. The norm of full-time jobs is plunging and the contingent workforce is growing ever greater. The global index of worker rights violations created by The International Trade Union Confederation includes the United States and Kenya on a list of 30 countries with *systematic violations* of worker rights.[1]

The Bureau of Labor Statistics' June 2014 survey of households showed that 1 million people were working part-time jobs, with 237,000 of them stating that they would prefer full-time jobs.[2] A 2015 government study shows that 48.3 percent of "on-call workers" would prefer a different type of employment.[3] At the same time, it shows that more than 85 percent of "independent contractors" would not prefer a different type of type of employment. So when pointing out that "freelancers" would prefer employment to freelancing, it is important to be precise about who exactly is meant by "freelancers."

Overview

In this chapter I will show that technological development outpaces regulatory efforts by the government and that current labor law inadequately reflects the shifts of labor markets to the Internet, thereby leaving an ever-growing segment of the working population unprotected.

1) What is the holdback for regulators?
2) Independent contractor, employees, or a third category of worker?
3) Widening the definition of employment
4) Lawsuits by workers
5) Toward a living wage
6) Toward a Bill of Rights for all platform workers
7) The French Internet tax proposal

A recent survey by the US Department of Labor showed that 53 million people work in contingent positions. "Contingent work" is a term used to describe temporary workers, independent contractors, as well as freelancers. It is important to note that we should not equate all these different group with freelancers. Contingent work is by no means new. Farmworkers have been contingent in the US. Domestic workers, janitors, and many healthcare workers do not have job security. It is stunning to observe that with platform capitalism, contingency is now spreading throughout the economy. A research report by the American software company Intuit predicted that by the year 2020, 40 percent of the American workforce will be "contingent workers."[4] Within that group of contingent workers, we also find those who toil for some of the more than 145 online outsourcing marketplaces. CrowdFlower has some 5 million registered workers and the Chinese online freelance platform Zhubajie/Witsmart claims close to 12 million workers.[5] Even when we calculate that not all of the registered workers are in fact active, this is a workforce of significant size.

Currently, outdated labor law and the legal gray zones of the Internet propel the blossoming of on-demand labor platforms. Over the long term, however, owners and policymakers need to understand that platform capitalism is not sustainable if it does not consider the social standards for workers.

Policymakers demonstrate a wait-and-see attitude. For them, uncertainty leads to forbearance. Even the enforcement of existing protections under the Fair Labor Standards Act is hardly a given.

For employers and platform owners who knock around workers, the chance of getting caught is very small. The Republican Party is waging a war on worker rights by not granting the Department of Labor the resources needed to employ a sufficient number of federal inspectors. Just consider that in 1941, there was one federal inspector for every 11,000 workers. As of 2008, one inspector was responsible for 141,000 workers. Three years later, in 2011, the Department of Labor had just 1,000 inspectors responsible for 130 million workers in 7 million enterprises. "The average employer has just a 0.001

percent chance of being investigated in a given year," political scientist Gordon Lafer estimates.[6] Strategic understaffing means that employers who violate labor regulations only have a very small chance of getting caught, and even if they do get busted, the worst that can happen to them would be that they have to return the wages owed. Robert Kuttner, co-founder of *The American Prospect*, puts it this way: "If you rob someone's house, you will probably go to jail. If you rob someone's wages, you might have to repay the wages. Or maybe not."[7]

The first part of this chapter is dedicated to crowd work. Importantly, the problems of crowd workers, online freelancers, and online marketplaces for physical services like Uber and TaskRabbit are very similar. All of them hover in the same legal gray zones of the Internet – they are deeply connected and should be considered in tandem. Without being a legal professional, I am identifying key regulatory issues in this chapter. These include: the classification of crowd workers as independent contractors vs. employees – I am discussing related class action suits brought about by workers, and the issue of a minimum wage (or living wage) floor; and an interpretation of crowd work as "industrial homework." I am suggesting that a broader, more inclusive definition of employment is needed to embrace more twenty-first-century workers. A second short-term approach would be to offer all citizens the same protections without tying them to a particular institutional work relationship. I'm also calling for a Bill of Rights for Digital Workers. A long-term proposal is, of course, Universal Basic Income, which is really getting some grassroots traction now, also in the United States.

The second part of this chapter is about legal interventions in the area of data labor. I'm arguing that regulators should revisit the French 2013 Colin & Collin tax proposal.[8]

In the conclusion, I will argue that Universal Basic Income would positively impact the future of crowd work and data labor. I'll show how Universal Basic Income could solve some of the problems of platform capitalism while not addressing others. This chapter is an invitation for activists, legal scholars, and policymakers to carry forward some of these discussions, proposals, and questions.

1) What is the Holdback for Regulators?

Since 2010, legal scholars like Miriam Cherry and Alek Felstiner have extensively written about digital labor. Alek Felstiner cautions: "our broken and outdated legal regime simply doesn't accommodate new labor models very well." He continues: "Our work laws are so far out of touch with the modern physical labor market, never mind virtual work that they quite simply don't function very well. We cannot afford to exacerbate this problem."[9] Miriam Cherry characterizes one of the consequences of the failure of the legal establishment to address the realities of twenty-first-century work: "The ultimate result is a fuzzy gray market for casual click work services, where there is practically no regulation."[10] But ethnographic work has shown that some Turkers are not in favor of government regulation of MTurk, as they are concerned that such interference may lead to the closure of the platform.[11]

Alek Felstiner does not sound hopeful about the prospect of the situation of digital workers changing any time soon. He writes, "there are virtually no cases and few indications in the literature as to how courts might approach regulation of the 'cyberspace workplace.'"[12] For the most part, Felstiner faults the "wait and see" group of legal scholars, who suggest that the phenomena associated with digital labor simply have not yet settled down in their development. Consequently, this group suggests that legal scholars should wait and see what the true nature of this work really is.

Internet exceptionalism is a variation on this theme – the suggestion that the Internet is a completely new and different "cyberspace" that exists outside of society and does not have to comply with the law. The concept refers to the separation of the roughly four-decade-old network from the daily struggles related to class, race, and gender. The language of Internet exceptionalism implies that legal "real world" frameworks do not apply online, and that the struggles of those who are powerless and exploited by platform owners are separate from those of baristas, adjunct professors, or nail salon workers. "The more we write about what takes place online as if it occurred in some other world, the more we fail to relate this communication system, and everything that happens through it, to the society around us. To understand the Internet, we have to destroy it as an idea," writes author Jacob Silverman.[13]

Internet exceptionalism is by no means a novel idea; it can be traced back to the early 1980s when cyberpunk science fiction author William Gibson coined the term "cyberspace," which was later associated with the Internet. Cyberspace seemed so excitingly separate from real life. Gibson, in his novel *Neuromancer*, described cyberspace as "a consensual hallucination experienced daily by billions of legitimate operators."[14] In 1996, John Perry Barlow, writer for the Grateful Dead, expressed this servse of separation in his Declaration of the Independence of Cyberspace: "Governments of the Industrial

World, you weary giants of flesh and steel, I come from Cyberspace, the new home of Mind. On behalf of the future, I ask you of the past to leave us alone."[15] In the same year, a judge described the Internet as "a unique and wholly new medium of worldwide human common occasion."[16] Also in the late 1990s, Republican politician Newt Gingrich warmly embraced cyber libertarian ideas projecting that they could pave the way for work environments that would be "unburdened" by government regulation. This has become eerily true, and the understanding of the Internet as a completely new medium, outside the gates of society, left its mark on policymakers. It's worth remembering that whether a worker toils in an Amazon warehouse or works for crowdSPRING, her body will get tired and hungry. She'll have to take care of car payments, medical bills for her children, and student debts, not to mention saving for retirement. Digital work makes the body of the worker invisible but no less real or expendable.

2) Independent Contractors, Employees, or What?

The question whether or not workers are independent contractors or employees is at the heart of the labor conflicts in the crowdsourcing industry. For the uninitiated, the question of misclassification might seem overly technical, inessential, or even esoteric. But as you will see, decisions about the classification of workers have far-reaching implications for them and for the companies, which might make themselves vulnerable to lawsuits.[17]

Some people prefer contract work because they value the schedule and location flexibility; but consider that only statutory employees, not contingent workers, qualify for protections under the Fair Labor Standards Act (FLSA) of 1938. Specifically, the FLSA requires employers to pay at least minimum wage and overtime. And there is more: following the Civil Rights Act of 1964, employers are prohibited from discriminating on the basis of race, color, religion, sex, or national origin. The Discrimination in Employment Act prohibits managers from showing bias based on the age of employees. Furthermore, there are protections against prejudicial behavior based on disability, as well as the Medical Leave Act. Lastly, let's not forget about The National Labor Relations Act, which grants employees the right to organize. While many of these legal rights have been undermined at a state level (just think of Wisconsin's "Right-to-Work" law), independent contractors are not protected by any of these laws. A recent survey of on-demand workers highlighted their desire for health insurance, retirements benefits, paid sick leave and vacation days, disability and unemployment insurance.[18] In the crowdsourcing sector, independent contractors are not only facing massive minimum wage violations, they are also entirely without rights.

The attorneys for the crowdsourcing company CrowdFlower are adamant about the claim that their workers are independent contractors, not employees. In the absence of a contract and control of the work process, this is a clear case, they argue. On the one hand, it is true that crowdsourcing is different than the forms of labor abuses that the US Congress sought to regulate with the Federal Labor Standards Act. Alek Felstiner cautions, however, that crowdsourcing companies shouldn't be too sure about the legality of their claim that their laborers are independent contractors, because that assertion has never been tested in the courts. "Contrary to the expectations of vendors such as Amazon, and many crowd workers, claims to employee status are not presumptively barred or inherently invalid."[19] On that point, legal scholar Miriam Cherry found that already "in June 2008, the Internal Revenue Service issued a private letter holding that greeters for the Electric Sheep Company in the virtual world Second Life were employees, rather than independent contractors."[20]

The question of how to classify workers doesn't only play out online; of course, it also impacts the realities of workers in Amazon's warehouses. Here, the German service worker union Ver.di wants Amazon workers to be classified as retail employees, while Amazon insists that they are logistics workers. These tensions surrounding employment classification have led to protests in various Amazon warehouses.

3) Widening the Definition of Employment

How does US federal law define employment? A person is generally an employee if the employer has the right to control that person's work process. In the case of an independent contractor, the employer does not control the process but prescribes the end result of the work process.

Federal Law offers four tests to distinguish between an employee and an independent contractor. A very abbreviated version of these tests states that in cases where the employer supplies the tools necessary to execute the work, and again, is able to control the work process, the relationship can be characterized as employment. In addition, employment is defined by a workplace that is provided by the employer. Lastly, the laborer only works for this one business; he or she has to be economically dependent on the particular company.

Independent contractors, by contrast, work without supervision; they are specialized and skilled. In the case of independent contract work, management has no control over the work process and the engagement with the company is only for a limited period of time.

Solo workers shoulder the material backbone for crowd work while platform owners provide the cloud-computing infrastructure. Crowd work is largely performed at home or in cafes, on an unprecedented scale, in real time, with workers providing their own means of production necessary to boot up their laboring activities.

But it is worth reminding readers that the Fair Labor Standards Act was established in response to the Great Depression/The New Deal, and that it was specifically designed at a time when workers toiled in physical, employer-owned workplaces. Almost 80 years later, the nature of work has changed for millions of workers in America and around the world, and these changes are not reflected in the law.

The US Department of Labor clearly recognizes the shortcomings of the current legal definition of employment: "in substance, the law is based on a nineteenth century concept whose purposes are wholly unrelated to contemporary employment policy."[21] Their recommendation for redefinition of employment is focused on the actual economic relationships on the ground, rather than the tests that I described above. Speaking to the situation of millions of contingent workers, however, the Office of the Secretary of the Department of Labor stated: "it is beyond [their] means to recommend a full policy program in this emerging area of concern."[22]

An additional site of contestation concerns the question of whether or not digital labor should be considered "industrial homework." If crowd work were to be accepted as "industrial homework," minimum wage and overtime laws would apply. The Department of Labor defines "industrial homework" as "production by any covered person in a home, apartment, or room in a residential establishment, of goods for an employer who permits or authorizes such production."[23] Whether or not digital labor would count as "industrial homework" would depend on the willingness of courts to accept that, today, digital services and goods are part of the labor landscape.

Companies interested in minimizing labor costs will rearrange their work processes in a way that deprives workers of the aforementioned protections under Federal law. One way to cover more workers by the traditional protections offered by the US government would be to test the legality of the classification in several courts. This will help workers who do indeed work under circumstances that resemble employment. If the FLSA were applied to crowd work, for example, time for setting up equipment and waiting periods in preparation for work would be compensable.

Rather than trying to argue that all of these workers are actually employees, which would be an uphill struggle, we might rather want to focus on broadening the definition of employment. Such definition would need to be cognizant of twenty-first-century work realities. When rethinking legal protections for today's workers, be they Uber drivers or crowd workers, we should keep a keen eye on the protections afforded to workers through employment.

By now, I have clarified how much hinges on the definition of employment, and how a nineteenth-century framing of the employment relationship will leave 40 percent of the American workforce without significant legal protections.

Jeff Howe, who coined the term crowdsourcing, wrote on his blog that Mechanical Turk "gives us a snapshot of a depressing future in which legions of click-slaves toil away at identifying duplicate webpages for less than minimum wage."[24] In 2009, Harvard law professor Jonathan Zittrain, wrote a Newsweek article titled "The Internet Creates a New Kind of Sweatshop." In the article, Zittrain noted that new forms of digital labor are cashing in on the post-financial crisis, and that they "could also usher in a new era of digital sweatshops."[25] But later, Zittrain put some distance between himself and the language of sweatshops, emphasizing that he did not pick the title of the article. The CEO of CrowdFlower, Lucas Biewald, wryly commented:

> the great thing about digital work is it's really hard to make a sweatshop out of digital work. It's really hard to force someone to do work, you can't beat someone up through a computer screen.[26]

Is the language of sweatshops really overstating the situation of workers on CrowdFlower or Mechanical Turk? The US Department of Labor defines sweatshops as a "place of employment that violates two or more federal or state labor laws governing minimum wage and overtime, child labor, industrial homework, occupational safety and health, workers' compensation ..."[27] On Mechanical Turk, minors are working to earn game credits, and they, along with all other workers, are denied a minimum wage or overtime payments. It is debatable whether calling AMT a sweatshop would be accurate, but doing so draws attention to workers who work under unethical conditions.

Various scholars, including Felstiner, have argued that legal intervention can only protect the organized efforts of crowd workers who
would have to complain and jointly help to alter the future of the
information economy.[28] As long as workers do not express their
outrage and organize, the chances of change are minimal.

4) Lawsuits by Workers

In June 2015, a judge in California ruled that an Uber driver was in
fact an employee, and not a contractor.[29] In October 2012, Christopher
Otey, a crowd worker for CrowdFlower filed a class action lawsuit
against the company in the United States, arguing that CrowdFlower,
one of the largest crowd sourcing companies, failed to pay minimum
wage – currently $7.25 an hour – to its American workforce under
the Fair Labor Standards Act.[30] As I have already mentioned,
CrowdFlower's lawyers insisted that none of their "cloud workers"
are employees; they are "free contractors." The company pays some
of their cloud workers no more than $2 per hour. In California, the
state where CrowdFlower operates, the minimum wage is $8 per
hour. In San Francisco, CrowdFlower's home city, the minimum wage
is $10.55; in Los Angeles it is $15. The case was pending a motion
to be dismissed because the court, situated in San Francisco where
this globally operating company was founded, might not have jurisdiction. In 2014, CrowdFlower has settled the class action lawsuit
for $585,000.[31] Consequently, the court did not rule on the question
of whether or not the workers were employees.

In addition, a class action suit was filed by a group of Yelp reviewers in October 2013. The reviewers claimed that their writing, their
uncompensated labor, is vital to the existence of this site, and that
therefore, they should be considered employees of Yelp.[32]

It is one matter whether or not the FLSA applies to crowd workers
such as Otey – that is for judges to decide – but a larger number of
such lawsuits would certainly draw more public attention to the dark
sides of digital labor.

5) Toward a Living Wage

At this point, it is also crucial to understand that workers, rather
than demanding minimum wage, should really press for living wages.
Minimum wage was meant as the minimum level of payment that
would protect particularly vulnerable workers from poverty. It was

designed to guarantee a basic standard of living. In theory, a minimum wage should reflect the needs of workers and their families as well as the cost of living.

The concept of a living wage refers to the minimum income necessary for worker to meet needs such as housing, closing, and nutrition. In the United Kingdom, the standard is generally in reference to a person working 40 hours a week without extra income. Based on a living wage, this person should be able to afford the basic quality of life, which includes payments for food, utilities, transportation, some recreation, childcare, and one course of continuing education. A living wage, following this definition, does not include saving for retirement or repaying any kind of debt.

The minimum wage, as cemented by law, does not currently cover those basic needs of many workers who are dependent on it. Instead, these workers have to rely on government programs to survive. A living wage calculator, designed at the Massachusetts Institute for Technology determined that in New York City, a family with two adults, one of them being the sole earner, and two children would need to make at least $10.60 an hour to live in poverty and $22.32 to earn a living wage. The minimum wage is currently $7.25.[33]

Currently, the majority of the workers who toil in labor platforms are based in the United States, Asia Pacific, and South America. It is clear that changes to the US legal system wouldn't directly bear on workers in those other countries, but before asserting the irrelevance of legal changes within the United States with regards to the digital labor situation, we also need to consider that most labor platforms like Amazon are headquartered in the US. If the American crowdsourcing industry were to accept minimum wage standards, this would positively affect the situation of workers worldwide.

Thus far, in this chapter, you have followed reflections about the here and now of digital work. What follows are more long-term goals. In this chapter, I'm thinking about government regulation and possible responses by policymakers. So far, I have reflected on the definition of employment and the role of Internet exceptionalism. I will continue with a short analysis of the Colin & Collin tax proposal, a fascinating French update for corporate tax law for the twenty-first century. Next, I will discuss why Facebook, Amazon, and Google should be treated as utilities, to be regulated just like gas and electricity companies. I will conclude with an introduction to the idea of Universal Basic Income, which would start to address many of the problems with data labor and crowd work.

I started out this chapter by pointing to an estimated 60 million Americans who will be without worker rights by the year 2020. Alek

Felstiner suggests mandatory and enforced wage floors for crowd-sourcing companies[34] but without the outrage of workers, little will happen. Companies would be wise to voluntarily establish more habitable, sustainable labor markets. They should commit to paying fair or living wages; satisfied workers are more productive.[35] Worker associations can lobby on behalf of crowd workers; they can attempt to establish benefits, handle disputes, inform crowd workers of their legal rights, and serve as a clearinghouse for campaign activities.[36]

Similarly, workers could – and should – file class action suits against large crowdsourcing companies. Workers can fight for recognition of their transnationally situated workforce as a "community of interest," for example. While they might not get a favorable decision, "pursuing an appropriate litigation strategy against a carefully selected target might yield groundbreaking new doctrines for virtual work."[37]

I am concluding this section on crowd work with a proposal.

6) Toward a Bill of Rights for All Platform Workers

In the spring of 2014, Tim Berners-Lee proposed a document that calls for accountability on the Internet where rampant privacy violations by large corporations and the National Security Agency (NSA) have been a common occurrence. In his proposal for a "Magna Carta of the Web," a Bill of Rights for the Internet,[38] Berners-Lee calls for affordable access, protection of personal user information, and the right to communicate in private. He evokes neutral networks that don't discriminate against content or users, freedom of expression, and decentralized open infrastructure.[39] Soliciting the support of groups and institutions, the inventor of the Web started a campaign under the title "The Web We Want."[40] While Berners-Lee's proposal comes with plenty of star power – Edward Snowden endorsed it and Sir Tim Berners-Lee himself is no stranger to social capital himself – it is by no means the first draft of such a document.

It is stunning, however, that over the past decade proposals for such a Bill of Rights relating to the Internet have been labor-blind. Brazil's President Dilma Rousseff signed a Brazilian proposal for a Bill of Rights for the Internet into law in 2014.[41] The proposal cements the principle of net neutrality, which means that network operators must treat all traffic equally. Brazil's "Internet law" also legally protects the privacy of Brazilian Internet users by prohibiting providers from abusing user data.[42]

Berners-Lee might consider amending his Magna Carta to accommodate a framework for dignity and justice for paid work in the deregulated marketplace of the Internet, broken down by nation-states corresponding to the legal jurisdiction. Adherence to such a Bill could become a point of competitive advantage for upstarts. But while asserting such basic rights is honorable, how would they ever be enforced, and by whom? One example of an enforceable document like that, in the European Union, is the Passenger Bill of Rights that defines the rights of passengers in the case of flight cancellations, delays, or overbooking. It also spells out enforcement mechanisms in case of non-compliance.[43]

But a Crowd Workers Bill of Rights, just like the Universal Declaration of Human Rights, could not be legally binding. Nonetheless, since 1948 the latter has been adopted by many national constitutions. National and international law has been influenced by this declaration, and many local institutions have adopted parts of it. While not directly enforceable, a Bill of Rights for the Internet could become a compelling instrument when applying moral pressure on governments and platform owners alike.

We can also take cues from the Domestic Workers' Bill of Rights that was passed in New York State in late 2010, granting nannies, housekeepers, and others working in private households basic legal rights such as a day of rest every seven days, and the right to overtime pay after 40 hours of work in a week.[44]

In a 2013 paper, Lilly Irani and M. Six Silberman elaborated how they arrived at a "Worker's Bill of Rights" by placing a task on Amazon Mechanical Turk asking workers to articulate such a Bill from their perspective. Some of the workers responded that they "felt that their work was regularly rejected unfairly or arbitrarily," and that such a Bill of Rights should include minimum wages, as well as fair and timely payment.[45]

In 2014, a group of Turkers and researchers authored a set of guidelines for ethical research on Amazon Mechanical Turk that could provide inspiration for a Crowdwork Bill of Rights. The section on fair payment is particularly eye opening.[46]

We might also take Ross Perlin's "Intern Bill of Rights" into consideration. Proposed in his book *Intern Nation*, Perlin asserts that all interns deserve fair compensation for their work, usually in the form of wages or dedicated training, and the same legal protection and basic workplace benefits – such as sick days and extra pay for overtime – as all other workers. Interns, Perlin writes, must not to be forced to take an unpaid internship and must not be required to pay in order to work. Interns should be treated with dignity and respect by coworkers and supervisors.[47]

A Bill of Rights for Crowd Workers should demand:

- Crowd workers, consignors, and platform owners should be able to communicate and treat each other with dignity and respect
- Fair payment starting with the establishment of a minimum wage floor
- The abolition of child labor
- Fair working conditions to include accurate classification, prompt payment, and protections against wage theft

Moving on from crowd work to data labor, let's consider the Electronic Frontier Foundation (EFF), which authored *A Bill of Privacy Rights for Social Network Users* in 2010. Here, EFF demanded the right to quit, exit a given platform completely, the right of control over one's data, and the right to informed decision making.[48] Before this, a group of Internet experts, academics, lawyers, journalists, activists, and students came together to phrase a Bill of Rights for Users of the Social Web, publicly asserting that all netizens are entitled to certain fundamental rights, which include the clarity of terms of service, the control of users over the sharing of their data, and the predictability of privacy change.[49,50]

A proposal by a group of scholars calls for a People's Terms of Service Agreement for Facebook. This narrower agreement would be a collectively negotiated contract that reflects some common consumer priorities. "Interested users and consumer advocates [would] publicly debate their consensus priorities and then drop them into a model contract."[51] The proposal further suggests that contracts could be unilaterally altered and that users have the right to have all of their materials permanently deleted. Users, they suggest, should have a right to compensation for commercial use of the user's names or likeness, and that they have "the right to confidentiality, meaning that companies promise not to disclose personal information to third parties unless users meaningfully opt into such disclosure for each party."[52]

The recent discourse about privacy has overshadowed the debate about the Internet as a portal for traditional labor exploitation – what I call crowd fleecing. While all of the mentioned proposals echo similar concerns about intellectual property, permanency, transparency, and security, an understanding of the situation of online workers is undoubtedly absent. Online workers should enjoy the same protections as workers who do not use the Internet as the exclusive interface for their daily toil. We need a common standard that would allow us to evaluate and improve digital labor.

The responses to these various proposals for a Bill of Rights for the Internet have been mixed. At first, the call for such a Bill may seem vague and possibly inconsequential. Could such expression of human consciousness in the digital age really change the power imbalance between users and intermediaries? Could there be sufficient public awareness of such a Bill of Rights?

In the second part of this chapter, I am investigating regulatory measures in relation to data labor. I'll first suggest that the French tax proposal that was issued in 2013 should be revisited, and then conclude the chapter with an introduction and discussion of the idea of Universal Basic Income.

7) The French Internet Tax Proposal

When I first read about the Colin & Collin tax proposal I was deeply moved. It focuses on a proposal by the French government, which targets Google, Amazon, Apple, and Facebook, asserting that these companies are profiting from the data of the French population without being taxed accordingly.

In 2007, in a blog essay with the title "What the MySpace Generation Should Know about Working for Free,"[53] I suggested that the data of users of social networking services like MySpace (if you still remember that) are being turned into profits. Two years later, this topic was much discussed at the Internet as Playground and Factory conference at The New School. While the idea of users being active agents in the digital economy is part of mainstream discussions today, few have offered realistic proposals in response to this expropriation scheme. What is proclaimed and offered as a free service is in fact exceedingly expensive in terms of its social costs; privacy intrusions exceed our wildest dreams. Some, including the artist Laurel Ptak, have called for wages for data labor but ultimately I don't think that Facebook would ever directly pay its users.

Ptak pays homage to the Wages for Housework campaign by the International Feminist Collective in Italy in 1972, which according to Kathi Weeks "sought to contest the invisibility of domestic work and its moralization, to redress both its devaluation as work and its overvaluation as labor of love."[54] In her book *The Problem with Work*, Weeks clarifies that it isn't at all certain that the campaigners for wages for housework really wanted what they were asking for.

The demand, quite literally, for wages for housework apparently only appears once and even there it is immediately put to question by the campaigners themselves. Weeks writes, "The demand for wages was conceived not only as a concrete reform, but as an opportunity to make visible, and encourage critical reflection on, the position of women in the work society – both in the wage labor system and in its satellite, the family."[55] In other words, the demand for wages should be understood as a provocation that leads to reflections that expose invisible labor. In similar ways, Ptak's piece could be simply understood as a way to contest the invisible labor of platform capitalism and point to the supporting role of digital laborers who are hidden behind the algorithm.

Highly relevant to this discussion is hypertext pioneer Ted Nelson, who suggested a system of micro-payments already in the 1960s, as part of his project Xanadu. Nelson's rule number nine for the project was: "every document can contain a royalty mechanism at any desired degree of granularity to ensure payment on any portion accessed, including virtual copies, called "transclusions," of all or part of the document."[56] The idea is fascinating: in a noncommittal world, people may not want to pay for a subscription to an entire magazine online; they may rather be willing to pay only for the amount of characters of a given text that they actually read. According to Nelson, the unit of payment would be "content scrolls," which would precisely refer to the amount of text that the reader actually scrolled through. Let's say, you could read the first paragraph of an article, decide that this is not for you, and then not pay for the rest of the piece. While the project has come to new prominence because Jaron Lanier promoted it in his book *Who Owns the Future*, such a micro-payment system would require a set-up other than the World Wide Web in its current form. It is therefore impractical and widespread adoption seems unlikely.

Another approach to paying for data labor would be to regulate companies like Facebook and Google. The way corporations are taxed needs to be brought more in line with twenty-first century realities. Mark Zuckerberg does not make a secret of the fact that "we think of [Facebook] as a utility."[57] This is by no means a new idea in other sectors of the economy such as telecommunications. When industries grow, they often start to get regulated. It is evident that Facebook, while being a publicly traded company, has not become more socially responsible. With far over one billion users, government protections for users of Facebook should start at the federal level. But what would such regulation look like? Rather than the demand for Facebook to pay its users, it would make more sense to call on governments worldwide to tax platform owners based on the value that citizens of given countries generate for them.

The French government asked Pierre Collin and Nicolas Colin to draft a report on the taxation of the digital economy. Colin and Collin write: "Inspiring startups or global corporations disrupt entire industries with the intensive use of IT, innovative business models, iterative design, and the powerful leveraging of data originated by user activity. And yet, official statistics utterly failed to measure all this."[58] Therefore, the report suggests to reform corporate tax, which its authors characterize as fair as it only taxes profitable companies.

In short, they suggest to tax platform owners like Facebook and Google based on the monetary value generated through data, which are produced by French citizens on French soil. With Marc Andreessen, Colin poses "the digital economy is eating the world." Collin and Colin compare this tax to the concept of a carbon tax, which grew out of the 1997 Kyoto Protocol on climate change. They would "tax any company that collects data through regular and systematic monitoring from lots of users based in France."[59] This proposed tax system would acknowledge that users in any particular country – France in this case – are part of the operation of companies that offer supposedly free services online. In other words, companies like Google, Apple, Facebook, and Amazon would be taxed based on the volume of data generated by the French population, which they ingest, as this data is part of the economic operation of these companies. It should be a relatively trivial task to distinguish data based on submissions that truly originate in France from all French-speaking content. Given the reality of social democracies in Europe, where taxes may indeed translate into social benefits for the population, such taxation of intermediaries would be a good starting point.

6

On Selective Engagement

When the Factory Turns Cold: A Manifesto

In certain periods, for instance when we learn that telcos and tech giants are making millions from their surveillance pact with the government, selling our location, and every word we write or speak, the will to resist gains momentum.

We won't answer your status updates. We will throw a switch and let bots do the data entries for us while we go for a stroll.[1] We will not cater to your expectations; we feel nothing but disdain for your conformism. We refuse to be stripped of our data. We will not submit to hours of tweaking of your privacy settings, or turning off Retweets, only to limit unwanted exposure and uncontrollable data leakage. Equally, opt-in defaults have become agents of forced labor. We lost interest and will no longer be caught in your web, enthralled and captured. When we refuse to perform ourselves, we will manage to break our attention away from your centralized hubs. We don't trust you and don't believe that somehow, suddenly, you'll act ethically and respect our relationships. We will seek new ways of coming together, not just temporarily but for the long haul. We don't boycott; we defect; we don't need your hall of mirrors. We don't have to look cool; we quit your reputation economy. We are tired of soliciting "likes" from our friends, which are then used to advertise to them. We are weary of being tagged in random photos and don't want to waste time thinking up authentic witticisms. We may not beat your mighty commerce and security apparatus but we can break away from your networked spectacle of self-promotion.

Various studies have shown that many users are feeling less satisfied with their lives when constantly reading about the highlights in the lives of others.[2] Let's put an end to Facebook Depression and social media dependency. Political theorist Jodi Dean even talks of the growing "constant-contact media addiction, birdlike attention-span compression, and vapidity to the point of depravity." Some propose "Internet usage disorder" as a new category of mental illness.[3]

We refuse the anxiety, envy, and loneliness that we feel because we are enthralled in your web. Our vitality is the sum of our fears.

Overview

1) Targeting the centers of power
2) Break off, switch off, disengage, unthink
3) A reprieve from monetized data labor
4) "There is no CLOUD, just other people's computers"
5) On withdrawal, defection, and refusal
6) Toward tactical refusal and selective engagement

Today, the data precariat no longer includes solely artists, musicians, and writers: it is now comprised of everybody who produces data. This chapter thinks through tactical refusal, defection, withdrawal, and selective engagement as possible responses to the monetization of data labor and cloud computing.

Which frustrations and disappointments instilled the desire for more ethically aligned alternatives to platform capitalism? Some of the urgency to build alternatives is rooted in the Global Recession, the "Uberization" of professional work, stagnating wages despite ever-increasing productivity, and a growing sense that capitalism is not good for most people.[4] The search for alternatives is also motivated by pervasive shifts of labor markets, the Internet of Things, sprawling automation, and cloud computing.

Tensions are increasing and questions about possible alternatives to platform capitalism are more urgently felt – just think of Los Indignados, Occupy, DebtStrike, Podemos, mass protests in Chile, the revolutionary upheavals in North African countries that were sometimes misconstrued as a "Twitter Revolution," the global antiwar protests on February 15, 2003, or the legendary defeat in the US House of Representatives of the Stop Online Piracy Act (SOPA) in 2012. Or, consider the rise of platform cooperatives that I introduce in chapter 7.

Add to that, the push for Universal Basic Income and the massive responses to disclosures of the whistleblower Edward Snowden, strategically analyzed, released, and distributed by Laura Poitras, Glenn Greenwald, and others. But government surveillance can also be profitable for platform owners. On the one hand, Snowden's revelations made some users turn away from giant platforms, but at the same time, telcos like AT&T, Sprint, T-Mobile, and Verizon are not only compelled to hand over user data, as it turns out, they are also making tens of millions of dollars from selling your phone records to the NSA. T-Mobile, for example, charges law enforcement a flat fee of $500 per target per wiretap. Or, take Sprint:

> *Sprint/Nextel – charges $400 per wiretap per "market area" and per "technology" as well as a $10 per day fee, capped at $2,000; it also charges $120 for pictures or video, $60 for email, $60 for voice mail and $30 for text messages; it also charges $50 per tower dump and $30 per month per target for location tracking.*[5]

1) Targeting the Centers of Power

When thinking about building alternatives, some predicate their vision on the end of capitalism as we know it, leading to a kind of wholesale criticism that leaves us without any alternatives. Contrary to this approach, *social visions* evaluate the current system and offer a guide to action that might lead to a new system.[6] For me, this discussion centers around my proposals for selective engagement and platform cooperativism.

Today, Apple, Goldman Sachs, Google, and even IBM are nothing but brands and their line segments can reach variable orientation in space. Apple calls production managers at the Taiwanese company Foxconn – the producers of the Xbox and Playstations – who then coordinate the production of objects, only to add the Apple brand sticker at the end of the manufacturing process. Naomi Klein taught us to think of the brand as the core meaning of the modern corporation, and advertising as one vehicle used to convey that meaning to the world.[7] Klein links the ever-growing cultural influence of multinational corporations to the innocuous ideas of development management theorists in the mid-1980s, which argued that successful businesses must primarily produce brands as opposed to products.

The author Matt Taibbi famously referred to the giant vampire squid that wraps itself around the face of humanity, relentlessly jamming his blood funnels into anything that smells like money.[8] This method of maintaining power is rooted in the ability of the overclass to spin and shift from one resource point to another.

To platform owners like Google or Facebook, what really matters is that their products become cultural magnets engineered primarily by "Internet users." Copyright of submitted material mattered only in so far as companies like Facebook want to be able to delete porn. But ownership of this content is not central to its business model. It is not based on the commoditization of knowledge; the benefits are indirect.

What is implicit in this, then, is also that the most important, value-generating class is not so much defined by the monetization of their knowledge labor, abstractions, and ideas but simply their raw life. Sheer life has become the source of profit. As Paolo Virno put it – "life itself is put to work." David Harvey writes: "What once was viewed as natural social behavior and pleasure-seeking has now been turned into labor."[9] The most significant participation in today's digital economy is not primarily intellectual; it is life itself.

If class is about property, then the vectoral class remains neatly defined. Consequently, the hacker class would be everyone else; the creative segment of the 99 percent. The ones who are productive are no longer merely researchers, authors, biologists, chemists, musicians, philosophers, or programmers, but also the 11-year-old on Facebook or the children who work on Amazon Mechanical Turk to feed their gaming habit with credit points.

Yet not all capitalists can be vectoralists. Thirty percent of the German economy, for example, is still based on manufacturing. Mercedes Benz, Daimler, and Caterpillar cannot spin their business around on a dime; they are not vectoral. They are not replacing the "productive capitalists;" instead, they are a segment of the merchant capitalists.

And the vectoral class no longer divests itself of direct productive processes either. Just think of the fact that Google inhaled all the leading companies that produce hardware and software in relation to the Internet of Things. And even more importantly, think of Google's acquisition of many leading robotics companies. Then consider Facebook's acquisition of Oculus, a manufacturer of virtual reality gear. These examples show the ways in which companies are moving from "cyber space" back into commodity space.

But one thing is clear, the search for non-commercial alternatives can't just be a discussion about gadgets, design interfaces, and back ends. To change everything you can't just click here. Ask Evgeny Morozov: technological solutionism is not the answer. But such disdain for techno solutionism cannot lead to a rejection of alternative social infrastructures online.

The figure of the politically-minded hacker used to be at the center of the discussion about digital alternatives. Former NSA Chief Michael Hayden has a rather burlesque take on hackers. For him, the term represents "nihilists, anarchists, activists, Lulzsec, Anonymous, twentysomethings who haven't talked to the opposite sex in five or six years."[10]

The loosely associated international network of activists Anonymous demonstrated the importance of what the author Gabriela Coleman calls *weapons of the geek*, not to be mistaken for *weapons of the weak*, a term introduced by James Scott to capture the unique clandestine nature of peasant politics – from foot dragging to minor acts of sabotage.[11] Network-centric actions like Distributed Denial of Service attacks are still part of their repertoire. In *Hacker Manifesto*, McKenzie Wark hailed hackers as the class of the dispossessed, the ones who produce abstractions. Hackers are not hackers of property but hackers of networks, he wrote. Today the hacker stands in for the deviant political subject whose aspirations, political insight, and tactical approaches vary widely. How useful is the hacker as the prototype of digital subjectivity today? Nishant Shah, director of The Centre for Internet & Society in Mumbai, India, wrote that it might be useful to look at the transformation of the hacker from the fringe to the mainstream, to step away from a defensiveness that justifies and explains the hacker.[12]

In the 1990s, the tactical media collective Critical Art Ensemble suggested that resistance should migrate to the network where power resides. Historically, activists targeted the centers of power: from the stock exchange to the headquarters of pharmaceutical companies. In the 1980s, the Coalition to Unleash Power (ACTUP) protested the apathetic approach of the US Food and Drug Administration to AIDS drug development by organizing the national "Seize Control of the FDA" demonstration, aiming to shut down the business of the FDA for a day.[13] In 2015, thousands of McDonald's employees and union activists went to the company's headquarters near Chicago to protest against the "poverty wages" paid to most of its 400,000 employees.[14]

Such protest against Amazon or Google rarely occurs at the physical headquarters of these companies in Seattle, Mountain View, and elsewhere. Despite a brief activist takeover of the Airbnb headquarters in San Francisco in 2016, there has not been much action in that vein. Where are the massive occupations of far out-of-the-way data centers? It is important not to overlook the validity of such direct action.

2) Break Off, Switch Off, Disengage, Unthink

Where to begin? Thinking about alternatives to the commercial regime of data labor could begin by giving priority to spending time with your own mind without distractions, and constant affirmative prompts. It could be about breaking off, switching off, and disengaging from the network. It could be about obscuring the network with fake data or unthinking the network altogether, as Ulises Mejias suggested in *Off the Network*.

On the post-Snowden Web, the network effect has run out of steam; hordes of users cut loose and backed out of Facebook when it became official that their parents and the NSA got on board. Who needs to see one billion faces anyway? Instead, let's foster thorny conversations, direct actions, and slowly growing friendships.

The search for new tactical approaches could find inspiration in the struggle of domestic workers and migrants in the 1960s, most notably the efforts of Hugo Chavez, who organized migrant farm workers and succeeded in raising wages with the help of consumer boycotts of grapes and lettuce.[15] A consumer boycott against platform owners would have to be a boycott by advertising agencies and all those others who purchase our user data.

Instead of hanging out on Facebook, Geert Lovink suggests, we should waste our time elsewhere. At a conference at the Volksbühne theater in Berlin in 2014, long-time Wird writer and Internet guru Bruce Sterling appealed to the audience: "It's time to move on, people, it's time to leave Apple, Google, Facebook, Microsoft, and Amazon!" When Facebook collides with an iceberg, only to sink (and it will sink, just like MySpace and Friendster) then where do we go? What are we joining when we are taking off?

3) A Reprieve from Monetized Data Labor

"In a media environment where everyone seems to be selling something and everything is for sale, the noncommercial model is more important than ever," writes Pat Mitchell, former director of the Public Broadcasting Society.[16] Alternative platforms can carve out greed-free spaces for shared humanity.

There is no lack of technical alternatives that take on platform owners like Facebook, but for the alternatives to succeed, Metcalfe's Law needs to kick into effect; it suggests that it is not only the number of people but also the possibility of their interaction that matters.

Therefore, the value of networks owned by telcos is proportional to the square of the number of connected users. The cognitive economy is driven by the network effect. It cannot only be geeks, post-Marxist theorists, artists, hackers, anarchists, and professional technologists who migrate to services like Diaspora.

It will be an exciting moment when liberal arts colleges and philosophy departments at major universities become concerned with digital labour and platform cooperativism. Academic work should at least try to help us to lead more meaningful and fulfilled lives. No longer should we remain punk-ish resistors on the page while leading conformist lives. The politics of our daily life choices matters just as much as our ideas and code.

Much of the success of alternatives hinges on addictive user experience (UX) design, system design, information management, ease of use, broad coalitions of support, and community organizing: the ability to convince large numbers of people to migrate. Ultimately, measuring the value of alternatives by asking how closely they resemble some purist ideal of human sociality does not help; they need to be assessed through comparison with existing options.

There is no shortage of examples: Crabgrass offers secure social networking for activists, while the self-identified Facebook successor Diaspora, and the decentralized social network Friendica offer alternative social networking services. For a short moment in 2014, the ad-free social network Ello with the motto "You Are Not a Product" became popular, but many users lost interest after the company accepted over $5 million in venture capital. Investors want to see a return on their money and it was unclear how that would sit with Ello's promise of never selling user data.[17] ownCloud offers secure, open source cloud services.[18] There is also FreedomBox,[19] an inexpensive computer in the making that can provide a platform for distributed applications. And lastly, there are cloud archives like Libgen and Monoskop that offer terabytes of free books.

Or, give Craigslist a second chance: not everybody knows that Craig Newmark is leaving at least $500 million a year on the table because he is not introducing advertising.[20] Craigslist has demonstrated that it is possible to make profits while also supporting the sociality of millions of users all over the world. It is offering a service that is free for almost all of its users. In the land of platform capitalism, Craigslist rules Sherwood Forest. The German upstart Fairmondo is another noteworthy example. At its core a cooperative, ethically run consumer-to-consumer business, it is a cooperatively run eBay of sorts.

After some initial thoughts about frustrations and some possible alternatives, I now turn to cloud computing.

4) "There is No CLOUD, Just Other People's Computers"

Just take a moment and delve into your own interactions with cloud-based services. Some of you might use Adobe's Creative Suite, Dropbox, Google Drive, Apple Cloud, and Evernote on a daily basis. Since the early 1990s, increased copyright protection and the so-called digital agenda attempted to expand the influence of copyrights to manage access to digital enclosures, thereby driving back copyright's historical and conceptual orientation.

In recent years, former CEO of Google Eric Schmidt wrote: "the network has become as fast as the computer, and the computer hollows out and spreads across the network."[21] Nicholas Carr refers to it as the *worldwide computer*. The introduction of cloud computing, then, has led to a move away from a general-purpose computer with sizeable hard drive to geographically distant, large data storage facilities. It's hard to imagine a better opportunity for a bait-and-hook business model. Samsung, HP, and others market a whole new generation of so-called Chrome books. These stripped down, two-hundred-something-dollar lightweight devices are nothing but gateways to production and data access, where, deprived of your own data, you can now conveniently buy back access to the data that used to be ours in the first place.

Now, a little bit more convenient, accessible on all your devices, the newest versions of all your äppäräti, in Gary Shteyngart's words, and in real time, you can get caught in what commons advocate David Bollier calls "the enclosure trap." It is incredibly convenient to rely on the cloud for your backups and data mobility from one device to the other. The cloud looks like a highway to heaven, but privacy concerns are very real. The cloud becomes the new playground for the vectoralists, but at its core, this is not about commoditized knowledge labor; it is merely about controlling nodal points of access in the Absurdistan of the Web.

The key problem with the vectoral mode of capital is conglomeration, consolidation, and centralization. If in doubt, ponder the moment when PayPal, Visa, and Mastercard decided to boycott donations for WikiLeaks. And while you are at it, don't forget about the electricity outages that affected Amazon.com's server farms, thereby shutting down dozens of core services on the Internet, including Netflix. Or, think of Apple's App Store that clearly defines how its users experience the web – no flash, no pornography, no political cartoons. For legal scholar Julie Cohen, the experience of the networked world is increasingly not one of freedom. There are fewer and fewer choices about the interactions with the online environment, she writes.[22] Cloud providers can completely reign over your web experience, and, therefore, they can expose you to as many advertisements as they wish.

In the post-post-Sputnik era, apologists in favor of centralization may argue that it might take the "Big Five" platform owners to manufacture driverless cars or restaurant service robots, for example. The same argument was made in fear of the powers of Communist centralized planning and its ability to focus enormous resources at a single objective. Are Google-Apple-Amazon-Facebook-Microsoft the modern day equivalent of the Communist Party? Is innovation, which has significantly eased off in the absence of Cold War competition, now the sole domain of platform owners? The resources that it might take to compete are certainly concentrated in their hands.

But from the outset, Internet users were promised an open and decentralized social environment. Wasn't that the whole point? Paul Baran was obsessed with distributed networks as a means of warding off the Red Menace.

So, if we don't manage to cut through the consensual defeatism, and the hypnosis of the convenience virus, we will wake up in the friendly fascism of the cloud to realize that we managed to mortgage from the ruling class the very data that was once ours.

Granted that the Internet, ruled by TCP/IP protocol, was never completely free from control, but today millions are caught in the suffocating grip of platform capitalists. Legal scholar David Lametti proposes a publicly delivered cloud, an alternative to the shortcomings of proprietary, privately owned cloud services that lock in their users.[23]

In light of all this, what really counts are our ideas and the partial alternatives: greed-free upstarts, emerging forms of solidarity, boycotts, and social movements. What matters are the initiatives that we are building and supporting, all the while acknowledging their shortcomings. What matters is that we don't stifle our outrage and protest, that we live aberrant lives.

5) On Withdrawal, Defection, and Refusal

"In this McJob era," Geert Lovink writes, "artists and cultural workers must prepare a range of parallel projects that may or may not become realized as paid labor. This is why it is not morally wise to dismiss participation on corporate platforms such as Facebook and Twitter."[24] For most people, being included in the Ferris wheel of the network society isn't something they have much control over. A growing number of companies like the IT consulting firm Appirio even mandate their employees to link their Facebook profiles to their employee identities. "In a society governed by economic trade-offs," Nick Carr writes, "the technological imperative is precisely that: an imperative. Personal choice has little to with it."[25] Pragmatically, workers justify their participation through the fear of losing their livelihood and social standing. Without privilege there is no lasting shelter from online sociality. No Facebook, no LinkedIn, no jobs.

Recalling days in the Hamptons, it is soothing to think of the smell of the trees, hikes, and the offline freedom, but all that is just a temporary reprieve. Those who are able to purposefully unhook themselves from media produsage will have to acknowledge their *privilege*.[26] Donald Knuth, a prominent computer scientist at Stanford University, put it this way.

> *I have been a happy man ever since January 1, 1990, when I no longer had an email address. E-mail is a wonderful thing for people whose role in life is to be on top of things. But not for me; my role is to be on the bottom of things.*[27]

The software freedom activist Richard Stallman confided that he rarely looks at any website, and never on his own computer. "This started as a personal penance," he wrote. "But nowadays [it] seems possibly advisable for reasons of privacy."[28] Let's not interpret Knuth's and Stallman's retreat as a boastful display of status and privilege; though these are life choices which are, no doubt, predicated on rare privilege, they should be respected as radical deviations from social norms.

It comes as no surprise that the 1 percent are not on Facebook; the only people not addicted to their smart phones, are the oligarchs.[29] Don't forget that the lack of a Facebook account does not only make you suspicious to love seekers who are deprived of the ability to find out more about you, it also makes you look dubious to the 1,200 intelligence agencies in the United States. Any behavior that falls outside of the grid of big data-induced predictive analysis, like the retreat of Knuth and Stallman, raises suspicion.

There are, however, options other than voluntary labor and servitude. The refusal of participation in corporatist platforms does not have to lead to the breaking of all social ties and professional relationships. If only the big blackout of 2003 lasted some more months, we would have learned how much the post-Snowden Web works us over; how much it shapes every moment of our lives, as McLuhan put it.

Some will start to engage with media platforms selectively, which does not mean opting out of urban life altogether, living in the deep dark forest like Henry David Thoreau or Ted Kaczynski, eating nothing but beans. The binary rhetoric for or against unplugging is missing the point.[30] There is more than the nuclear option; this is not about an all-out refusal of technology or a romantic, posing withdrawal to "Betterworld Island" in "Real Life." The German author Michael Seemann calls it "multi homing." Seeman explains that in order to avoid the lock-in effect, applications, services, or data resources should be stored on several platforms at once. It's a "strategy to make users less dependent on individual platforms," he writes.[31] It's not about finding the ultimate form of resistance or critique that works for all. It's not about a social media diet versus staggering gadget-addiction. It's not about detox versus addiction. It's not about stylized self-help for the well-to-do. This is about respect for selective engagement, alternative modes of being and inconvenient life choices. To paraphrase Geert Lovink: To live a tweetless life should not be constructed as not living.[32]

The will to refuse is also born from the impulse to acknowledge the plentitude of alternatives and the possibilities for protest. Coleman writes, "Just as there are many ways to hack, there are many ways for hackers to enter the political arena. From policymaking to running political parties like the pirate party, from reinventing the law through free software to engaging in personally risky acts of civil disobedience, the geek and hacker are not bound to one single type of politics and they certainly don't agree on how such politics should be accomplished."[33] Some of us will fight from within by working with civil liberties groups and human rights organizations. They will write to Congress, and promote secure and alternative social networking software.[34] Others will obfuscate their data by adding noise to the networks, with everything from random "likes" to fake searches that used to pollute the stream of signals that marketers collect, analyze, and sell.[35]

In an effort to figure out what technology works for us, we remain open and perform small experiments with it all the time. Then, there is also the e-mail sabbatical,[36] "technology diet," and offline "detox."[37] Some responses are technical, with software such as No-Social, Freedom, Self-Control, or plugins like AdBlock Plus, and NoScript.[38] Freedom, for example, allows you to block the Internet connection on your computer for a defined period of time.

Boycott is not the only way to protest against unfair digital labor, but it is surely one option. After years of continuous privacy blunders, the Electronic Privacy Information Center filed complaints with the Federal Trade Commission suggesting that Facebook deceived users about the way their data is shared.[39]

While some people wait for a Katrina-like event to prompt them to turn their backs to platform owners, there is already an opt-out movement against the effects of the real-time Web. It started on May 31, 2010 when Quit Facebook Day was declared and an estimated 38,146 people signed an online pledge committing to delete their Facebook account. The organizers pointed out that the average Facebook user does not have many fair choices when it comes to the management of their data and that the service isn't aligned with any positive future for the Web, which is reason enough to leave, they suggest.[40]

While authors like danah boyd, Alice Marwick, Nancy Baym, Zeynep Tufekci, and Don Tapscott have argued in favor of a public discussion rather than boycott of Facebook, Geert Lovink joined the Facebook "exodus" in 2010 to question the growing role of centralized Internet services. "What we need to defend," he wrote, "is the very principle of decentralized, distributed networks."[41] Media theorist Douglas Rushkoff writes that he surrendered his Facebook account because his participation on the site simply became inconsistent with the values to which he espouses in his work. Facebook is entitled to be paid for delivering users to advertisers, Rushkoff explains, but now you're supposed to pay to "promote" your posts to your friends and if you pay even more, to their friends, and that wasn't the deal going in. "The promotional leverage that Facebook affords me is not worth the price....Facebook isn't the Internet. It's just one website, and it comes with a price."[42]

Surely, not being on Facebook makes us harder to reach. Some may even find such withdrawal a bit presumptuous. But how will dissent ever get any traction if all we care about is blending in? This is about what kind of person we want to be in the world.

6) Toward Tactical Refusal and Selective Engagement

Discussions about refusal, withdrawal, or defection from platform capitalism must account for the privilege of participation, but also the privilege of defection, given the drastically different life situations of people worldwide. Considering the social costs of our participation, it only makes sense that those who can afford it choose to opt out. Defection from platform capitalism is not only about the refusal of data labor, it could denote a refusal of work altogether.

In 1883, The French revolutionary Paul Lafargue, who also happened to be Karl Marx's son-in-law, wrote in "The Right to be Lazy" that the "proletariat has allowed itself to be seduced by the dogma of work." He refuses the configuration of the work society, and speaks out against the ideology of work as the highest calling. In his provocative tribute to the merits of laziness, Lafargue refuses to privilege work over all other pursuits.[43] Kathi Weeks, a Duke University professor and author of *The Problem with Work*, explains that Lafargue's extravagant refusal of work is not a refusal of all productive activity. Data labor outside of the confines of platform capitalism would not be an issue at all. Weeks points to the autonomist Marxist critique that not only focuses on alienation and exploitation, but also on the overvaluation of work itself.[44] How could we possibly unlearn our extreme work habits, our overvaluation of work? The refusal of work is really a refusal of the way work is organized. For Weeks, the problem with work would not disappear if invisible labor would be more visible and appropriately compensated. The problem is not only about the degradation of skill, low wages, exploitation, and discrimination: it's about "securing not only better work, but also the time and money necessary to have a life outside of work."[45] Do you remember the times when people still had hobbies and knew how to take a vacation?

A small cadre of people also finds ways of subverting the system. Take Kevin Killian, a poet living in San Francisco. As an active Amazon reviewer, he is not exclusively honing in on books. With his reviews, Killian found a creative way of establishing an audience for his autobiographical fiction; he reviews everything from sweet potato baby foods to films like Doctor Zhivago.[46] In recent months, whenever I feel low, or in a funk because of the depressed, gray state of the world today (not excluding the poetry community from my strictures either!), I have been fueled by the raw energy of Peter Valente's Artaud Variations, surely the best book on the subject. Here is an excerpt from one of his reviews about an oil painting in his mother's living room.

As an American boy growing up in France, I became mesmerized by an enchanting painting of an ancestor that hung never very far from the hearth. The painting, smudged by smoke and damaged by Vichy occupation of the chateau, showed a very thin and angular woman, her face like something reflected in the bowl of a spoon, festooned in bright stones that gleamed out still bright after the passage of many decades. "Who is this woman," I used to wonder out loud, until one

*evening, as my grandmother passed through the room looking for our
vanished cat, "Gateau," I noticed that she wore the same diamond and
ruby necklace as the ancestor in the old damaged painting.... Amazon's
14K Ruby and Diamond "Dynasty" necklace looks a lot like my family
jewels; the resemblance is shocking enough to have made me drop my
cocoa while leafing through the jewel pages this morning in an attempt
to bring back, madeleine-style, the vanished days of yesteryear.*[47]

You can have the necklace delivered in a day or two with Amazon
Prime.

An equally challenging proposal is Ulises Mejias' suggestion to not
only refuse but *unthink* the network logic, to become aware of those
who are left out by the network, loosen up our habitualized network-
centric thinking, and form subjectivities that are not created in reference to the network. That is, of course, easier said than done, given
that the real-time Web is a professional imperative for most people
in the overdeveloped world; it's hard to imagine a job that does not,
in some way, involve the network.

It would be a false dichotomy to present the option as either being
connected or being unplugged, as either signing my life away to platform capitalism or giving it a pass. I can loosen my device dependency
through "email sabbaticals" or a day without social media each
week. I can engage selectively, actively seek out and experiment with
emerging alternative platforms; I can deactivate Facebook for a few
weeks or months, and, of course, I can ultimately quit altogether. We
are just beginning to imagine what tactical refusal and defection
could look like.

7

The Rise of Platform Cooperativism

Among all the problems with twenty-first-century work – the ballooning of the low wage service sector, economic inequality – the main problem really is that there are so few realistic alternatives. What has been missing from the debate about the future of work is an approach that offers people a realistic alternative. This is what this chapter is about.

First, I will reflect on the opportunities, pitfalls, and consequences of the sharing economy, to then think about possible futures of work. Whoever thinks that there is just one possible future of work ignores the fact that workers are everything but despondent when facing the crisis of twenty-first-century work.

Second, I will ask who, in the face of the Uber-ization of everything from transportation and haircuts, to medical services, stands in solidarity with the poorest, most exploited workers? This section includes discussions of the use of social media for worker mobilization, design interventions that connect otherwise anonymous workers, new guilds, and inventive unions; it stresses the importance of the involvement of young people in electoral politics – pushing for worker-friendly and environmentally sustainable legislation.

This will be followed by an important structural proposal for democratic ownership models for the Internet. I will illustrate the rise of what I am calling platform cooperativism, to conclude with examples of platform co-ops and ten principles for decent labor platforms.

Overview

1) Consequences of the Sharing Economy

They called it the gig economy, the peer economy, the collaborative economy, the sharing economy. It took a while to acknowledge that the sharing economy was really an on-demand service economy that set out to monetize services that were previously private. It is true that there are undeniable opportunities for students, educated workers between jobs, and everyone who owns a second home. Now, it's easier for college graduates to land a gig assembling furniture or renovating someone's house. Consumers, raised with a keen appreciation of low prices and uber-convenience above all else, welcome these upstarts.

In *Who Owns the Future?*, Jaron Lanier suggests that, while the Internet is poised to rid American society of its middle class, micro-payments could become its savior.[1] In the 1990s, right-wing acolyte Newt Gingrich welcomed the upward spiral of the Internet as a way to "empower elites and reevaluate forms of government." If companies like Work Market have it their way, they will become the middlemen when traditional employees at corporations like IBM are replaced by "independents." Their five-year plan is to achieve a sweeping turn away from waged employment: shifting a market characterized by full employment – jobs for life – to a market that is "liberated" from employment, and dominated by freelancers, part-timers, and independent contractors. Should we understand the sharing economy as a road sign pointing to a better, more flexible future of work? What has this economy really brought us?

Welcome to the Potemkin Villages of the "sharing economy," where you can finally sell the fruit from the trees in your garden to your neighbors, share a car ride, rent a tree house in Redwood Forest, or visit a Kinkbnb. Your friendly convenience is, for many workers, a low-wage, precarious trap. But you, on the other hand, can listen to your very own Spotify account in an Uber taxi. No longer do you have to suffer from what economist George Akerlof penned as a "market for lemons;"[2] these new platforms are introducing new checks and balances. You are promoted to middle management, entitled to fire your driver. Companies behind the "Internet of Things" even found a way to suck financial value out of interactions with everyday objects, recruiting them as informants for surveillance capitalism.

Hip labor companies like Handy, Postmates, and Uber celebrate their Andy Warhol moment, their 15 billion dollars of fame. They revel in the fact that they launched their platform monopolies in the absence of a physical infrastructure of their own. Just like AOL and AT&T didn't build the Internet, and Mitt Romney did not build his business all by himself,[3] the firms in the on-demand economy did not build their empires either. They are running off your car, your apartment, your labor, your emotions, and importantly, your time. They are logistics companies that require participants to pay up to the middleman. We are turned into assets; this is the financialization of the everyday 3.0. In *What's Yours is Mine*, the Canadian researcher Tom Slee sums it up:

> *Many well-intentioned people suffer from a misplaced faith in the intrinsic abilities of the Internet to promote egalitarian community and trust, and so have unwittingly aided and abetted this accumulation of private fortune, and the construction of new and exploitative forms of employment.*[4]

At the Platform Cooperativism conference,[5] John Duda of the Democracy Collaborative stated that:

> *The ownership of the institutions that we depend on to live, to eat, to work is increasingly concentrated. Without democratizing our economy we will just not have the kind of society that we want to have, or that we claim to have, we are just not going to be a democracy. The Internet is certainly not helping! It is fueled by short-term thinking, corporate profits; it is directed by venture capital and it's contributing to the concentration of wealth in fewer and fewer hands. Wherever the tech economy is rampant, housing becomes totally unaffordable. We need to reverse that trend.*[6]

Occupations that cannot be off-shored – the pet walker or home cleaner – are becoming subsumed under what Sascha Lobo[7] and

Martin Kenney call platform capitalism. Baby boomers are losing sectors of the economy like transportation, food, and various other sectors, to millennials who fiercely rush to control demand, supply, and profit by adding a thick icing of business onto apps-based user interactions. They are extending the deregulated free market into previously private areas of our lives.

The "sharing economy" is portrayed as a harbinger for the post-work society – the path to ecologically sustainable capitalism where Google will conquer death itself, and you don't have to worry about a thing. With the slogan "What's Mine is Yours," the Trojan horse of the sharing economy rids us of Jurassic forms of labor while unleashing a colossal union-busting machine; passing over especially aging workers. The German author Byung-Chul Han frames the current moment as Fatigue Society.[8] We are living, he writes, in an achievement-oriented society that is allegedly free, determined by the call of "yes we can." Initially, this creates a feeling of freedom but soon it is accompanied by anxiety, self-exploitation, and depression.

Importantly, we cannot have this discussion without first acknowledging that the "sharing economy" is not some sort of isolated shrink-wrapped cube in "cyber space," it's just another reflection on capitalism and the massive atlas of digital labor practices. Consequently, we cannot have a conversation about labor platforms without first conceding that they depend on exploited human lives all along their global supply chains, starting with the hardware without which this entire "weightless" economy would sink to the bottom of the ocean.

All the Apple devices cannot be considered without first reminding ourselves of the labor conditions at what Andrew Ross called "Foxconn's suicide mills" in Shenzhen, China. Or take the rare earth minerals in the Democratic Republic of the Congo; it is essential to follow the supply chains that facilitate all those outwardly clean and glamorous digital life styles.

There is a mass of bodies without a name, hidden behind the screen, exposed to workplace surveillance, crowd fleecing, wage theft, and proprietary software. As the free software activist Micky Metts cautioned: "When building platforms, you cannot build freedom on someone else's slavery."[9]

When responding to a political critique of the on-demand economy, some scholars pose that, well, the terrible results of unfettered capitalism are well understood; that whole spiel does not need to be asserted yet another time. But perhaps, as McKenzie Wark claimed: "This is not capitalism, this is something worse." He suggested, "the mode of production we appear to be entering is one that is not quite capitalism as classically described."[10]

As I argued in chapter 4, the digital economy isn't merely a continuation of pre-digital capitalism as we know it, there are notable discontinuities – new levels of exploitation and concentration of wealth for which I penned the term "crowd fleecing." Crowd fleecing is a new form of exploitation, put in place by four or five upstarts, to draw on a global pool of millions of workers in real time.

The current situation needs to be discussed at the intersection of intensified forms of exploitation online and also older economies of unpaid and invisible work – think of Silvia Federici, Selma James, and Mariarosa Dalla Costa's "Wages for Housework" campaign and, in the 1980s, cultural theorist Donna Haraway discussing ways in which emerging communication technologies allowed for "home work" to be disseminated throughout society.

2) Possible Futures

Twenty or thirty years from now, when we are possibly facing the end of professions and ever more people's jobs will be "uberized," we may well wake up and wonder why we did not protest these shifts more forcefully. Despite all the scrumptious, home-cooked convenience of the "sharing economy," we may end up sharing the scraps, not the economy. We may feel remorseful about not seeking out alternatives earlier on. But we cannot change what we do not understand. So, I am asking, what does the "sharing economy" stand for?

Every uber has an unter

The sharing economy indicates a massive, global push in favor of "digital bridge builders" who insert themselves between those who offer services and others who are looking for them, thereby embedding extractive processes into social interactions. The on-demand economy indicates that digital labor is not a niche phenomenon. Upwork (formerly ODesk and Elance) claims to have some 10 million workers; Crowdwork 8 million; CrowdFlower 5 million. In 2015, 160,000 drivers are on the road for Uber if you trust their numbers. Lyft reports 50,000 drivers. TaskRabbit states that it has 30,000 workers.[11]

In Germany, unions like ver.di concentrate their efforts on defending the rights of employees, while in the United States I see little chance for a return of the 40-hour workweek for those in the contingent sector. The question then becomes, how we can make it better for one-third of the workforce that is not traditionally employed.

Today's extractive platform-based business models make some of the earlier Internet money schemes look like Socialist experiments. Douglas Rushkoff, author of *Throwing Stones at the Google Bus*, points out that "Instead of creating truly distributive businesses, we are just putting industrial economics on steroids, creating more extreme divisions of wealth and more extreme forms of exploitation. We are making all these new technologies like Bitcoin or blockchain but we are not really asking what we are programming these things for."[12] The benefits of platform capitalism for consumers, owners, and stockholders are apparent, but the value added for vulnerable workers and the long-term value for consumers is unclear at best.

New dependencies and new command

It is about the shift from the employee – with his or her W-2 tax document,[13] working a 40-hour workweek – to a more contingent worker, the freelancer, or independent contractor, also sometimes referred to as 1099,[14] gig worker, or "gigster." In the process, workers are losing minimum wage, overtime, and protections through employment anti-discrimination laws. Employers also don't have to contribute to Medicare, unemployment insurance, workers' compensation, or social security payments.

"Whereas traditional employment was like marriage," legal scholar Frank Pasquale writes, "with both parties committed to some longer-term mutual project, the digitized work-force seeks a series of hookups."[15] Energetically projected myths about employment suggest that working as an employee means that you have to give up all flexibility and that working as an independent contractor somehow inherently means that your work is flexible. But this "innate flexibility" of low-income freelancers should be put to question because workers do not exist in a vacuum; they have to adapt to the schedules of their virtual bosses, too.

Using the language of entrepreneurship, flexibility, autonomy, and choice, the burden of the biggest risks of life – unemployment, illness, and old age – have been lifted onto the shoulders of the workers. Platform owners refer to workers as "rabbits," "turkers," "gigsters," or "providers"! I wonder if Leah Busque, CEO of TaskRabbit, would feel insulted if you called her a rabbit. She's a head. The trouble is that she owns her mind and the platform.

Who will be willing to offer employee-like rights to all freelancers, temps, and contract workers? Senator Mark Warner of Virginia[16] and notably Princeton economist Alan Krueger, among others, have suggested a third category of worker that is neither an independent contractor nor an employee: the independent worker.[17] This category of worker would receive many of the protections that come with employment.

A different response to the loss of bargaining power on the side of workers in the on-demand economy comes from the computer programmer and writer Steve Randy Waldman who suggested that the classification of independent contractors should be made contingent on the requirements for workers to "multi-home," work using several platforms, thereby avoiding the trappings of single, dominant platforms like Uber. Waldman understands "multi-homing" as bargaining power when it comes to mitigating the power of monopolies.[18]

The sharing economy is Reaganism by other means

Taking a step back, I argue that there is connection between the effects of the "sharing economy" and the deliberate shockwaves of austerity that followed the financial crash in 2008. Tech billionaires jumped right in, riding on the back of those desperately looking for work, thereby not only increasing inequality but also restructuring the economy in a way that makes this new way of working, deprived of all worker rights, livable, survivable, or, as they would put it, "sustainable."

The "sharing economy" grew out of the lineage of Reagan and Thatcher who, in the 1980s, not only shut down the strikes of miners and flight traffic controllers, they damaged the belief in the ability of unions to watch out for workers; they weakened the belief in the possibility of solidarity, and created a framework in which the restructuring of work, the cuts in welfare checks, and the decoupling of productivity from income became more plausible.[19]

Meanwhile, from April to June 2013, Bank of America, Citigroup, Wells Fargo, JP Morgan Chase, Goldman Sachs, and Morgan Stanley had their highest ever quarterly profits: a combined $42.2 billion.[20]

Demands for qualifications are getting ever higher and anxiety, the fear of unemployment, and poverty have become central life themes for many young people today. All of this led to a world where for millennials, the end of the world seems more plausible than the end of capitalism and their career paths look like autonomous vehicles heading towards Armageddon.

It's Elia Kazan's film *On the Waterfront* on steroids; digital day laborers are getting up every morning only to join an auction for their own gigs. According to the economist Juliet Schor, the sharing economy increasingly provides access to low-level work for the educated middle class who can now drive taxis and assemble furniture in people's houses while simultaneously displacing low-income workers from these occupations.[21]

One in three laborers in the American workforce is now an independent contractor, day laborer, temp, or freelancer. Voluntarily and forced, people trade their lives as "wage slaves," exposed to hierarchy and authority in the workplace for a life that they can allegedly organize as they wish. The jury is still out whether or not they would rather return to a world with a regular paycheck, a 40-hour work-week, and decent social protections.

Generating profits for the few

With the creation of new occupations in the 1099 economy, businesses like Intuit started to blossom because their software helps freelancers to report their taxes. The software that propels the sharing economy is wrapped up in addictive interface design. On the screen, the ant-sized icon of a taxi approaching your location is as seductive and treacherous as the Sirens who lured Odysseus; it's design for extraction and scale. On the business side, entrepreneurs and software engineers have created new markets, but is this innovation or is there a factory behind the playground? Should innovation be just about profits for the few while leaving in its wake a workforce that is predominantly without sufficient social protections? Is innovation geared for value extraction and growth or is it about the circulation of this value between people?

Efficiency, in the same way, is not a virtue when it is, most of all, built on the extraction of value for shareholders and owners. It is in this sense of taking away value from people that labor companies like Amazon, crowdSPRING, and Taskrabbit are neither genuinely effective nor innovative. Platform capitalism, so far, has been highly ineffective in addressing the needs of the commonwealth. In fact, what initially looked like innovation eventually cranked up the volume on income inequality.

Illegality as a method

In the United States, illegality is a feature of the "sharing economy," not a bug. So far, the Federal government has not intervened, leaving much of the responsibility for regulation to municipalities and states. The sharing economy has been criticized for its "nullification of Federal law,"[22] a lack of dignity for workers, the elimination of worker rights, and democratic values like accountability and consent. Firms in the sharing economy failed to pay taxes and violated other federal laws. Their modus operandi follows a pattern. First, companies like Uber disregard various laws – anti-discrimination laws, for instance – to then point to a growing and keen consumer base whose demand for legal changes is only proof of their success. In 2015, Airbnb spent over $8 million to lobby in San Francisco when residents voted on regulating their operations. Uber spends more money on lobbyists than even Walmart. Significantly, both Uber and Airbnb are using their apps as political platforms that can be used to activate their client base to oppose any regulatory efforts against them.

When you learn that Uber drivers in Los Angeles are making below minimum wage; when you know that workers on CrowdFlower and Mechanical Turk earn no more than $2–3 an hour; when you understand that much (if not most) of Airbnb's revenue in New York City comes from hosts who rent out entire apartments for less than thirty days;[23] when you are told that startups are sailing around the definition of employment by restructuring work in such a way that the people who are working for them are categorized as independent contractors instead of employees; when you understand that the status of the independent contractor voids the protections afforded to workers by the Fair Labor Standards Act; when Uber, Lyft, and Airbnb continue to run their businesses in cities that shut down their operations; then you will understand why the government and/or municipalities have to act against this "nullification of federal law."[24] In 2015, a Princeton study showed that Uber drivers in 20 cities are netting about $17.50 an hour, which, according to drivers, comes out to anywhere between $10 and $13 an hour after subtracting the cost of gasoline, insurance, auto payments, and auto maintenance.[25] Los Angeles approved a $15-an-hour minimum wage, which puts Uber in violation of this law. Now, anyone with basic awareness of the Fair Labor Standards Act of 1938 would say that such payments must be illegally low; they don't meet minimum wage standards.

Considering the significant attrition rates among Mechanical Turk workers and Uber drivers (half of all Uber drivers do not stay longer than one year),[26] it is clear that these businesses, in their current form, are not sustainable. In the US, not doing right by workers comes at a very low legal risk for business owners.

But there's some hope. In one decision, a Federal judge found that an Uber driver was an employee and not an independent contractor, for example.[27] And also Lyft and even Yelp workers are filing lawsuits to become recognized as employees.[28] In the fall of 2015, the city of Seattle opened the door for the unionization of Uber drivers. And around the same time, an unlikely coalition of startups and organized labor published a document outlining necessary social protections for workers that are needed for the digital economy to thrive.[29] Whether the Federal government has the political will to introduce new worker protections remains to be seen.

On the local and state level, some regulatory efforts are under way. In Montgomery County, for instance, the Maryland General Assembly decided to regulate Uber and Lyft by imposing a $0.25 charge for each trip with those companies. The revenue will then be used to offer more accessible taxicab services for eligible senior citizens and low-income residents.[30] Mayor De Blasio is working to curb the size of the Uber fleet on the streets of New York City, while New York governor Cuomo is ready to override any such regulatory effort.

Amazon.com is rapidly joining the "sharing economy." Despite the fact that the company is barely above the legal drinking age, it is one of the oldest companies in this digital economy. Amazon's book section started in 1994 and their Mechanical Turk in 2005, but today, Amazon, not unlike Uber, has become a template for countless other businesses. The cruel genie is out of the bottle; companies like CrowdFlower, 99Designs, and hundreds of others are now adapting the business logic of crowdsourcing systems like Amazon Mechanical Turk. Amazon entered the sharing economy with enterprises like Flex, a crowdsourced delivery service that uses regular people, not legacy couriers, to deliver packages.[31] It also launched HomeServices, which places the company squarely in the middle when you order an electrician or plumber and HandMade-at-Amazon, directly taking on Etsy. In chapter 1, I discussed Amazon Mechanical Turk, where workers can log on to pick from long listings of tasks. Often well-educated, novice workers are making between $2 and $3 an hour in this environment. Just like migrant workers, barristers, or temps in the fast food industry, they are working long hours, are underpaid, and treated poorly by their virtual bosses, and have few or no benefits.

Yet a different future of work is possible; a People's Internet is possible! A coalition of designers, workers, artists, cooperatives, developers, inventive unions, and labor advocates can shift structures so that everybody can reap the fruits of their own labor.

3) Solidarity

Workers
Unpaid interns
Adjunct professors
Uber drivers
TaskRabbits

Independent contractors with a criminal record
Logistics workers in Amazon's warehouses
Crowd workers at Mechanical Turk with a disability
Fast food cooks
Miners of rare earth crystals in Nigeria, China, and the Congo
Migrant workers in ports
Starbucks Baristas
Day laborers outside Home Depot
Women in Foxconn's Shenzhen factories
Designers or developers at Upwork, 99designs, or Fivver
Freelancers
Workers!

Just a few years ago, who would have predicted that IKEA, Walmart, and Amazon would be hit by waves of strikes and walkouts? Or that New York City would introduce paid sick leave and the city's taxi drivers would form the NYC Taxi Association? Who would have believed that in May 2014, fast-food workers from New York City to Mumbai, Paris, and Tokyo, would coordinate a global strike, picketing McDonald's, Burger King, and Pizza Hut, fighting just-in-time scheduling and demanding a $15 minimum wage floor and benefits. For hackers, "long tail workers," and labor activists, now is the time for solidarity. This is the time to form or join inventive unions, and support design interventions that allow for moments of solidarity among geographically dispersed digital workers. Robotic abundance, layoffs, and wage stagnation do not just appear out of the blue. These are orchestrated developments that can be resisted.

A society that wants to call itself a democracy should not tolerate workplace exploitation in any form. Who stands in solidarity with the poorest, most exploited workers? Historically, capitalist owners were faced with a mass of workers, frequently represented by a union. But today workers are, in many cases, anonymous individuals facing off against anonymous employers. At present, unions cannot easily represent most workers through firm-by-firm collective bargaining: workers often have contracts with more than one company at a time, and many of these companies are skeptical of unions.

What do we make of the steady decline of unions over the past 60 years? In 2012, union membership in the United States reached its lowest point in over 100 years: only 11.3 percent of public sector employees and 6.6 percent of those in the private sector belonged to a union. The implosion of the Soviet bloc around 1989 was one reason for this decline; it removed the only living comparison to another social system and opened up global markets. The class of owners no longer needed to fear a mass exodus of organized workers who would descend on their suburban cottages.

Canadian sociologist Vincent Mosco, and the Wobblies before him, discussed the dream of one big union of unions, capable of converging various forms of solidarity worldwide. Why couldn't American and Indian workers connect online and stand united as they face Amazon's CEO Jeff Bezos?

American unions are too busy with their own problems to take on the plight of digital laborers; I'm not aware of a single American union that has taken on the issue of digital labor explicitly. In contradistinction, the German Association of Unions proclaimed, in reference to "digital McJobs," that they "will not passively watch a modern form of slavery emerge, which drives competition to the bottom." While such a reference to slavery is unwise, it is commendable that this association of unions has put the issue of exploitative digital work practices on the table. The largest German union, IG Metall, issued a press release suggesting that there has been a pervasive moral decline in the workplace due to digital labor.[32] Consequently, in 2015, IG Metall published the edited volume *Crowd Work: Zurück in die Zukunft (Crowd Work: Back to the Future)*.[33]

Social media for worker mobilization

These are not the days of *On the Waterfront*, a film showing how unions controlled the hiring on the New Jersey docks in the mid-twentieth century. Today's digital laborers cannot be reached in cafeterias during lunch break, or outside the gates of the factory. The character Terry Malloy, played by Marlon Brando, would instead be on LinkedIn. He could use apps like LabourLeaks, which, taking the spirit of WikiLeaks and Anonymous, calls on would-be whistleblowers to publicize nuts-and-bolts accounts of underpaid and dangerous work. Or he could crowdfund and gamify worker organizations, handing out badges for talking to other workers instead of rewarding workplace efficiency. Terry Malloy could use Coworker.org, a platform for labor organizing that convenes around worker rights. Why not "napsterize" the Teamsters with peer-to-peer technology, anonymity gear like Tor, or LiquidFeedback, the free software tool for political opinion formation?

Where is the 4chan – the /b/ board – for viral labor memes? Workers at Foxconn in Shenzhen are using social networking platforms like Qzone and Renren to inform other workers about union campaigns; but by doing so, they are also making themselves visible, easily identifiable by their employer.

"Tough day at work? Are you feeling overworked, underpaid, unsafe or disrespected by your boss? You are not alone – and you don't have to just put up with it." The American Federation of Labor and Congress of Industrial Organizations (AFL-CIO) asked these questions and now offers its own toolkit, including the online platform http://www.fixmyjob.com – also accessible through http://www.organizewith.us. With the help of these tools, workers can clarify their grievances and discover possible routes for collective action.

The Italian media theorist Tiziana Terranova, in her contribution to the New School's Digital Labor conference in 2014, wrote: "the old forms of blocking production are obsolete, if not impossible." Instead of these forms, she reframes the traditional general strike as the "social strike" – a permanent experiment of invention which diffuses forms of striking practicable even by those who would, according to the traditional model, be incapable: the unemployed, the precarious, the domestic worker, the crowd worker, the migrant without official documents. The social strike aims to redeploy, reconnect, and reinvent all forms of strike: "The general strike of those who cannot strike, net strikers, strikers within the spaces of education, the gender strike."[34]

Electoral politics and the materiality of platform capitalism

Beyond this kaleidoscope of strategies, I'd like to add physical protest and electoral politics. Take the great victory of 2012, when the Stop Online Piracy Act (SOPA) was defeated in the US House of Representatives. SOPA's objective was to control and censor Internet users, to prevent them from violating the copyrights of third parties. Netizens cooperated with large businesses to force their point: on January 18, 2012, thousands of websites, including Google and Wikipedia, went dark or offline for 24 hours to make a clear point that such copyright enforcement would be a gross act of censorship. It was not only the millions of e-mails, countless phone calls, and letters, but also street protests that led elected officials in Washington, DC to realize that SOPA could become a voting issue. The SOPA example could inspire a new species of electoral politics, one led by associations, new guilds, and driven by the pursuit of worker demands. If enough people clamor for better working conditions – based on their own sense of dignity and the right to speak authoritatively of their own lived experience – this may sway some politicians. In the case of SOPA, new media companies worked with activists to challenge the Bill. But who will stand with the digital laborers? Perhaps the most promising response to this question would be the founding of worker cooperatives.

Inspiration could also come from the activist strategies of ACT UP, a coalition of AIDS activists formed in the 1980s when Reagan ignored the deaths of countless gay men who had contracted the immunodeficiency virus. Activists illegally entered the press offices of the firm that produced the murderously priced HIV drugs and faxed out press releases stating that the company would substantially lower the price of the drugs.

Digital labor brokers have headquarters, too – possibly in your city. Protests held right there – outside the offices of Bezos and Biewald – might be a promising way to think about worker pushback. Amazon's headquarters is located at 1516 2nd Avenue in Seattle, Washington.

Inventive unions, guilds, and design interventions

Freelancers Union, founded in the United States by Sara Horowitz in 2001, offers health insurance to each of its 250,000 members: temps, freelancers, part-timers, and other workers who are not insured by their employer. Horowitz sees upsides of freelancing in the freedom from authoritarian workplaces, the autonomy to set one's own work schedule, and the freedom to make alliances with like-minded people. A setback for Freelancers Union has been the introduction of the Affordable Care Act, which led to a $2,000 average increase in annual premiums for members after the initial one-year waiver. Nevertheless, the union provides a client rating system, insurance plans, networking opportunities, and now also a primary care prac- tice for freelancers in New York City.

Many MTurk workers are outspoken about their lack of interest in unions. Friends recommend to friends that they try out MTurk, and they recommend each other better paying tasks. But Turkers also join worker-run forums like TurkerNation, CloudMeBaby, MTurkGrind, and the Reddit subreddit (/r/mturk), to chat, seek emo- tional support, and direct each other to "lucrative" tasks. On TurkerNation, workers express frustration with particular employers – but such disproval is distinguished clearly from any broad dismissal of Amazon, the company that sustains or contributes to their livelihood.

Design interventions

Lilly Irani, a professor at UC San Diego, asks how to build a system that can support collective action online. How can you gather people, gain critical mass, and mobilize? Together with Niloufar Salehi, Michael Bernstein, Ali Al Khatib, and Eva Ogbe, she built a platform called Dynamo that allows workers to safely post and discuss ideas for actions. One such proposal was to start an e-mail campaign to Jeff Bezos with the intention of humanizing the workers on MTurk.

Irani is also the co-creator of a rating system, Turkopticon,[35] which allows Turkers to flag companies for bad behavior. Early in 2015, Irani's tool, a Firefox plug-in, was already used by roughly 22,000 workers in any given month. Turkopticon – named a bit tongue-in-cheek after Jeremy Bentham's Panopticon – is designed as a social support system for MTurk workers. It helps them to identify subcontractors/quasi-employers who don't pay, subcontractors who severely underpay, and subcontractors who don't respond to workers whose work has been rejected. If sufficient numbers of workers were to join the platform, employers might have to care about their reputation within the workforce. Design interventions like Turkopticon aim to bring fairness and social peace to platforms like MTurk.

New guilds

In his book *A Precariat Charter*, University of London professor and labor activist Guy Standing calls for new guilds to fight for more than just better working conditions.[36] It is not sufficient to fight for higher wages; the very structures of production should be under scrutiny. Following the model of social movement unionism, guilds and associations could engage in wider political struggles for social justice and democracy. Digital labor associations, like TurkerNation, could coalesce with existing movements such as the National Domestic Workers Alliance and its equivalents in the fast food industry. While there are, of course, vast differences, precarity unites these groups. As I'll argue later in this chapter, TurkerNation could build a worker-owned, app-based labor platform. Beyond that, TurkerNation could fight for the recognition of invisible sites of work, and support campaigns for guaranteed basic income, which would secure the future for crowd labor. Such new guilds could inform workers of their rights, challenge their status as independent contractors through coordinated campaigns and class-action law suits, celebrate ethical companies that pay a living wage to their workers; call for international codes of good practice, and a restructuring of social protections for the contingent workforce. As advocated by Guy Standing, they could document, as well as publicize, unfairness, lobby for the application and enforcement of Federal labor law. Such guilds could also advocate for more time to rethink life, rest, live in our bodies, and reflect on what we are doing at work. What follows is a call to place the people who most rely on labor platforms at the center and turn profits into social benefit. Silicon Valley loves a good disruption, so let's give them one.

4) The Rise of Platform Cooperativism

We need to build an economy and an Internet that works for all. How can we take lessons from the long and exciting history of cooperatives and bring them into the digital age?[37]

Where shall/should you/one start/begin? Fifty-one percent of Americans make less than $30,000 a year and 76 percent have no savings at all.[38,39] From 2000 to 2010, the median income in the United States declined 7 percent when adjusted for inflation.[40] In terms of social wellbeing and environmental sustainability, for more and more people, capitalism is no longer working out. So, let's think about how the Internet could be owned and governed differently and how solidarity could be strengthened in the process. My collaborator Nathan Schneider asked, "can Silicon Alley do things more democratically than Silicon Valley?"

Whether you are thinking about secure jobs, minimum wage, safety, health insurance, and pension funds – none of these issues can be addressed fundamentally without the reorganization of work, without structural change. None of these issues can be addressed effectively until we reinvigorate solidarity, change ownership, and introduce democratic governance.

"Old school" companies typically give workers as little as they can get away with. The distrust in the willingness of owners and stock-holders to watch out for the workers, the distrust in the old, extractive model, the economics of surveillance, and monopoly, and the proliferation of the workplace without borders, led many people to revive the spirit of cooperativism. What are the long-term prospects for platform cooperatives? Aren't cooperatives an outlived organizational model for work? Anybody who is making that claim should first consider that worldwide, the solidarity economy is growing; cooperatives employ more people than all multinationals combined.[41] Democratic Presidential candidate, US Senator Bernie Sanders of Vermont is promoting worker-ownership as one practicable way to move forward.[42] In today's United States, 900,000 people are employed by co-ops.[43]

In her book *Collective Courage*, Jessica Gordon Nembhard describes the Black experience in cooperatives in the US as one of activism, grounded in the experience of the struggle for human rights. The Japanese consumer cooperative union serves 31 percent of the nation's households and Mondragon, Spain's seventh largest industrial corporation is a network of cooperatives that in 2013, employed 74,061 people. Emilia Romagna, an area in Italy that encouraged employee ownership, consumer cooperatives, and agricultural cooperatives, has lower unemployment than other regions in Italy.[44]

Forty percent of agriculture in Brazil and 36 percent of retail markets in Denmark are made up of cooperatives, according to Kelly. Forty-five percent of the GDP of Kenya and 22 percent of the GDP of New Zealand come from cooperatives. Despite many setbacks, it would be hard to successfully argue that the cooperative model is done with.[45]

In the United Kingdom, for example, there are currently 200,000 people working in more than 400 worker cooperatives. In Berlin, citizens are currently forming utility cooperatives to buy and operate the city's power grid.[46] In the German city of Schönau, another such consumer cooperative runs and operates both the power grid and the gas supply for that city.

For 2016, New York City Council Member Maria del Carmen Arroyo reports that New York City approved a $2.1 million Worker Cooperative Business Development Initiative for the city.[47] In 2015, women almost exclusively operated the coalition of 24 worker-owned cooperatives in New York City. Low-wage workers who joined these cooperatives saw their hourly rates increase from $10 to $25 over the past two years.

Undoubtedly, the challenges for all co-ops are vast. Just think of Walmart, which is, after the US Department of Defense and China's Liberation Army, the third largest global organization.[48] For cooperatives, to compete with such giants is no walk in the park. But still, in this struggle about the imagination of the future of work, who should be the driving agents of change? Is it the platform owner, shareholder, CEO, and VC, or do we focus on the collective of workers alongside a citizen-led movement? The answer could be: all of the above.

But for me, the problem begins when change is sought mainly in the boardrooms of Silicon Valley. Tim O'Reilly convened the Next:Economy in November 2015,[49] for instance, which was vastly dominated by Silicon Valley business leaders. And if the selection of speakers – who, despite two or three labor advocates, were predominantly corporate leaders – did not make it clear who was identified as agents of change, the conference registration fee of $3,500 clarified that once and for all.

Former Secretary of Labor Robert Reich pointed out that in order to "save capitalism," workers have to have minimal social protections; otherwise there will be a rebellion. Robin Chase, co-founder of ZipCar, echoed Reich's sentiment. And sure enough, if you want to retain social peace, you have to give workers something. You can appeal to the best in corporate leaders, as Tim O'Reilly does perhaps, you can hope for their goodwill, but the question remains if such pleas can change the core mission of these enterprises. It is true that workers need solid protections and somebody who really cares for their long-term welfare. Being "realistic" also means to realistically assess whether platform owners will go beyond handing out small concessions to workers. Being realistic means acknowledging the historical successes and failures of the extractive "sharing economy" and the solidarity economy. You cannot counter economic inequality with the benevolence of owners; together we must redesign the infrastructure with democracy at its core.

As part of this redesign, it is also worth re-examining the history of building structures for cooperativism and mutualism in the United States. Here, spiritual communalism and co-operative movements play a central role. The German Mennonites, including the Amish, started coming to the US as early as 1684. In the spring of 1825, Robert Owen opened the doors of the New Harmony community in Indiana. In the 1930s, The Nation of Islam as well as the Catholic Worker Movement set up hundreds of communal projects. The Catholic social teaching of distributism is influential in that context. It suggests that communities could co-own property and tools. Three decades later, the Hindu Kripalu Yoga Ashram and the Buddhist Karme-Choling Center were founded. Spiritual communities and co-ops have often proven to have more staying power than secular cooperative businesses.

Since the first modern cooperative in Rochdale in 1844, there has been enough time to talk about worker cooperatives, critics argue, and in their minds the evidence shows that the model isn't working. And partially, they are right; most worker-owned cooperatives in the United States did not succeed. But it also worth keeping in mind, as the author John Curl observes, that

> The very existence of cooperatives challenges corporations and capitalism; corporations have always worked hard to weaken, discredit, and destroy [cooperatives] through waging price wars, enacting legislation that undercuts their viability, labeling them in the media as subversive and a failure, and using several other stratagems.[50]

Also Rosa Luxemburg was cautious when it came to thinking about cooperatives as all-out alternatives to capitalism.

The workers forming a co-operative in the field of production are thus faced with the contradictory necessity of governing themselves with the utmost absolutism. They are obliged to take toward themselves the role of capitalist entrepreneur – a contradiction that accounts for the usual failure of production co-operatives which either become pure capitalist enterprises or, if the workers' interests continue to predominate, end by dissolving.[51]

All methods that enable an enterprise to stand up against its competitors in the market are used, Luxemburg wrote.[52] There is, however, the undeniable and important effect that co-ops have on the workers in those systems. Existing cooperatives have been shown to offer more stable jobs and reliable social protections than traditional extractive models. It would be unhelpful to see co-ops as rosy alternatives; they function within a capitalist context where they are forced to compete. Networks of cooperatives like Mondragon cannot truly decouple themselves from the exploitative supply chains that fuel capitalism.

One common objection to cooperatives is that they are just as much bound to market pressures as any other capitalist enterprise, which makes self-exploitation unavoidable. Eventually, co-ops too can resort to the gambit of unpaid internships and uncompensated volunteers. Co-ops are exposed to the pitiless competition of the market, but in the light of the 20–30 percent profit that companies like Uber are taking, one approach would be for platform cooperatives to offer their services at a lower price. They could run on 10 percent profit, which could then be partially translated into the social benefit of workers. Cooperatives could also flourish in niche markets, taking on low-income clients/consumers as their target groups.

Co-ops have been important instruments for building economic power for marginalized groups. Karla Morales of the childcare cooperative Beyond Care describes the simple benefits of working in a co-op: "In my work now I have sick leave, vacations, and employment entitlements."[53] Beyond this co-op in New York, it has been the southern states where agricultural co-ops have built economic and social self-determination, especially for African American communities. At times, though, co-ops have reinforced hierarchies of race and gender, reproducing rather than challenging the practices of the broader society. Juliet Schor pointed out that:

If you are interested in social justice, then you should know that in non-profit spaces, there are high levels of race, class, and gender exclusion. People act in ways that reinforce their own class position or their own racial position. These spaces are often more problematic from the perspective of race, class, and gender than many for-profits. So if you want to build a platform that attracts people across class, race, and gender, you need to start with the group of people that you want to attract to your platform.[54]

Skeptics bemoan the fact that credit unions haven't really transformed the economy as a whole and that worker-owned cooperatives have not become the beachheads of socialism that they were promised to be. But then there is the indisputable long-term benefit for the workers in those enterprises; and, doesn't that count for anything? Here, workers control their own work in a fashion that contributes to their own wellbeing. Cooperatives, however small, can function as ethical, self-managed counterparts that provide a model for businesses that don't have to rely on the exploitation of their workers. Cooperatives can bring creativity not only to the consumption of products but also to the reorganization of work.

There have been frequent references recently to Hannah Arendt who observed that a stray dog has a better chance of survival when it is given a name. So, welcome to platform cooperativism.

> *Together we will grow old we will hold*
> *each other close and we will hold each other closer*
> *We will hold each other as the country changes; we will hold each*
> *other as the world changes.*
> *– Anonymous*[55]

The concept of platform cooperativism has three parts: First, it is about cloning or creatively altering the technological heart of the sharing economy. It embraces the technology but wants to put it to work with a different ownership model, adhering to democratic values, so as to crack the broken system of the "sharing economy"/on-demand economy that only benefits the few. It is in this sense that platform cooperativism is about structural change, a change of ownership.

Second, platform cooperativism is about solidarity, which is sorely missing in this economy driven by a distributed, and sometimes anonymous workforce. Platforms can be owned and operated by inventive unions, cities, and various other forms of cooperatives, everything from multi-stakeholder and worker-owned co-ops to produser-owned platform cooperatives.

And third, platform cooperativism is built on the reframing of concepts like innovation and efficiency with an eye on benefiting all, not just sucking up profits for the few. Platform capitalism is amazingly ineffective in watching out for people. I am proposing ten principles of platform cooperativism that are sensible to the critical problems facing the digital economy right now.

The concept of platform cooperativism, or at least part of it, was hard to understand. People understood the "cooperativism" bit but the "platform" part remained mysterious. What do you call the places where you hang out and generate value after you switch on your phone? A platform, in the context of this chapter, is a term used to describe an environment in which digital intermediaries offer their services or content.

Right from the outset, when explaining the concept of platform cooperativism, let me clarify that this is not about a technological aurora borealis; it can't be about the Western infatuation with advancements in technology. Platform cooperativism is a mindset. Evgeny Morozov and Siva Vaidhyanathan are absolutely right in their stance against "technological solutionism" and Internet centrism.

Platform cooperativism is a term that describes technological, cultural, political, and social changes; it's a rectangle of hope. It is as much Ernst Bloch's concrete utopia as it is an emerging economy. Below, I will describe some models, none of them older than a few years, some prototypes, some experiments, some still merely imagined, but all of them imbued with alternative values. After this introduction to various types and principles for platform co-ops, I will discuss objections, challenges, and the co-operative ecosystem.

5) Toward a Typology of Platform Co-Ops

Some examples of platform cooperatives already exist. Naming them here inevitably excludes other important projects, but not introducing concrete instances would leave us open to the suggestion that platform cooperativism is nothing but a pipe dream.

Cooperatively owned online labor brokerages and marketplaces

Quite likely, you're familiar with the model of the online labor brokerage. Just think of companies like TaskRabbit where you can schedule someone to assemble your IKEA furniture in 20 minutes. The app on your smartphone serves as an intermediary between you and the worker. It's trickle-up economics with TaskRabbit extracting a cut from each transaction.

The "sharing economy" lawyer and cartoonist Janelle Orsi notices a decisive uptick in the interest in cooperatives. She reports that dozens of tech startups and traditional businesses like florists or landscapers have reached out to her Sustainable Economies Law Center[56] because they are interested in "crowd leaping," the migration of their business to the co-op model.

In San Francisco, Loconomics[57] is a freelancer-owned cooperative where members-freelancers own shares, receive dividends, and have a voice in running the company. There is no bidding and no markup. Loconomics offers massages and other services that are locally in demand. Membership in Loconomics costs $29.95 per month. The founders tested the app in the San Francisco Bay Area early in 2016 and expanded to other cities shortly after that.

Ali Al Khatib, a Stanford PhD student in Computer Science, started to work on the design of a "generalizable, worker-centric peer economy platform" that would allow workers to own, operate, and control the software.[58] The project, still in its early stages, is co-shaped by the workers.

In Germany, Fairmondo, started as a decentralized online marketplace owned by its users, is a cooperative alternative to Amazon and eBay. With its 2,000 members, it aspires to eventually become a genuine alternative to the big players in e-commerce while at the same time staying true to its values. The site promotes a smaller number of fairtrade and ethically sourced companies. In the process of transferring their model from Germany to other countries, they are aiming for a decentralized global online marketplace that is collectively owned by all local co-ops.

Coopify[59] is a student-built labor platform that connects low-income workers to the digital economy. Workers using Coopify are low-income New Yorkers who are under- or unemployed and who do not have sufficient credit rating or documentation that would allow them to participate in existing online markets. The platform, which will likely include its own referral system and multilingual support, may also offer support with taxes and allow workers to be paid in cash. The Center for Family Life (CFL) in Sunset Park, New York, is a social support agency that is testing Coopify. Melina Diaconis, an MBA candidate who helped develop Coopify, said that the business removes the middleman; it "won't have to rely on the bottleneck of office managers for bookings" and "the money is going to the worker, not the business of the Coopify platform."[60] Coopify should "bring a face and a sense of community to the app-based booking world," said Emma Yorra of the CFL.

CFL has been incubating worker cooperatives as a way to provide living wages and dignified working conditions to low-income immigrants since 2006. The center supports nine co-ops and a total of 180 worker-owners – mostly Latina women. Coopify will help these nine co-ops to compete more effectively with the likes of Handy and Amazon Flex.

City-owned platform cooperatives

After talking about cultural producers, now let me make a big leap and discuss public ownership, which has an image problem in the United States. The political economist and founder of democracy collaborative, Gar Alperovitz, writes that there are more than 2,000 publicly owned electric utilities that, along with cooperatives, supply more than 25 percent of the country's electricity.[61] Alperovitz points to the long history of cities like Dallas owning various hotels, and municipalities all over the United States owning hospitals, and apparently, contrary to public opinion, this model has been working rather well.

Janelle Orsi has detailed ideas about ownership and the Internet. Corresponding to my proposal to repurpose and creatively change technologies of the "sharing economy" with democratic values in mind, Orsi suggests a city-designed software similar to Airbnb, that could serve as an online short-term rental platform owned and democratically controlled by the city or the residents themselves. One such project is already under way in Seoul (South Korea). It is proposing to create a Cities Alliance for the Platform Economy (CAPE) that would build such a rental platform. Orsi calls such collaboration between a large number of cities "Munibnb." The idea is that cities would pool their resources to create a software platform for short-term rentals. These cities could then mandate that short-term rentals in their municipalities have to go through this portal. Fees could largely stay with the hosts or partly go to the city goverment, which could then use it to serve its residents or maintain infrastructure. Orsi asks:

> Why should millions of traveler dollars leak from our cities into the hands of wealthy corporate shareholders especially if it wouldn't be all that hard to run these operations through something like Munibnb.[62]

Another model, suggested by Orsi, Allbnb, would secure a dividend that would be paid to residents from the profits of such rental platform. Allbnb could be comparable to the Alaska Permanent Fund, which pays residents of the state a few thousand dollars each year, a percentage of the profits that Alaska makes from selling oil. These apps seem ultimately feasible to implement; they would allow cities to not only play a role in the regulation of the on-demand economy; they could actively co-share it.

Produser-owned platforms

I am using the term "produser," which is not a typo but a portmanteau of user and producer.[63] Produser-owned platforms are a response to monopolistic platforms like Facebook and Google that are luring users with the promise of the "free service" while monetizing their content and data.

What if we owned our own version of Facebook, Spotify, or Netflix? What if the photographers at Shutterstock.com owned the platform where their photos are being sold? Sites like Member's Media, Stocksy, and Resonate are a step in the direction of answering this question. They offer produsers the opportunity to co-own the site through which they are distributing their artwork. Produser-owned platforms allow artists to build careers by co-owning the platforms through which they are selling their work.

The Berlin-based Resonate, is a cooperative streaming music system owned by the people who use it.[64] Stocksy[65] is an artist-owned cooperative for stock photography. The co-op is based on the idea of profit sharing and co-ownership with the artists who are contributing photos to the site. Artists can apply to become members and when accepted, license images and receive 50 percent commission on sales as well as profit sharing at the end of the year. The objective of the cooperative is to create sustainable careers for its members. By 2014, their revenues had reached $3.7 million dollars, and since their founding they've paid out several million dollars in surplus to their artists.

Member's Media[66] is a cooperatively-owned media platform that is dedicated to producers and fans of independent, narrative film. The people using and producing for this site – the produsers – own the majority of the platform along with the original founders and investors.

Union-backed labor platforms

There are several examples from Denver to Newark where cabbies and unions started to work together, build apps, and organize the taxi sector. And if companies are smart, they would welcome the unions because studies show that unionized workers have a better retention rate and at least the same productivity.[67]

In Newark, New Jersey, Transunion Car Service started as a non-for-profit taxi service with drivers being part of the United Transportation Alliance of New Jersey and affiliates of the

Communications Workers of America (CWA) local 1039. Drivers benefit from the union's many protections such as credit unions, immigration support, and healthcare, as well as pension benefits. The company is planning to expand to Atlantic City, Elizabeth (New Jersey), and Hoboken.

Already in 2007, taxi drivers joined the CWA local 7777 and two years later, they managed to kick off Union taxi, the first driver-owned cooperative in Denver. They are also getting support from the organization 1worker1vote.org that supports unionized cooperatives by helping them figure out how to negotiate wages, benefit plans, and training programs. The upfront capital costs, often a big challenge for cooperatives, are less of an issue here because drivers already own the equipment.

The California App-Based Drivers Association (CADA)[68] is a not-for-profit membership organization that unifies drivers from Uber, Lyft, and Side-car and other apps-based companies. CADA's drivers are not employees and therefore they cannot become full members of the union. However, the Teamsters Local 986 in California can lobby for driver-friendly regulation. They make sure that drivers working for companies like Lyft and Uber are speaking with a unified voice.

Cooperatives as a result of antitrust legislation

Another alluring if imaginary proposal is the idea of worker cooperatives forming inside the belly of the sharing economy. Uber drivers could use the technical infrastructure of the company to run their own enterprises. Such hostile takeover by workers could be imaginable as a result of an antitrust lawsuit comparable to the one brought forward against Microsoft after its launch of Internet Explorer.

The platform as protocol

Perhaps then, the future work will not be dictated by centralized platforms, even if they are operated by co-ops. Perhaps, it will be peer-to-peer interactions facilitated by protocols that enable business. In Israel, for instance, La'Zooz[69] is a distributed peer-to-peer ride rental network. Where Members Media wanted you to think of them as Netflix for filmmakers and fans, owned by those produsers, La'Zooz could be likened to the Bittorrent of ride sharing. Anyone driving around a city can earn crypto tokens by taking in fellow travelers. Unlike the systems previously described, La'Zooz is built merely on peer connections; there is no central business.[70]

6) Ten Principles for Platform Cooperativism

A technical discussion of values, rules, and guidelines for platform co-ops is, no doubt, for the already committed. First must be the creation of a longing for cooperative solutions. Astra Taylor holds up the wisdom of Elaine Browne, former leader of the Black Panther Party: "You never organize or mobilize around abstract principles."[71] Of course! But once people are committed, once they are moved, once they are on board, principles and values associated with a project matter a great deal. Juliet Schor conducted 200 interviews with workers in the sharing economy. Her suggestion is:

> *Make sure that you get the value proposition right. What you are offering needs to be of economic value to the people that you want to attract. In the non-profit space this is often missing. The for-profit space is getting that right more often.*[72]

Beyond Schor's points, informed by the thinking of the German service worker union ver.di,[73] I'm proposing the following principles for platform co-ops.

1. Ownership

One of the main narratives of what used to be called the sharing economy was about the rejection of ownership. Millennials, we were told, are not interested in physical possessions; they just want access to "stuff." They don't download their music; they stream it. They don't buy a car; they are fans of ride sharing. Our narrative, in contrast, is about a people-centered Internet.

The Internet was designed as a military scientific network in 1969. But from 1990 up to 1994, the National Science Foundation planned to pass the network to private companies who would now own the cables and routers. In 1995, the publicly funded Internet infrastructure – The National Science Foundation Network (NSFNET) – was officially handed over to the private sector. Since then, the Internet has brought us much in almost every area but it has left the question of shared ownership untouched.

This is not about cute kittens on Reddit; it is about an Internet of ownership. Collectively owned platform co-ops, owned by the people who generate most of the value on those platforms, could reinvigorate this early, public minded history without. Platform cooperativism can change the ways average people think about their relation to the Internet.

2. Decent pay and income security

In 2015, crowdsourcing systems like Amazon Mechanical Turk novice workers – who are well educated – are paid between \$2 and \$3 an hour, which is a disgrace in a country as rich as the United States. Just as domestic workers were tucked away in people's houses, digital workers remain invisible, tucked away in between algorithms. The Domestic Workers Alliance pushed back. At the White House Worker's Voice event, they introduced a Good Work Code with demands including: "Everyone needs fair pay and benefits to make a living."[74]

3. Transparency and data portability

Transparency isn't only about operational transparency. The cooperatively owned online marketplace Fairmondo, for instance, emphasizes that it makes most of the budget of the co-op publicly available. But transparency is also about the handling of data, especially the data on customers. It should be transparent which data are harvested, how they are collected, how they are used, and to whom they are sold.

4. Appreciation and acknowledgment

A good working atmosphere should be part of this discussion, too. Workers deserve the acknowledgment and appreciation of owners and operators. The ability of workers to communicate with platform operators or owners is central in this context. When workers are paid late[75] or fired, they must have the enforceable right to get an explanation.

5. Co-determined work

The design process of labor platforms should involve workers from the first moment and throughout the platform's existence. This way, too, operators will learn much more about the workflow of workers. As Juliet Schor said, "Start with the people that you want to end up with." From day one, involve everyone that you eventually want to use your platform.

6. A protective legal framework

Platform co-ops require legal help because they are deemed unusual, but your help is also necessary when it comes to defending

cooperatives against adverse legal actions. The triumph of the shareholder enterprise has been achieved through their control of the
political, legal, and economical system. US laws subsidize corporations over the wellbeing of all people. Frank Pasquale has observed
that there is a bizarre inconsistency in US antitrust law based on the
difference between monopolies and co-ops.[76]

While monopolies can get a free pass in the US if they vaguely
play by the rules, a federation of co-ops trying to take on a dominant
incumbent firm might be liable under antitrust law if it tries to
set prices or even standards of conduct. The legal system in the
United States is mostly welcoming of monopolies but unaccepting
when it comes to cartels. The powers of the government promote
the system of corporate rule and the marginalization of the middle
classes.

7. Portable worker protections and benefits

Both contingent as well as traditional economy workers should be
able to take benefits and protections with them in and out of changing work scenarios. Social protections should not be tied to one
particular workplace. The French government is testing this idea and
in the United States, Steven Hill, a San Francisco-based author, is one
of the people who made this proposal in his latest book *Raw Deal:
How the "Uber Economy" and Runaway Capitalism Are Screwing
American Workers*. Each worker would be assigned an Individual
Security Account into which every business that hires that worker
would make a small pro-rata "safety net fee" payment based on the
number of hours a worker is employed by that business. Those funds
would be used to pay for each worker's safety net, steering the funds
into already established infrastructure such as Social Security,
Medicare, injured worker and unemployment compensation funds,
and health care through the Affordable Care Act. In addition, this
plan would provide a minimum of 5 days each of paid sick leave and
paid vacation for every worker.[77]

An important consequence of this proposal is that, by putting
nearly all workers on a similar footing, we would greatly reduce the
incentives for employers to resort to contingent workers as a way of
avoiding paying benefits for workers. These changes can be implemented at the local or state level; Americans don't have to wait for
a dysfunctional Congress to move forward. But much would depend
on the "small print " of such a program, which could just as easily
become a cover-up for more deregulation.

8. Protection against arbitrary behavior

Uber is known for its arbitrary disciplining and firing practices. Without warning, drivers may be left without an income.[78] Reasons for the firing of drivers are often unclear as the company refuses to respond to the enquiries of drivers demanding an explanation, a problem that is also facing workers at other platforms.[79] On Uber, if drivers fall below a 4.6 rating, they will be "deactivated." Consumers take on managerial powers over workers' lives, which comes with an enormous responsibility.

And if this was not enough, Uber's reputation system faults drivers for fat-fingered passengers who simply hit the wrong button when evaluating a driver, thereby putting the driver's livelihood in jeopardy.[80] Uber's worker reputation system is hosted in the "cloud," on Amazon's web services. Just like with other upstarts in the sharing economy, this makes it impossible for workers to capitalize on their reputation. When they are moving to another platform, they are starting from scratch. Consequently, it is essential that workers establish their own, decentralized reputation and identity systems. Projects like Traity[81] and Crypto Swartz[82] are working in that direction.

9. Rejection of excessive workplace surveillance

Excessive workplace surveillance along the lines of oDesk's (now Upwork's) worker diaries[83] or the constant reviews on TaskRabbit need to be rejected. Where is the dignity of work in such systems? How would you like to get up every morning, only to leverage some quantitative measure of your worth in competition for that day's work? How would you like to be evaluated every four hours by people you don't know at all? Such surveillance practices leave workers without much dignity.

10. The right to log off

Workers also need to have the right to log off. Decent digital work should have clear boundaries, platform cooperatives need to leave time for relaxation, lifelong learning, and voluntary political work.

It is important to articulate such a vision, guided by such lofty principles. It will take us a very long time to get closer to this vision. Our inability to imagine a different life, however, would be capital's ultimate triumph.

It will not come as a surprise when I say that platform cooperativism is also faced with enormous challenges, from the self-organization and management of workers, to technology, user experience (UX) design, education, long-term funding, scaling, wage scales, competition with multinational corporate giants, and public awareness. Other challenges include the screening of core members of a co-op, insurance, competition with multinational corporate giants, and importantly, public awareness. Thinking through obstacles clearly matters. Naivety and enthusiastic arm waving are not enough. Jodi Dean has a point when she poses that "Goldman Sachs doesn't care if you raise chickens" but corporate owners will become interested if they get wind of the growth of chicken cooperatives, powered by online marketplaces, all across North America. To make decent digital labor a reality, like-minded people will escape the rat race and fight for democratic ownership and rights.

Another challenge is that of worker mobilization: so-called 1099 workers don't meet their colleagues for lunch break, they don't get to hang out in union halls. Instead, they are, for the most part, isolated from each other. "If these people have to gain ownership and decision-making power, enhancement of their social networks must be part of the project," economist Paola Tubaro emphasizes in response to the idea of platform cooperativism.[84]

There have been some attempts to create new forms of worker solidarity, including design interventions like Turkopticon and Dynamo, which I mentioned earlier. But neither of these projects should be mistaken for a union. The challenge remains: how do you organize distributed workers and empower them with real bargaining power?

7) The Cooperative Ecosystem

Platform co-ops are not islands, entire of themselves. Every co-op is part of an ecosystem. Neal Gorenflo writes:

> Part of the magic of tech startups is that there's a well-understood organizational structure, financing method, and developmental path for entrepreneurs to use. In other words, there's a template. Platform co-ops need templates too, but the ones that support a diversity of organizational patterns. What's needed is a small number of incubators in different global cities working together to give birth to the first wave of platform co-ops. The trick is to get the first few platform co-ops off the ground, and then develop a global ecosystem that encourages replication of working models across industry verticals and geographies.[85]

Platform co-ops depend on other cooperatives, funding schemes, software engineers, lawyers, workers, and designers. Alliances between co-ops are essential. They need to be based on standards, a commitment to the open commons, shared strategies, goals, and values: a shift of mentality from Ayn Rand to Robert Owen, supported by a political platform.

Financing

Platform cooperatives and co-ops in general are calling for a different funding scheme than traditional enterprises. Many of the traditional avenues for funding are not available to platform co-ops and regulators eagerly guard against experiments. What are financing options that broaden the financial power of the many?

On the one hand, the upfront capital costs that often present the biggest challenge for co-operatives are not the biggest obstacle in this case. At least when you think of transportation, the drivers already own their major assets. In Spain, Mondragon, the world's largest industrial cooperative, is functioning like a development bank. In Germany, banks also play an important role in the development of small business, which makes up a large part of that country's economy.

Projects like Seed.coop are helping co-ops to get off the ground.[86] Crowdfunding drives can be successful. The Spanish crowdfunding site GOTEO is worth highlighting here because it only allows projects to seek funding that follow a commons-oriented set of values.[87]

In his article, "Owning is the New Sharing,"[88] Nathan Schneider reported about the world's first experiment in "crypto equity" called Swarm,[89] a crowdfunding site that relies on a "swarm" of small investors rather than big venture capitalists. The site runs on a crypto currency, not dollars, but as part of its first drive, it raised more than $1 million.

But regulators don't make things easier. In 2011, Brewster Kahle, founder of archive.org, attempted to start a credit union but was faced with a barrage of regulatory audits and the bureaucracy eventually led him to give up.[90] Silicon Valley, which is built on speculation, short-term returns, and jumping ship through initial public offerings, is not the right funding model for cooperatives, which grow slowly and are designed for sustainability.

The philanthropy platform External Revenue Service aims to help non-profits so that they are not spending all of their time on begging for money. With External Revenue Service, users pledge a particular amount per month, which is then divided up among their favored organizations.[91] Max Dana of External Revenue Service writes:

In order to receive pledges from others, a person must first make a pledge of their own annual income and allocate it to at least one other person.[...] The external revenue service is not owned by anyone. It is a distributed network of contributors and users invested in the maintenance and development of the system.[92]

In the United Kingdom, Robin Hood Minor Asset Management is a co-op hedge fund that acts conservatively in the stock market. It simply operates a data-mining algorithm that mimics the moves of Wall Street's top investors and invests the profits into co-ops. They ask, "What if capital was P2P?"[93]

In the United States, Slow Money stands out as a national nonprofit organization that catalyzes investment in sustainable food and farms in particular. FairShares supports farming co-ops and The Workers Lab is the nation's first union-backed innovation accelerator. Institutional investor Kanyi Maqubela states that the most important thing for the cooperative movement is scalability. At Collaborative Fund, Maqubela is trying to help platform co-ops to create scale by providing them with enough liquidity so that they can attract large pools of capital. "We need all hands on deck, including investors to create a more cooperative world," Maqubela said.[94]

Platform cooperativism for the commons

The Internet has been associated with the commons and non-market exchanges since Richard Barbrook's *Hi-Tech Gift Economy*, Yochai Benkler's *Wealth of Networks*, David Bollier's *Spiral Viral*, Dmytri Kleiner's *Venture Communism*,[95] as well as Michel Bauwens' work with the P2P Foundation. Over ten years ago, Dmytri Kleiner coined the term "venture communism" to describe the possibility of federated cooperatives creating communication platforms that can overcome some of the centralized, capitalist, very controlled and privacy-violating platforms that have emerged recently. He calls on us to investigate how the Internet, which was started out as a decentralized and cooperative network became centralized and corporate.[96]

Platform co-ops build on the commons; they rely on open design, and open source hardware licenses for 3D printing; they facilitate the cooperative ecosystem. Michel Bauwens is currently working on the commons-based reciprocity license,[97] which would, for instance, allow cooperatives to share pieces of code in the commons. Cooperatives could freely use the code while others would have to pay for it.

Free software for platform co-ops

The backend of platform co-ops needs to be free software. Not only must the code be accessible to the workers so that they can understand the parameters and patterns that govern their working environment, the software also needs to be developed in consultation with the workers from day one.

In the transportation sector, for example, we're talking about at least four apps. There's one app for the passenger and one for the driver, and these have to be programmed for Android and the iPhone; and those would have to be kept constantly updated and usable, as operating systems and phones are frequently changing. This also means that funding for the developers needs to be ongoing. Platform co-ops cannot be built based on one-time crowdfunded initiatives.

Free software developers could publish core protocols and then allow various independent open source projects to build their own different backend and front-end components. This would accommodate the various service sectors – from crowdsourcing, undocumented migrants, and domestic cleaners, to babysitters.

Blockchain technology as algorithmic regulator?

As co-ops start to take part in online labor markets, they become more distributed, more international. The trust among members that existed in local organizations is no longer a given. Blockchain technology is one way to address the problem of trust.

Blockchain is the protocol underlying the virtual currency Bitcoin. But the most relevant developments for platform co-ops are not solely about Bitcoin itself; "blockchain" has applications well beyond cash and currency. "The blockchain is a distributed ledger that runs under the Bitcoin currency," Irish researcher Rachel O'Dwyer explains. Blockchain technology can constitute a public database that can then be used for all kinds of transactions that require trust. Governments, for instance, experiment with blockchain technology for voting applications. The Honduran Property Institute has asked Factom, an American startup, to provide a prototype of a blockchain-based land registry, for example.[98] O'Dwyer cautions that while there is lots of positive potential, currently most of the applications of blockchain technology are closer to venture capitalism than venture communism: Think better sharing between private banks and "improved" forms of digital rights management.

But this technology also allows for middle-man-free peer-to-peer marketplaces. Imagine "decentralized autonomous organizations" and virtual companies that are basically just sets of rules for transactions executed between peers.[99] Where would one turn if something goes wrong? Blockchain-based programming is also used as a "consensus mechanism" for platforms/tools that facilitate democratic decision making in cooperatives. Here, bylaws, membership, shares, and voting records could be irrevocably stored.

On the other hand, "blockchain technology is based on the idea of delegating trust away from centralized institutions like the state, but also social institutions, and putting that instead into a technical architecture. Some people call this trust in the code but this trust also presumes that we no longer have trust in each other. Instead, you are asked to trust some kind of algorithm. Some have even called this a form of algorithmic regulation," O'Dwyer said.[100] There is also the concern that blockchain-enabled marketplaces could make it easier to avoid paying taxes, for instance.

A consortium focused on the creation of a template of platform co-ops

In our experience working to connect people interested in cooperatives and the Internet, we noticed that developers across the country are working on similar projects.

Underfunded system designers on the West Coast would set up an online labor market while an East Coast project does something similar, but neither of them would consider joining forces.

My proposal is for various developers worldwide to work under the auspices of a platform co-op consortium that would be able to raise funds for the ongoing development of the kernel of such free software projects. Contrary to Jeremy Rifkin's proposal of a marginal cost society, it is still extremely expensive to program and constantly update an online labor market and such a foundation could assist.

Democratic governance

Cooperative structures call for collective decision making, conflict resolution, consensus building, and the managing of shares and funds in a transparent manner. Then there is also the overall management of workers. One of the central questions in this discussion is how its abuses of power can be kept at bay. One of the essential questions is governance. How could the platform govern itself in a distributed, truly democratic way? Convincing tools based on blockchain technology have emerged over the past few years: Backfeed, D-CENT, and Consensys.

Loomio, also sometimes referred to as "the Facebook of the citizen web," is a worker-owned cooperative based in Wellington, New Zealand, and New York City[101] that produces open source software, very much guided by the values of Occupy. It is a web app that features communication and polling tools that make it easier to facilitate democratic communities.[102] In Spain, 27,000 citizens joined Loomio to connect a nationwide grassroots network to the rapidly growing political party Podemos. Altogether, 100,000 people in 93 countries are already using Loomio.

Backfeed.cc is a distributed collaborative organization based on blockchain technology; it supports coordination within a self-organized network.[103]

D-CENT was born out of recent activism work in Catalonia, Iceland, and Greece. A suite of tools is being created to be used for rapidly implementing democracy and other cooperative platforms. The goal is to give political power to people who are able to propose policies, debate options, draft and scrutinize the proposal, vote, and make decisions.[104]

ConsenSys[105] is a venture production studio building decentralized applications and various developer and end-user tools for blockchain ecosystems, focusing primarily on Ethereum.

Designing for convenient solidarity

All too often, technologists belittle the importance of front-end design. This is unfortunate because on the level of UX design, free software platforms have to rival the habit-creating seductiveness of the approaching Uber taxi on the screen of your phone. Or, at least, designers need to decide how much of a consumer mentality they want to integrate. Cameron Tonkinwise, Director of Design Studies at Carnegie Mellon University, cautions that:

> A lot of these platforms enable interactions between people. Political decisions are being made at the level of software design, at the level of interface design, and the sorts of people who are making these decisions are designers and they are very ill-equipped about the political ramifications of what they are doing. Politics is now happening at the level of micro interactions and it's very important that designers are understanding the sociology and anthropology of what they are doing.[106]

What can design for platform co-ops do differently? Cameron Tonkinwise calls for a design that facilitates "convenient solidarities," a design that makes small acts of solidarity easier and more seamless.[107] He proposes, for example, that design should literally provoke solidarity with a worker. If I can see that worker A has three children,

is more expensive than worker B, and that she is about to be termi-
nated by Taskrabbit or Uber, I am faced with the decision whether
or not I want to support her. While making solidarity a bit more
convenient, such an approach would also bring about obvious privacy
issues.

Good design for platform cooperatives begins with the development of a relationship between the designers and their clients. UX
design for platform co-ops presents a great opportunity. The interface
of these platforms could instruct users about the fair labor standards
of the co-op and contrast it with the social protections that are
lacking in the sharing economy. In other words, such platforms could
visualize the unfairness of the established on-demand economy.

I'm also suggesting the use of Mozilla's badge technology[108] to
certify that the particular platform follows the principles that I out-
lined above. Not unlike the fair trade coffee that, for all its shortcomings, has captured a segment of the market, these badges could certify
ethical labor practices behind the screen.

Scale

In order to build an economy that is socially fairer and ecologically
sustainable, cooperatives have to move beyond the growth imperative. Cooperatives don't always have to scale up. Democratically
controlled businesses such as worker cooperatives could target
smaller, local niche markets without having to focus on scaling up.
Such efforts could start in cities like Paris, Berlin, or Rio de Janeiro,[109]
and other municipalities that have banned Uber. If your priority is to
take care of your workers, then scaling up is not an immediate
imperative. In contrast to countless startups, the goal isn't to jump
ship by way of acquisition, but to build lasting businesses over
decades to come.

Learning and education

One of the reasons that Mondragon is so successful in Spain is that
they have a cooperative university that directly feeds into their
network of businesses. Various universities set up centers dedicated
to the preparation of students for cooperative work: University of
Wisconsin (1962), Kansas State (1984), UC Davis (1987), and North
Dakota State (1994). Currently, The Labor Studies Program at the
City University of New York is offering a graduate course on worker
cooperatives.[110] In Boston, MIT's Sasha Costanza-Chock teaches a
project-based co-design course with worker-owned cooperatives.[111]

Teaching cooperative design and values is one approach, another would be to think up and build a college that is build on cooperative principles, a Black Mountain College 2.0.

How could alternative learning institutions better prepare youth for cooperative working and living today? Again, the work of Janelle Orsi is quite essential here. In her co-authored book, *The Sharing Solution*, Orsi demonstrates in a practical, hands-on manner, the various ways in which sharing can become part of our everyday life: everything from sharing housing, household goods, space, tasks, childcare, transportation, and even work. *The Sharing Solution*, The Whole Earth Catalog of genuine sharing, lays out the practical ground rules that could orient college students to a more cooperative approach to life.

8) For All People

We must invent a new Web in the service of a viable macroeconomic model, rather than developing a completely ruinous economy of data.[112]

Right now, platform capitalism is getting defined top-down by decisions being made in Silicon Valley, executed by black box algorithms. What we need is a new story about sharing, aggregation, openness, and cooperation; one that we can believe in.

The cooperative movement needs to come to terms with twenty-first-century technologies. It will take some work to make the notion of online cooperatives as American as apple pie. It will also take discussions in various national and local contexts, from Peru, Germany, and Italy, to the UK, South Korea, and India.

The importance of platform cooperativism does not lie in "killing death star platforms."[113] It does not come from destroying dark overlords like Uber but from writing them over in people's minds, incorporating different ownership models, and then inserting them back into the mainstream. In the late 1960s and early 1970s, counterculturalists formed utopian communities; they left the cities for the mountains to force their idea of the future into existence by living it. Frequently, these experiments failed.

To successfully develop platform cooperatives, it does take more than practical wisdom and giddy enthusiasm. An anti-theory stance, a rejection of critical self-reflection, will – as we saw with American counterculture – become an impediment. We need to study the failures and successes of the past to identify the areas in which platform cooperatives are most likely to succeed. We need to spread an ideology of felt mutualism, communitarian ideals, and cooperation that makes all of this possible. Platform cooperativism can invigorate a genuine sharing economy, the solidarity economy. It will not remedy the corrosive effects of capitalism but it can show that work can be dignifying rather than diminishing for the human experience.

Platform cooperativism is not, first of all, about the next device or "platform;" it is about envisioning a life that is not centered on the shareholder enterprise. Making change is not always about a dinner party, or about writing an essay, or convening a conference; it's not so convenient: platform cooperativism is also about confrontation.

To strengthen and build out platform co-ops, it is essential for like-minded people to organize. Yochai Benkler encouraged this movement, "If you can imagine it, it can happen, if you do it in time and capture a market."[114]

We cannot waste any more time. Politicians and platform owners have been promising social protections, access, and privacy, but we need to make ownership a reality. It's time to realize that they will never deliver. They can't. But we must. Through our collective effort we can build political power for a social movement that will bring these ideas into existence.

Epilogue

Over the course of these chapters, I have tried my best to locate, explain, and elaborate narratives that may illuminate the landscape of digital work. If you have come this far, you will understand that this book refuses to accept a future of work that is characterized by deregulation and a lack of enforcement of legally guaranteed labor standards. I chose the title for this book carefully with a view toward an emerging movement of workers that is starting to take back the digital economy. In 2014, at the Digital Labor conference at The New School in New York City, Amazon Mechanical Turk workers started a discussion about worker-owned and -governed online labor platforms. In the same period, I noticed the launch of cooperative platforms in Germany and the United States. It was in this context that I framed the idea of platform cooperativism.

A year later, more than a thousand people attended the Platform Cooperativism: The Internet, Ownership, Democracy event. The platform cooperativism primer has since been translated into German, Italian, Dutch, Chinese, Spanish, and Portuguese. In 2016, together with Nathan Schneider, I edited a handbook on platform cooperativism in collaboration with OR Books, and now platform cooperativism events are in the works from Vancouver, Berlin, London, Bremen, Paris, Bangkok, Barcelona, New York, Austin, Boulder, Oakland, the San Francisco Bay Area to Adelaide. A foundation to support the ecosystem of online cooperatives is also under way.

Platform co-ops don't want to copy the likes of Uber; the companies that came before us. Instead, they embrace a vision for decent digital work, democratic governance, creativity, and worker ownership. Silicon Valley loves a good disruption. Let's give them one.

Notes

Introduction: Why Digital Labor Now?

1 United States Department of Justice, "FBCI: Prisoners and Prisoner Re-Entry." Available at: http://www.justice.gov/archive/fbci/progmenu_reentry.html.

2 Alan Pyke, "Almost Half The Country Can't Afford The Basics," ThinkProgress, September 18, 2013. Available at: http://thinkprogress.org/economy/2013/09/18/2641301/half-country-afford-basics/.

3 https://loconomics.com.

4 https://www.stocksy.com.

5 By 2014, their revenues had reached $3.7 million dollars, and since their founding they've paid out several million dollars in surplus to their artists.

6 Tyler Cowen, *Average Is Over: Powering America Beyond the Age of the Great Stagnation* (E P Dutton & Co, 2013).

7 "In Mexico for instance, I have met large numbers of people who live on less than $10,000 a year, or maybe even on less than $5,000 a year. They hardly qualify as well-off but they do have access to cheap food and very cheap housing. They cannot buy too many other things. They don't always have money to bring the kid to the doctor or to buy new clothes. Their lodging is satisfactory, if not spectacular, and of course the warmer weather helps" (Cowen, *Average Is Over*, 240).

8 Natasha Singer, "In the Sharing Economy, Workers Find Both Freedom and Uncertainty," *The New York Times*, August 16, 2014. Available at: http://www.nytimes.com/2014/08/17/technology/in-the-sharing-economy-workers-find-both-freedom-and-uncertainty.html?_r=0.

9 Seth D. Harris and Alan B. Krueger, "A Proposal for Modernizing Labor Laws for Twenty-First-Century Work: The 'Independent Worker,' " The Hamilton Project, December 7, 2015. Available at:

http://www.hamiltonproject.org/papers/modernizing_labor_laws_
for_twenty_first_century_work_independent_worker.

10 Moshe Z. Marvit, "How Crowdworkers Became the Ghosts in the
    Digital Machine," *The Nation*, February 5, 2014. Available at: http://
    www.thenation.com/article/how-crowdworkers-became-ghosts-digital-
    machine/.

11 It is not at all surprising that the US was included in a global index of
    worker rights violations, which included the US on a list of 30 countries
    including Kenya that showed *systematic* violations of worker rights.

12 Vanessa Barth and Florian Schmidt, "Interview with Spam Girl," in
    Crowd Work: Zurück in die Zukunft, ed. by Christiane Benner (Bund
    Verlag, 2014).

13 Lawrence Lessig, *Remix: Making Art and Commerce Thrive in the
    Hybrid Economy* (Penguin, 2008), 178.

14 Steve Lohr, "Customer Service? Ask a Volunteer," *The New York
    Times*, April 26, 2009. Available at: http://www.nytimes.com/2009/04/
    26/business/26unbox.html.

15 Stéphane Hessel, *Time for Outrage* (Quartet Books, 2011).

16 http://digitallabor.org/2009. You can access over 170 interviews with par-
    ticipants in these conferences at https://vimeo.com/mobilityshifts/videos/.

17 Trebor Scholz, *Digital Labor: The Internet as Playground and Factory*
    (Routledge, 2012).

18 Conferences that have helped shape this discourse include *Digital
    Labor: The Internet as Playground and Factory* (New School, New York
    City, United States, 2009), *Digital Labour: Workers, Authors, Citizens*
    (Western University, London, Ontario, Canada, 2009), *Invisible Labor
    Colloquium* (Washington University Law School, 2013), *Towards Critical
    Theories of Social Media* (Uppsala University, Uppsala, Sweden, 2012),
    Re:Publica conference (Berlin, Germany, 2013), and the *Chronicles of
    Work* lecture Series at Schloss Solitude (Stuttgart, Germany, 2012/2013).
    Exhibitions like *Arbeidstid* in Oslo (2013), MASSMOCA's exhibition
    The Workers (2012) and artworks and films by Alex Rivera, Stephanie
    Rothenburg & Jeff Crouse, Xtine, and Aaron Coblin were also crucial.

19 "Platform Cooperativism: The Internet, Ownership, Democracy" was
    convened by Trebor Scholz and Nathan Schneider (platformcoop.net).

20 Trebor Scholz, "Platform Cooperativism vs. the Sharing Economy."
    Available at: https://medium.com/@trebors/platform-cooperativism-
    vs-the-sharing-economy-2ea737f1b5ad#.e886o8hmj.

21 Ian Shapiro, *The Flight from Reality in the Human Sciences* (Princeton
    University Press, 2007), 179.

Chapter 1: Waged Labor and the Creative Wrecking of Employment

1 Bob Black, "The Abolition of Work," available at: http://www.primi-
   tivism.com/abolition.htm.

2   Yann Moulier Boutang, *Cognitive Capitalism*, 1st edn (Polity, 2012).
3   Darrell Jones, "Introducing Upwork – the Evolution of Elance and oDesk," Company Blog, *Elance Blog*, May 4, 2015. Available at: https://www.elance.com/q/blog/introducing-upwork-%E2%80%93-evolution-elance-and-odesk.
4   Jeff Howe, "The Rise of Crowdsourcing," *Wired*, June 1, 2006. Available at: http://www.wired.com/wired/archive/14.06/crowds.html.
5   Don Tapscott and Anthony D. Williams, *Wikinomics: How Mass Collaboration Changes Everything*, exp. edn (Portfolio Trade, 2010).
6   Rachel Emma Silverman, "Big Firms Try Crowdsourcing," *Wall Street Journal*, January 17, 2012. Available at: http://online.wsj.com/article/SB10001424052970204409004577157493201863200.html.
7   Tapscott and Williams, *Wikinomics*, 63.
8   David Mattin, "The World of Wiki," *Think Open*, October 2012. Available at: https://www.thinkwithgoogle.com/intl/en-gb/article/the-world-of-wiki/.
9   Armin Medosch, "Crowdsourcing: Vielfalt in Der Masse," *OE1 ORF*, February 25, 2013. Available at: http://oe1.orf.at/artikel/332592.
10 Chris Anderson, *The Long Tail: Why the Future of Business Is Selling Less of More*, rev. edn (Hyperion, 2008), 219.
11 Panos Ipeirotis, "Why People Participate on Mechanical Turk, Now Tabulated," *Behind Enemy Lines. A Computer Scientist in a Business School*, September 11, 2008. Available at: http://www.behind-the-enemy-lines.com/2008/09/why-people-participate-on-mechanical.html.
12 Adam DuVander, "Amazon Proves It Remembers Mechanical Turk," Wired.com, December 3, 2008. Available at: http://www.wired.com/business/2008/12/amazon-proves-i/.
13 "Soylent: A Word Processor with a Crowd Inside," available at: http://projects.csail.mit.edu/soylent/.
14 Mary L. Gray, "Facing the Crowd: Past, Present, and Futures of Digital Labour," Closing Keynote Address. The Internet, Policy, and Politics Conference at Oxford Internet Institute, Oxford, UK, 2014). Available at: https://www.youtube.com/watch?v=sqr62QTiZvA.
15 Joel Ross, Lilly Irani, M. Six Silberman, Andrew Zaldivar, and Bill Tomlinson, "Who Are the Crowdworkers? Shifting Demographics in Mechanical Turk" (CHI 2010: Imagine All the People, Atlanta, GA, USA, 2010), 231.
16 Frank Pasquale, *Black Box Society: The Secret Algorithms behind Money and Information* (Harvard University Press, 2015), 3.
17 Alex Rivera, *Cybracero Systems*, available at: http://cybracero.com.
18 Aaron Koblin, "The Sheep Market," available at: http://www.aaronkoblin.com/work/thesheepmarket/index.html.
19 Jeff Krouse, "Crowded," available at: http://jeffish.com/projects/crowded.html.
20 P2P Foundation, "The State of Distributed Labour," available at: http://blog.p2pfoundation.net/the-state-of-distributed-labour/2009/12/25.

21　James Marcus, "The Mercenary Position: Can Amazon Change Its Predatory Ways?," *Harper's Magazine*, December 2013. Available at: http://harpers.org/archive/2013/12/the-mercenary-position/.

22　Jodi Kantor and David Streitfeld, "Inside Amazon: Wrestling Big Ideas in a Bruising Workplace," *The New York Times*, August 15, 2015. Available at: http://www.nytimes.com/2015/08/16/technology/inside-amazon-wrestling-big-ideas-in-a-bruising-workplace.html?smid=tw-nytimes&smtyp=cur&_r=0.

23　Flora Wisdorff and Michael Gassmann, "Amazon Schüchtert Mit 'Inaktivitätsprotokollen' Ein," *Welt Online*, March 13, 2015. Available at: http://www.welt.de/wirtschaft/article138353783/Amazon-schuechtert-mit-Inaktivitaetsprotokollen-ein.html.

24　By 2015, Amazon had already introduced 15,000, 16-inch-tall robots in their warehouses. They can carry over 300 lb and speed up the processing of Amazon orders. Amelia Smith, "Amazon Reveals Robot Army in Its Warehouses," *Newsweek*, December 1, 2014. Available at: http://www.newsweek.com/amazon-reveals-robot-army-its-warehouses-288124.

25　Alison Griswold, "Supreme Court Decides Amazon Workers Don't Need to Be Paid While Waiting for Mandatory Security Screenings," *Slate*, December 9, 2014. Available at: http://www.slate.com/blogs/moneybox/2014/12/09/supreme_court_rules_against_paying_workers_for_security_screenings_amazon.html.

26　Matthew Lease et al., "Mechanical Turk Is Not Anonymous" (Social Science Research Network, March 6, 2013). Available at: http://papers.ssrn.com/sol3/papers.cfm?abstract_id=2228728.

27　Ned Resnikoff, "Invisible Data Janitors Mop up Top Websites behind the Scenes," Al Jazeera America, May 1, 2015. Available at: http://america.aljazeera.com/articles/2015/5/1/invisible-data-janitors-mop-up-top-websites-behind-the-scenes.html.

28　"Amazon Mechanical Turk Participation Agreement," *Amazon*, December 2, 2014. Available at: https://www.mturk.com/mturk/conditionsofuse.

29　Gregory M. Lamb, "When Workers Turn into 'Turkers,' " *Christian Science Monitor*, November 2, 2006. Available at: http://www.csmonitor.com/2006/1102/p13s02-wmgn.html.

30　Katharine Mieszkowski, "'I Make $1.45 a Week and I Love It,'" *Salon*, July 24, 2006. Available at: http://www.salon.com/2006/07/24/turks_3/.

31　Michael Pooler, "Crowdworkers Form Their Own Digital Networks," *Financial Times*, November 3, 2014. Available at: http://www.ft.com/cms/s/0/2c23a880-5df3-11e4-bc04-00144feabdc0.html#axzz3ORZ6raA3.

32　Joel Ross et al., "Who Are the Turkers?," 2863–72.

33　Rachael King, "Mechanical Serfdom Is Just That," *Bloomberg Business*, February 1, 2011. Available at: http://www.bloomberg.com/bw/stories/2011-02-01/mechanical-serfdom-is-just-thatbusinessweek-business-news-stock-market-and-financial-advice.

34 Rochelle LaPlante, "MTurk," March 15, 2015.
35 Nathan Schneider, "Intellectual Piecework," *The Chronicle of Higher Education*, February 16, 2015. Available at: http://chronicle.com/article/Intellectual-Piecework/190039/?key=SWh7JFRvYXYbYHFjY2 5HYTdTaHM7Zk0nNyNJPXotbllREA==.
36 Lilly Irani, "Justice for 'Data Janitors,' " *Public Books*, January 15, 2015. Available at: http://www.publicbooks.org/nonfiction/justice-for-data-janitors.
37 Ibid.
38 Ross et al., "Who Are the Crowdworkers?"
39 Ibid., 232.
40 Christiane Benner, *Crowd Work – zurück in die Zukunft* (Bund-Verlag, 2014), 100.
41 Ipeirotis, "Why People Participate on Mechanical Turk."
42 "MTurk CENSUS," *AWS Developer Forums*, January 2011. Available at: https://forums.aws.amazon.com/thread.jspa?threadID=58891.
43 Karën Fort, Gilles Adda, and K. Bretonnel Cohen, "Amazon Mechanical Turk: Gold Mine or Coal Mine?," *Computational Linguistics* 37, no. 2 (2011), 413–20.
44 Neil Stewart et al. "The Average Laboratory Samples a Population of 7,300 Amazon Mechanical Turk Workers," *Judgment and Decision Making* 10 (2015), 479–91.
45 David Martin, Benjamin V. Hanrahan, Jacki O'Neill, and Neha Gupta, "Being a Turker," *CSCW'14*, February 15–19, 2014, Baltimore, MD, 6.
46 Trebor Scholz, ed., "Digital Labor Notebook" (The New School, August 2014).
47 Open Society Foundation's Final Report on the "Future of Work" Project, December 2015.
48 Stanley Aronowitz and William DiFazio, *The Jobless Future*, 2nd edn (University of Minnesota Press, 2010), 93.
49 Final report about the Future of Work Project commissioned by the Open Society Foundation.
50 Iris Dorbian, "LeadGenius Racks up $6 Mln," *PE Hub*, October 8, 2014. Available at: https://www.pehub.com/2014/10/leadgenius-racks-up-6-mln/.
51 Pooler, "Crowdworkers Form Their Own Digital Networks."
52 David Carr, "Plentiful Content, So Cheap," *The New York Times*, February 8, 2010. Available at: https://www.nytimes.com/2010/02/08/business/media/08carr.html.
53 Florian Schmidt, "For a Few Dollars More," February 10, 2013. Available at: http://florianschmidt.co/for-a-few-dollars-more/.
54 *Threadless*, 2009. Available at: https://www.youtube.com/watch?v=9 VKRbmnqXR4&feature=youtube_gdata_player.
55 Mike Davis, *Planet of Slums* (Verso, 2007).
56 "InnoCentive," Wikipedia, the Free Encyclopedia. Available at: http://en.wikipedia.org/wiki/InnoCentive.

57 Eric von Hippel, *Democratizing Innovation* (The MIT Press, 2006).
58 Miriam A. Cherry, "A Taxonomy of Virtual Work," *Alabama Law Review*, May 14, 2012, 3.
59 Cory Doctorow, *For the Win* (Tor Teen, 2010), 27.
60 Ibid., 19.
61 Lisa Nakamura, "Don't Hate the Player, Hate the Game: The Racialization of Labor in World of Warcraft," *Critical Studies in Media Communication* 26, no. 2 (2009): 128–44.
62 Julian Dibbell, "The Life of the Chinese Gold Farmer," *The New York Times*, June 17, 2007. Available at: http://www.nytimes.com/2007/06/17/magazine/17lootfarmers-t.html.
63 Jack Linchuan Qiu, *Working-Class Network Society: Communication Technology and the Information Have-Less in Urban China* (The MIT Press, 2009), 185, 105.
64 Peter Ludlow and Mark Wallace, *The Second Life Herald: The Virtual Tabloid That Witnessed the Dawn of the Metaverse* (The MIT Press, 2007).
65 Cherry, "A Taxonomy of Virtual Work," 2.
66 Danny Vincent, "China Used Prisoners in Lucrative Internet Gaming Work," *The Guardian*, May 25, 2011. Available at: http://www.guardian.co.uk/world/2011/may/25/china-prisoners-internet-gaming-scam.
67 If not strictly in-game labor, a related practice is that of "cherry blossoming." Sometimes also referred to as "crowd turfing," it refers to people being hired to perform small digital tasks such as "liking" a firm's Facebook page or following its Twitter account, all aimed at improving the online presence of a particular brand.
68 Alek Felstiner, "Working the Crowd: Employment and Labor Law in the Crowdsourcing Industry," *SSRN eLibrary*, August 16, 2011. Available at: http://papers.ssrn.com/sol3/papers.cfm?abstract_id=1593853.
69 "The Workforce in the Cloud," *The Economist*, June 1, 2013. Available at: http://www.economist.com/news/business/21578658-talent-exchanges-web-are-starting-transform-world-work-workforce.
70 Mayo Fuster Morell, "The Unethics of Sharing: Wikiwashing," *International Review of Information Ethics*, 15 (2011), 9–16.
71 Alison Griswold, "In Search of Uber's Unicorn," *Slate*, October 27, 2014. Available at: http://www.slate.com/articles/business/moneybox/2014/10/uber_driver_salary_the_ride_sharing_company_says_its_drivers_make_great.html.
72 Paul Resnick, "Estimating Uber Driver Pay, Net of Expenses: $12.76 in Boston," Personal Blog, *Paul Resnick's Occasional Musings*, January 25, 2015. Available at: https://presnick.wordpress.com/2015/01/25/estimating-uber-driver-pay-net-of-expenses-12-26-in-boston/.
73 "5-Year Anniversary Remarks from Uber CEO Travis Kalanick," *Uber Global*, June 3, 2015. Available at: http://newsroom.uber.com/2015/06/5-years-travis-kalanick/.
74 Lauren Weber and Rachel Emma Silverman, "On-Demand Workers: 'We Are Not Robots,' " *Wall Street Journal*, January 27, 2015.

Available at: http://www.wsj.com/articles/on-demand-workers-we-are-not-robots-1422406524.

75 Andre Gorz, *Reclaiming Work: Beyond the Wage-Based Society*, 1st ed. (Polity, 1999), 89.

76 Ibid., 93.

77 Sascha Lobo, "Sascha Lobo: Sharing Economy Wie Bei Uber Ist Plattform-Kapitalismus," *Spiegel Online*, March 9, 2014, http://www.spiegel.de/netzwelt/netzpolitik/sascha-lobo-sharing-economy-wie-bei-uber-ist-plattform-kapitalismus-a-989584.html.

78 US Department of Labor, "Technical Note – Bureau of Labor Statistics," US Department of Labor, October 2012. Available at: http://www.bls.gov/news.release/pdf/empsit.pdf.

79 Josh Constine, "Uber's Denial of Liability in Girl's Death Raises Accident Accountability Questions," *TechCrunch*, January 2, 2014. Available at: http://techcrunch.com/2014/01/02/should-car-services-provide-insurance-whenever-their-driver-app-is-open/.

80 "Beating the Winter Slump – Price Cuts with Guaranteed Earnings," *Uber Blog*, January 8, 2015. Available at: https://blog.uber.com/PriceCut2015.

81 Brishen Rogers to Trebor Scholz, "Sharing Economy," June 2015.

82 Frank Pasquale, "Low-Wage Work: Getting By & Fighting Back," Digital Labor Conference, November 15, 2014. Available at: http://digitallabor.org/schedule/low-wage-work-getting-by-and-fighting-back.

83 "Uber," *Crunchbase*, accessed April 27, 2015. Available at: https://www.crunchbase.com/organization/uber.

84 "Lobbyist Activity Report" (Government of the District of Columbia Board of Ethics and Government Accountability, January 2015). Available at: https://efiling.bega-dc.gov/efs/pdf_files/lob/611b46e0-199e-41f3-8608-65853deb20d0.pdf.

85 Rebecca Tushnet, "Violating Taxi Regulations Isn't Unfair Competition in Pa.," *Rebecca Tushnet's 43(B)log*, March 9, 2015. Available at: http://tushnet.blogspot.com/2015/03/violating-taxi-regulations-isnt-unfair.html.

86 Casey Newton, "Temping Fate: Can TaskRabbit Go from Side Gigs to Real Jobs?," *The Verge*, May 23, 2013. Available at: http://www.theverge.com/2013/5/23/4352116/taskrabbit-temp-agency-gig-economy.

87 Ibid.

88 Erin Hatton, "The Rise of the Permanent Temp Economy," *New York Times*, January 26, 2013. Available at: http://opinionator.blogs.nytimes.com/2013/01/26/the-rise-of-the-permanent-temp-economy/.

89 Ibid.

90 Ibid.

91 Ibid.

92 David Weir, "TaskRabbit Threatens to Disrupt Traditional Temp Agencies," *7x7*, May 23, 2013. Available at: http://www.7x7.com/tech-gadgets/taskrabbit.

93   Joshua Brustein, "In the Future We'll All Be TaskRabbits," *Bloomberg Business*, May 24, 2013. Available at: http://www.businessweek.com/ articles/2013-05-24/in-the-future-well-all-be-taskrabbits.
94   "Zirtual – What We Do," *Zirtual*. Available at: https://www.zirtual. com/what-we-do/.
95   Weber and Silverman, "On-Demand Workers."
96   Winnie Rebecca Poster, "Saying 'Good Morning' at Night: The Reversal of Work Time in Global ICT Service Work," *Research in the Sociology of Work* 17 (2007), 62.
97   Ibid., 68–9.
98   Greg Grandin, *Fordlandia: The Rise and Fall of Henry Ford's Forgotten Jungle City*, 1st edn (Picador, 2010), chapter 2.
99   Daniel Jackson, "1000 Workers," personal project, *1000Workers*, May 1, 2014. Available at: http://1000workers.com/.
100   To learn more about Maslow's theory, read Abraham H. Maslow, *Hierarchy of Needs: A Theory of Human Motivation* (American Psychological Association, 2011).
101   William Thies, Aishwarya Lakshmi Ratan, and James Davis, "Paid Crowdsourcing as a Vehicle for Global Development," ACM CHI 2011 Workshop on Crowdsourcing and Human Computation (May 2011).
102   Jeffrey Brown, Lisa Lynch, and Andrew McAffe, "Is New Technology Chipping Away at Scope of the American Workforce?," *PBS Newshour*, April 5, 2013. Available at: http://www.pbs.org/newshour/bb/business-jan-june13-jobs2_04-05/.
103   Susan Buck-Morss, *Dreamworld and Catastrophe: The Passing of Mass Utopia in East and West* (The MIT Press, 2000), 105.
104   Jonathan V. Last, "Capitalism's Brave New World," *The Weekly Standard*, July 16, 2012. Available at: http://www.weeklystandard. com/print/articles/capitalism-s-brave-new-world_648222.html.
105   Kent Greenfield, *The Myth of Choice: Personal Responsibility in a World of Limits* (Yale University Press, 2011).
106   Eric Mack, "The Lawsuit That Could Help Undo (or Cement) Crowdsourcing in the U.S.," www.crowdsourcing.org, January 7, 2013. Available at: http://www.crowdsourcing.org/editorial/the-lawsuit-that-could-help-undo-or-cement-crowdsourcing-in-the-us/22968.
107   Martin Oetting, "Digitale Arbeit: Eine Positive Vision für die Sozialdemokratie," D64 Zentrum für Digitalen Fortschritt, June 20, 2012. Available at: http://d-64.org/digitale-arbeit-eine-positive-vision-fur-die-sozialdemokratie/.
108   Ibid.
109   Mike Davis, *Planet of Slums* (Verso, 2007), 170.
110   Alek Felstiner, "Working the Crowd: Employment and Labor Law in the Crowdsourcing Industry," *Berkeley Journal of Employment and Labor Law*, 32, no. 1 (2011), art. 3.
111   Aniket Kittur et al., "The Future of Crowd Work," *16th ACM Conference on Computer Supported Cooperative Work (CSCW 2013)*.

112   Mary L. Gray, "Crowds Are People, Too!" Closing Keynote Address, 2014 Microsoft Research Faculty Summit, Redmond, Washington, July 14, 2014.
113   Kittur et al., "The Future of Crowd Work."
114   Benner, Crowd Work – zurück in die Zukunft, 121.

Chapter 2: Playbor and Other Unpaid Pursuits

1   Lawrence Lessig, Remix: Making Art and Commerce Thrive in the Hybrid Economy (Penguin, 2008), 178.
2   Clay Shirky, Cognitive Surplus: Creativity and Generosity in a Connected Age (Penguin, 2010).
3   Scott Rettberg, "Corporate Ideology in World of Warcraft," Institute for Distributed Creativity, September 11, 2009. Available at: https://lists.thing.net/pipermail/idc/2009-September/003870.html.
4   Franco "Bifo" Berardi, The Soul at Work: From Alienation to Autonomy, trans. Francesca Cadel and Giuseppina Mecchia (Semiotext(e), 2009), 99.
5   Tiziana Terranova, "Free Labor: Producing Culture for the Digital Economy," Social Text 18, no. 2 (2000), 74.
6   John W. Budd, "What Is Work?" (Invisible Labor Colloquium, Washington University School of Law, 2013).
7   Andrew Crabtree, Tom Rodden, Peter Tolmie, and Graham Button, "Ethnography Considered Harmful," in Proceedings of the SIGCHI Conference on Human Factors in Computing Systems, CHI '09 (ACM, 2009), 879–88.
8   Suely Rolnik, "The Geopolitics of Pimping," EIPCP, October 2006. Available at: http://eipcp.net/transversal/1106/rolnik/en.
9   Ulises Ali Mejias, Off the Network: Disrupting the Digital World (University of Minnesota Press, 2013), 6.
10   Lessig, Remix, 92–93.
11   Nick Carr coined the term "data mine crowd." Nick Carr, "Rough Type: A Typology of Crowds," March 4, 2010. Available at: http://www.roughtype.com/archives/2010/03/a_typology_of_c.php.
12   Olivia Katrandjian, "Hurricane Irene: Pop-Tarts Top List of Hurricane Purchases," ABC News, August 27, 2011. Available at: http://abcnews.go.com/US/hurricanes/hurricane-irene-pop-tarts-top-list-hurricane-purchases/story?id=14393602.
13   Burak Arikan, Meta-Markets, 2007, available at: http://burak-arikan.com/meta-markets.
14   Chris Catiglione, "Yann Moulier Boutang Asks, 'Are We All Just Google's Worker Bees?,' " Society of the Query Conference, November 13, 2009. Available at: http://networkcultures.org/wpmu/query/2009/11/13/yann-moulier-boutang-asks-are-we-all-just-googles-worker-bees/comment-page-1/#comment-439.

15 "GWEI – Google Will Eat Itself," available at: http://gwei.org/index. php.

16 http://digitallabor.org/2009

17 Katie Hafner, *Where Wizards Stay Up Late: The Origins of the Internet* (Simon & Schuster, 1998), 176.

18 Johnny Ryan, *A History of the Internet and the Digital Future* (Reaktion Books, 2010), 77.

19 Michael Hauben, Ronda Hauben, and Thomas Truscott, *Netizens: On the History and Impact of Usenet and the Internet* (Wiley-IEEE Computer Society Press, 1997), 124.

20 Chip Morningstar and F. Randall Farmer, "The Lessons of Lucasfilm's Habitat," The First International Conference on Cyberspace, May 1990, University of Texas at Austin. Available at: http://www.fudco. com/chip/lessons.html.

21 Rob Hornig, "Escape from Love Jail," *The New Inquiry*, March 7, 2013. Available at: http://thenewinquiry.com/blogs/marginal-utility/ escape-from-love-jail/.

22 Alice E. Marwick, *Status Update: Celebrity, Publicity, and Branding in the Social Media Age* (Yale University Press, 2013), 117.

23 Jonathan Crary, *24/7: Late Capitalism and the Ends of Sleep* (Verso, 2014), 98.

24 "[loveMachine] Like Everything Your Friends Do on Facebook," available at: http://lovemachine.cc/.

25 Arlie Russell Hochschild, *The Managed Heart: Commercialization of Human Feeling*, 3rd rev. edn (University of California Press, 2012).

26 Arlie Russell Hochschild, *The Commercialization of Intimate Life: Notes from Home and Work* (University of California Press, 2003).

27 Ibid., 87.

28 http://www.apple.com/watch/health-and-fitness/

29 Daniel J. Solove, *The Future of Reputation: Gossip, Rumor, and Privacy on the Internet* (Yale University Press, 2008), 38.

30 Gary Shteyngart, *Super Sad True Love Story: A Novel* (Random House, 2010).

31 Adrian Chen, "The Laborers Who Keep Dick Pics and Beheadings Out of Your Facebook Feed," Wired, October 23, 2014. Available at: http://www.wired.com/2014/10/content-moderation/.

32 This also reminds me of Manuel Castells who argued that people "give life" to a city not only through their labor in the service industries but also through their music, dance, food, and festivals. Clearly, Facebook is not a public space but a similar dynamic unfolds in this enclosure too.

33 George Yúdice, *The Expediency of Culture: Uses of Culture in the Global Era* (Duke University Press, 2004), 19.

34 Mejias, *Off the Network*, 8.

35 "Suddenly Snowden Comments on "Just Days Left to Kill Mass Surveillance under Section 215 of the Patriot Act. We Are Edward Snowden and the ACLU's Jameel Jaffer. AUA." Available at: https://

www.reddit.com/r/IAmA/comments/36ru89/just_days_left_to_kill_
mass_surveillance_under/crglgh2.

36 Matt Sledge, "CIA's Gus Hunt On Big Data: We 'Try To Collect
Everything And Hang On To It Forever,' " March 20, 2013. Available
at: http://www.huffingtonpost.com/2013/03/20/cia-gus-hunt-big-data_
n_2917842.html.

37 Anne Flaherty, "What the Government Pays to Snoop on You," *USA
Today*, July 10, 2013. Available at: http://www.usatoday.com/story/
money/business/2013/07/10/what-government-pays-to-snoop-on-
you/2504819/.

38 Just peel off the sticker on the back of a shampoo bottle to find a little
dot with a spider-like pattern around it. The dot in the middle is the
radio and the mesh surrounding it constitutes an antenna.

39 "Fence Systems," *PetSmart*, available at: http://www.petsmart.com/dog/
fence-systems/cat-36-catid-100015?utm_source=MSN&utm_medium=
cpc&utm_term=petsmart+invisible+fence&utm_content=Pet_Fences-
PetSmart&utm_campaign=US_Merch_Search_DTM_Near_
Hardgoods_Containment_nv&OVMTC=b&OVKEY=petsmart+invisi
ble+fence&url_id=161951464&device=c.

40 And sure enough, if I had a 94-year-old grandfather who suffers from
dementia, I would be happy to pay DigitalAngel to keep track of him
on his urban wanderings, at least during the times when I'm not able
to look after him.

41 Bruno Waterfield, "Tom Tom Sold Driver's GPS Details to Be Used
by Police for Speed Traps," The Telegraph, April 28, 2011. Available at: http://www.telegraph.co.uk/technology/news/8480702/Tom-
Tom-sold-drivers-GPS-details-to-be-used-by-police-for-speed-traps.
html.

42 With the PayPass you can pay with a slight gesture of the hand,
tapping the card against the machine, seamlessly scratching any con-
sumerist itch. At Prada's flagship store in Manhattan, shoppers (the
1%, really) can register for a program that allows them to enter the
store, grab whatever they like and simply leave. Their purchases will
be automatically charged to their accounts.

43 Margaret Jane Radin, *Boilerplate: The Fine Print, Vanishing Rights,
and the Rule of Law* (Princeton University Press, 2014), 88.

44 Julianne Pepitone, "Instagram Can Now Sell Your Photos for Ads,"
CNN Money, December 18, 2012. Available at: http://money.cnn.
com/2012/12/18/technology/social/instagram-sell-photos/index.
html?iid=s_mpm#comments.

45 Michel Bauwens in Trebor Scholz, ed., *Digital Labor: The Internet as
Playground and Factory* (Routledge, 2013).

46 Kathi Weeks, *The Problem with Work: Feminism, Marxism, Antiwork
Politics, and Postwork Imaginaries* (Duke University Press, 2011), 29.

47 Yochai Benkler, *The Wealth of Networks: How Social Production
Transforms Markets and Freedom* (Yale University Press, 2007), 19.

48 http://civichall.org/

49 "Projects at the Center for Civic Media," *MIT Center for Civic Media*. Available at: https://civic.mit.edu/projects?page=2.

50 Golan Levin and David Newbury, "Moon Drawings," *The Frank-Ratchye STUDIO for Creative Inquiry at Carnegie Mellon University*, 2015. Available at: http://www.moondrawings.org/.

51 lhamilton, "28,000 Unique Titles Preserved!," *Distributed Proofreaders*, August 16, 2014. Available at: http://www.pgdp.net/phpBB2/view-topic.php?t=56977.

52 Brandi Grissom, "Web Traffic to Texas Border Cameras Dropping," *The Texas Tribune*, November 11, 2009. Available at: http://www.texastribune.org/2009/11/11/web-traffic-to-texas-border-cameras-dropping/.

53 Ushahidi, "Crowdmap," 2010. Available at: https://crowdmap.com/welcome.

54 "OpenStreetMap Wiki," available at: http://wiki.openstreetmap.org/wiki/Main_Page.

55 Maps were originally published under a Creative Commons license but are now licensed under an Open Database License.

56 Shteyngart, *Super Sad True Love Story*, 90.

57 http://content.yardmap.org

58 On the site it reads: "The Library of Babel is a place for scholars to do research, for artists and writers to seek inspiration, for anyone with curiosity or a sense of humor to reflect on the weirdness of existence."

59 "r/LibraryofBabel/," Forum, *Reddit*, available at: http://www.reddit.com/r/LibraryofBabel.

60 "Flickr," *WolframAlpha*, available at: http://www.wolframalpha.com/input/?i=flickr.

61 Kathleen Kuehn and Thomas F. Corrigan, "Hope Labor: The Role of Employment Prospects in Online Social Production," *The Political Economy of Communication*, 1, no. 1 (2013). Available at: http://www.polecom.org/index.php/polecom/article/view/9/64.

62 Ta-Nehisi Coates, "Lucrative Work-for-Free Opportunity," *The Atlantic*, March 9, 2013. Available at: http://www.theatlantic.com/national/archive/2013/03/lucrative-work-for-free-opportunity/273846/.

63 The Daily Dish, "The HuffPo Model: Rich Liberals Exploiting Blog-Serfs for Millions," *The Atlantic*, February 14, 2011. Available at: http://www.theatlantic.com/daily-dish/archive/2011/02/the-huffpo-model-rich-liberals-exploiting-blog-serfs-for-millions/175808/.

64 Alexandra Steigrad, "Condé Nast Settles Intern Lawsuit," *WWD*, April 4, 2014. Available at: http://wwd.com/business-news/fashion-memopad/cond-nast-settles-intern-lawsuit-7630782/.

65 Ross Perlin, *Intern Nation: How to Earn Nothing and Learn Little in the Brave New Economy* (Verso, 2012).

66 Phil Gardner, "The Debate Over Unpaid College Internships," Michigan State University Collegiate Employment Research Institute,

n.d. Available at: http://www.ceri.msu.edu/wp-content/uploads/2010/
01/Intern-Bridge-Unpaid-College-Internship-Report-FINAL.pdf.

67   Columbia University School of General Studies, "Internship Credit."
     Available at: http://bulletin.columbia.edu/general-studies/undergradu-
     ates/additional-academic-opportunities/internship-credit/.

68   "The Best Reviews: Harriet Klausner," available at: http://
     thebestreviews.com/user5.

69   Mayo Fuster Morell, "The Unethics of Sharing: Wikiwashing,"
     International Review of Information Ethics, 15 (2011).

70   Over one million scanned public domain books are also available at
     https://archive.org/details/googlebooks.

71   "reCAPTCHA," available at: https://www.google.com/recaptcha/
     intro/index.html.

72   For a critical discussion of reCAPTCHA, go to https://encyclopedi-
     adramatica.se/CAPTCHA#Types_of_CAPTCHAs

73   Alan Connor, "Are You Google's Gopher?," *BBC News*, September
     13, 2006. Available at: http://news.bbc.co.uk/2/hi/uk_news/maga-
     zine/5336284.stm.

74   https://en.wikipedia.org/wiki/Duolingo.

75   Rosalyn Baxandall and Linda Gordon (eds), *Dear Sisters: Dispatches
     from the Women's Liberation Movement* (Basic Books, 2001), 259.

76   Samuel Osborne, "China Has Made Obedience to the State a Game,"
     Independent, December 22, 2015. Available at: http://www.independ-
     ent.co.uk/news/world/asia/china-has-made-obedience-to-the-state-a-
     game-a6783841.html.

77   Miriam A. Cherry, "Working for (Virtually) Minimum Wage: Applying
     the Fair Labor Standards Act in Cyberspace," *Alabama Law Review*
     60, no. 5 (2009), 854.

78   Ian Bogost, "Gamification Is Bullshit," Ian Bogost blog, August 8,
     2011. Available at: http://www.bogost.com/blog/gamification_is_bulls-
     hit.shtml.

79   "Luis von Ahn's Research," available at: http://www.cs.cmu.edu/
     ~biglou/research.html.

80   "Chore Wars:: Claim Experience Points for Housework," available at:
     http://www.chorewars.com/.

81   Heather Chaplin, "I Don't Want To Be a Superhero," *Slate*, March 29,
     2011. Available at: http://www.slate.com/articles/technology/
     gaming/2011/03/i_dont_want_to_be_a_superhero.single.html.

82   Moira Lavelle, "What Did 'Generation Like' Think of 'Generation
     Like'?," *FRONTLINE*, August 5, 2014. Available at: http://www.pbs.
     org/wgbh/pages/frontline/media/generation-like/what-did-generation-
     like-think-of-generation-like/.

83   Ibid.

84   Kenneth Goldsmith, *Uncreative Writing: Managing Language in the
     Digital Age* (Columbia University Press, 2011), 7.

85   Julian Kücklich, "Precarious Playbour: Modders and the Digital
     Games Industry," *The Fibreculture Journal* 5 (December 5, 2005).

Available at: http://five.fibreculturejournal.org/fcj-025-precarious-playbour-modders-and-the-digital-games-industry/.

86   *The Internet as Playground and Factory*, The Internet as Playground and Factory Conference (The New School, NYC, 2009), available at: http://vimeo.com/7994620.

87   Robinson Meyer, "90% of Wikipedia's Editors Are Male – Here's What They're Doing About It," *The Atlantic*, October 25, 2013. Available at: http://www.theatlantic.com/technology/archive/2013/10/90-of-wikipedias-editors-are-male-heres-what-theyre-doing-about-it/280882/.

88   Robinson Meyer, "Facebook's Mood Manipulation Experiment Might Have Been Illegal," *The Atlantic*, September 24, 2014. Available at: http://www.theatlantic.com/technology/archive/2014/09/facebooks-mood-manipulation-experiment-might-be-illegal/380717/.

89   In *Tom Sawyer*, Tom manages to convince Ben to whitewash Aunt Polly's 810 square foot fence. You might recall how at the outset, Ben mocks Tom about the dreadful job that he has ahead of him. Tom digs deep in his pockets, but he does not have enough toys to pay Ben to do it for him. Famously, Tom turns the conversation around by posing: "You call that work? Well, maybe it is work, and maybe it ain't. All I know is, it suits Tom Sawyer. I mean, when does a boy ever get the chance to white-wash a fence?" Tom is quite persuasive and Ben wants to give it a try but no, no, there's no way Ben could be involved, he insists. You know the story, this isn't any old fence, the argument continues, this one belongs to Aunt Polly, and she surely is very particular about who is allowed to paint it. By now, a few more boys had joined them, begging Tom for permission to take over this prestigious task. They can only just imagine how their neighbors would enjoy the sight of this freshly painted fence, and how they would praise them for a job well done.

90   The sociologist Barry Glassner demonstrates how media in American society use fear to regulate everyday practices. Barry Glassner, *The Culture of Fear: Why Americans Are Afraid of the Wrong Things*, rev. edn (Basic Books, 2009).

91   Ray Oldenburg, *The Great Good Place: Cafes, Coffee Shops, Bookstores, Bars, Hair Salons, and Other Hangouts at the Heart of a Community*, 3rd edn (Marlowe & Co., 1999), 282.

92   Yochai Benkler, *The Wealth of Networks: How Social Production Transforms Markets and Freedom* (Yale University Press, 2007), 96.

93   Andrew Ross, "In Search of the Lost Paycheck," in *Digital Labor: The Internet as Playground and Factory*, ed. Trebor Scholz (Routledge, 2012), 14–24.

94   Ibid., 93.

95   "Precarious Workers Brigade Homepage," Blog, *Precarious Workers Brigade*, (November 2010), http://precariousworkersbrigade.tumblr.com/.

96   "Carrotworkers' Collective Homepage," *Carrotworkers' Collective*, 2009, https://carrotworkers.wordpress.com/.

97 "Fund Our Future Demo Nov 10th 2010," *Carrotworkers' Collective*, available at: https://carrotworkers.wordpress.com/2010/11/10/fund-our-future-demo-nov-10th-2010/.

98 United States Census Bureau, "Income, Poverty and Health Insurance Coverage in the United States: 2013." Available at: http://www.census.gov/newsroom/press-releases/2014/cb14-169.html.

99 André Gorz, *Reclaiming Work: Beyond the Wage-Based Society*, 1st ed. (Polity, 1999), 73.

100 "Household Wealth Trends in the United States, 1962–2013: What Happened over the Great Recession?," accessed January 1, 2016, http://www.nber.org/papers/w20733.

101 Why keep a virtual assistant or intern if a bot could do as good a job? Everyone from truck drivers, doctors, lawyers, waiters, delivery drivers, gas station attendants, to chefs, and journalists is slowly elbowed out of their jobs; even farmers are losing their salary to cow-milking robots.

102 Adam Boult, "Finland Is Considering Giving Every Citizen €800 a Month," *The Telegraph*, December 6, 2015. Available at: http://www.telegraph.co.uk/news/worldnews/europe/finland/12035946/Finland-is-considering-giving-every-citizen-800-a-month.html.

103 Nathan Schneider, "Why the Tech Elite Is Getting Behind Universal Basic Income," *VICE*, January 6, 2015, http://www.vice.com/read/something-for-everyone-0000546-v22n1.

104 Jefferson R. Cowie, *Stayin' Alive: The 1970s and the Last Days of the Working Class* (The New Press, 2012).

105 Gorz, *Reclaiming Work*, 83.

106 Weeks, *The Problem with Work*, 13.

107 Gorz, *Reclaiming Work*, 74.

Chapter 3: The Vocabulary of Digital Labor

1 William A. Galston, "Visions of a Permanent Underclass." *The Wall Street Journal*, October 1, 2013. Available at: http://www.wsj.com/articles/SB10001424052702303918804579107754099736882.

2 Della Bradshaw, "Sharing Economy Benefits Lower Income Groups." FT.com, April 22, 2015. Available at: http://www.ft.com/cms/s/2/7afde9b0-d95a-11e4-a8f1-00144feab7de.html#axzz3qQCu3s8T.

3 Andrew Ross, *The Exorcist and the Machines: 100 Notes, 100 Thoughts: Documenta Series 044*, Bilingual, vol. 44 (Hatje Cantz Verlag, 2012), 16.

4 Ayhan Antes, "iDC Digest, Vol 59, Issue 23," Archive of the mailing list of the Institute for Distributed Creativity, *iDC Mailing List* (November 21, 2009). Available at: http://www.mail-archive.com/cyberinternational@ml.free.fr/msg00962.html.

5 Maurizio Lazzarato, "Immaterial Labor," *Generation Online*, May 13, 2012. Available at: http://www.generation-online.org/c/fcimmateriallabour3.htm.

6   Andre Gorz, *Reclaiming Work: Beyond the Wage-Based Society* (Polity, 1999), 39.

7   Raymond Williams, *Keywords: A Vocabulary of Culture and Society*, rev. edn (Oxford University Press, 1985), 335.

8   Lewis Hyde, *The Gift: Creativity and the Artist in the Modern World*, 25th Anniversary edn (Vintage, 2007), 51.

9   Ibid.

10   Ibid., 52.

11   Kathi Weeks, *The Problem with Work: Feminism, Marxism, Antiwork Politics, and Postwork Imaginaries* (Duke University Press, 2011), 14.

12   Andrew Ross, "In Search of the Lost Paycheck," in *Digital Labor: The Internet as Playground and Factory*, ed. Trebor Scholz (Routledge, 2012), 14–24.

13   Karl Marx, *Capital: Volume 1: A Critique of Political Economy*, trans. Ben Fowkes (Penguin Classics, 1992), 137.

14   Karl Marx, *Grundrisse: Foundations of the Critique of Political Economy*, trans. Martin Nicolaus, reprint (Penguin Classics, 1993), 305. Marx writes: "if it's not crazy that the piano maker is a productive worker, but not the piano player, although obviously the piano would be observed without the piano player. But this is exactly the case. The piano maker produces capital, the pianist only exchanges his labor for revenue. But doesn't the pianist produce music and satisfy our musical ear, does he not even to a certain extent produce the latter? He does indeed, his labor produces something but that doesn't make it productive labor in the economic sense, no more than the labor of the madmen who produces delusions is productive. Labor becomes productive only by producing its own opposite" (Marx, *Grundrisse*, 305).

15   Andrew Ross, *Nice Work If You Can Get It: Life and Labor in Precarious Times* (New York University Press, 2009), 6.

16   Mario Tronti, "Factory and Society," *Operaismo in English*, June 13, 2013. Available at: https://operaismoinenglish.wordpress.com/2013/06/13/factory-and-society/.

17   Mario Tronti, *Operai e Capitale* (DeriveApprodi, 2006).

18   Mario Tronti, "Factory and Society."

19   Dallas Smythe, "On the Audience Commodity and Its Work," in *Media and Cultural Studies: Keyworks*, ed. Meenakshi Gigi Durham and Douglas M. Kellner, 2nd edn (Wiley-Blackwell, 2012), 238.

20   Sut Jhally, "The Factory in the Living Room: How Television Exploits Its Audience," Distinguished Faculty Lecture, University of Massachusetts, March 8, 2007. Available at: http://www.sutjhally.com/audiovideo/videothefactoryint/.

21   Trebor Scholz, "What the MySpace Generation Should Know about Working for Free | Re-Public: Re-Imagining Democracy – English Version." Available at: http://www.re-public.gr/en/?p=138.

22   Christian Fuchs, *Internet and Society: Social Theory in the Information Age* (Routledge, 2008).

23 Michael Hardt and Antonio Negri, *Empire* (Harvard University Press, 2001).
24 Yann Moulier-Boutang, *Cognitive Capitalism* (Polity, 2012), 72.
25 Paolo Virno, *A Grammar of the Multitude: For an Analysis of Contemporary Forms of Life*, trans. Isabella Bertoletti, James Cascaito, and Andrea Casson, 1st US edn (Semiotex(e), 2004), 154–5.
26 Daniel Bell, *The Coming of Post-Industrial Society* (Basic Books, 1973), 20.
27 *McKenzie Wark, The Internet as Playground and Factory*, The Internet as Playground and Factory Conference (The New School, NYC, 2009). Available at: http://vimeo.com/6428602.
28 "DIRTY PROJECTORS LYRICS – Drilling Profitably," available at: http://www.azlyrics.com/lyrics/dirtyprojectors/drillingprofitably.html.
29 Jefferson R. Cowie, *Stayin' Alive: The 1970s and the Last Days of the Working Class* (The New Press, 2012).

Chapter 4: Crowd Fleecing

1   In 1908 Lewis Hine started a series of photographs that contributed to changes to child labor laws in the United States. Lewis Wickes Hine, *Home Work*, Photographic Print, August 1912, available at: http://www.loc.gov/pictures/item/ncl2004002032/PP/.
2   http://www.ima.org.au/mierle-laderman-ukeles-maintenance-art-works-1969-1980/
3   Geert Lovink, "What Is the Social in Social Media?," *E-Flux*, December 2012. Available at: http://www.e-flux.com/journal/what-is-the-social-in-social-media/.
4   Geert Lovink, ed., *Unlike Us Reader: Social Media Monopolies and Their Alternatives* (Institute for Network Culture, 2012), 15.
5   TurkerNational, "MTurkers Are Doing Just Fine – Don't Boycott Anyone on Our Behalf. No One Is Exploited, We Choose to Turk," Twitter, *Kristy@TurkerNation*, May 7, 2013. Available at: https://twitter.com/TreborS/status/331821017615970304.
6   Alan Wertheimer, *Exploitation* (Princeton University Press, 1999), 305.
7   Ibid., 271.
8   Melissa Gregg, *Work's Intimacy* (Polity, 2011), 167.
9   Brian Holmes, "The $100bn Facebook Question: Will Capitalism Survive 'Value Abundance'?," *Nettime*, March 1, 2012. Available at: http://permalink.gmane.org/gmane.culture.internet.nettime/6552.
10 Do not pollute these affordances of the Internet by associating them with the Web 2.0 brand. "The Arab Spring" should not be portrayed as a win for Web 2.0.
11 Nicholas Carr, "Sharecropping the Long Tail," Personal Blog, *Rough Type*, December 19, 2006. Available at: http://www.roughtype.com/?p=634.
12 Ibid.

13   Julian Kücklich, "[iDC] Exploitation, ..." June 11, 2009. Available
      at: https://lists.thing.net/pipermail/idc/2009-June/003501.html.
14   Michel Bauwens, "The Economics of Intimacy and Their Financial
      Valuelessness: Divesting from the Money Economy," P2P Foundation
      blog archive, June 14, 2012. Available at: http://blog.p2pfoundation.
      net/the-economics-of-intimacy-and-their-financial-valuelessness-
      divesting-from-the-money-economy/2012/06/06.
15   Dominic Rushe, "Facebook Profits Triple as Revenues Surge on Mobile
      Platform Success," *The Guardian*, April 23, 2014. Available at: http://
      www.theguardian.com/technology/2014/apr/23/facebook-quarterly-
      earnings-soar-mobile-success.
16   Matt Petronzio, "How Much Is the Average Facebook User Worth?,"
      MashableUK, April 25, 2014. Available at: http://mashable.com/2014/
      04/24/facebook-average-worth-chart/#6KmviO0GJEq5.
17   Cotton Delo, "How Much Are You Really Worth to Facebook and
      Google?," Adage, May 7, 2014. Available at: http://adage.com/article/
      digital/worth-facebook-google/293042/.
18   Mike Davis, *Planet of Slums* (Verso, 2007), 186.
19   Asawin Suebsaeng, "Steve McQueen Dedicated His '12 Years a Slave'
      Best Pic Oscar to Victims of Modern-Day Slavery," *Mother Jones*,
      March 3, 2014. Available at: http://www.motherjones.com/mixed-
      media/2014/03/12-years-slave-best-picture-steve-mcqueen-speech-
      modern-day-slavery.
20   Guardian Editorial, "Slavery Is a Violent and Cruel Trade That the
      World Must Finally Stamp Out," *The Guardian*, March 1, 2014.
      Available at: http://www.theguardian.com/commentisfree/2014/mar/
      02/slavery-oscars-12-years-a-slave.
21   Davis, *Planet of Slums*, 178.
22   Ibid., 190.
23   Ibid., 174.
24   Jon Evans, "TxtEagle Raises $8.5 Million To Give 2.1 Billion A
      Voice," *TechCrunch*, April 12, 2011. Available at: http://techcrunch.
      com/2011/04/12/txteagle-raises-8-5-million/.
25   Ellen Huet, "Larry Page's Plan For People Whose Jobs Are Replaced
      By Tech: Work Less," *Forbes*, July 7, 2014. Available at: http://www.
      forbes.com/sites/ellenhuet/2014/07/07/larry-page-robot-jobs/.
26   Dillon Mahmoudi and Anthony Levenda, "Beyond the Screen: Uneven
      Geographies, Digital Labour, and the City of Cognitive-Cultural
      Capitalism," *tripleC* 14, no. 1 (2016).
27   Christian Fuchs, "Dallas Smythe Today: The Audience Commodity,
      the Digital Labour Debate, Marxist Political Economy and Critical
      Theory. Prolegomena to a Digital Labour Theory of Value," *tripleC*
      10, no. 2 (2012) 692–740.
28   Graham Murdock, "Political Economies as Moral Economies:
      Commodities, Gifts, and Public Goods," in *The Handbook of Political
      Economy of Communications*, ed. Janet Wasko, Graham Murdock
      and Helena Sousa (Wiley-Blackwell, 2011), 30f.

29   Nicholas Carr, "Rough Type: Nicholas Carr's Blog: Sharecropping the Long Tail," July 2008, http://www.roughtype.com/archives/2006/12/sharecropping_t.php.

30   Irani is leaning on Donna Haraway's *When Species Meet*: "Try as we might to distance ourselves, there is no way living that is not also a way of someone, not just something, else dying differentially." I am not sympathetic to Irani's approach. Gray is not the new black and relationships of ownership and yes, gender, very well still dictate the way in which people are taken advantage of. Lilly Irani, "[iDC] Exploitation ...," June 11, 2009. Available at: https://lists.thing.net/pipermail/idc/2009-June/003502.html.

31   Howard Rheingold, "[iDC] Introduction Re: 'The Internet as Playground and Factory,'" *Institute for Distributed Creativity*, June 5, 2009. Available at: https://lists.thing.net/pipermail/idc/2009-June/003448.html.

32   Wertheimer, *Exploitation*, 248–9.

33   Ibid., 271.

34   Patrice Flichy, *The Internet Imaginaire* (The MIT Press, 2007), 94.

35   Geert Lovink, *Dark Fiber: Tracking Critical Internet Culture* (The MIT Press, 2003), 236.

36   Turner, *From Counterculture to Cyberculture*, 9.

37   The quality of their writing, their political allegiance, and even the size of their readership didn't matter as much as the hope that people would walk through their everyday lives with the perception that they could intervene in some way, that they could become more active, engaged citizens.

38   A March 2008 study found that 184 million people worldwide had started a blog, out of which 26.4 million were in the United States. Japan and South Korea, Brazil, Iran, Italy, and India all have their own sprawling blogospheres. China had some 47 million blogs in 2008 alone (Scott Rosenberg, *Say Everything: How Blogging Began, What It's Becoming, and Why It Matters* (Broadway, 2010), 311).

39   Eric Hobsbawm, *The Age of Extremes: A History of the World, 1914–1991* (Vintage, 1996), 414.

40   Jonathan Crary, *24/7: Late Capitalism and the Ends of Sleep* (Verso, 2014), 7.

41   Ibid.

42   Crary describes studies of migratory white-crowned sparrows that migrate seasonally from Alaska to Northern Mexico on the West Coast of the United States. The birds have the rare ability to stay awake for up to seven days. These studies are funded by the US Department of Defense and are focused on the production of a combatant who can go for a minimum of seven days without sleep. Eventually, however, such activity-enhancing drugs would trickle down into the civilian sector and make 24/7 activity a question of competitive advantage. Ibid., 7.

43   Theodor W. Adorno, "Free Time," in *The Culture Industry: Selected Essays on Mass Culture*, ed. J. M. Bernstein (Routledge, 1991).

Chapter 5: The Legal Gray Zones of Digital Labor

1 Observers with a libertarian streak might wring their hands in joy; they wouldn't trust government to get it right in any case. More progressive-leaning forces are distressed by this war against worker rights. They are disappointed by the United States government's neglect of millions of people who punch in and out of work through iPhone or Android apps. For a segment of the left, any attempt at reform means that capitalism becomes more bearable, which merely postpones the ultimate goal of its demise. "New ITUC Global Rights Index – The World's Worst Countries for Workers," May 19, 2014. Available at: http://www.ituc-csi.org/new-ituc-global-rights-index-the.

2 Randall W. Forsyth, "Slim Pickings, Indeed," *Barron's*, July 26, 2014. Available at: http://online.barrons.com/articles/SB5000142405311190 4780504580043362746332330.

3 Patty Murray and Kirsten Gillibrand, "Contingent Workforce: Size, Characteristics, Earnings, and Benefits," US Government Accountability Office, April 20, 2015, 24. Available at: http://www.gao.gov/assets/670/669766.pdf.

4 In 2011, the number of crowd workers in developing countries alone was estimated to be 2.4 million. San Jose Mercury News, "Online Labor Pool: New Work Model or Digital Sweatshop?," *Portland Press Herald*, May 16, 2012. Available at: http://www.pressherald.com/2012/05/16/new-work-model-or-digital-sweatshop__2012-05-16/.

5 Siou Chew Kuek et al., "The Global Opportunity in Online Outsourcing," The World Bank ICT Unit, June 2015, 18. Available at: https://www.dropbox.com/s/iq1ch2e0lv6pc3s/The%20World%20Bank%20-%20The%20Global%20Opportunity%20in%20Online%20Outsourcing.pdf?dl=0.

6 Corey Robin, "The Republican War on Workers' Rights," *The New York Times*, May 18, 2014. Available at: http://opinionator.blogs.nytimes.com/2014/05/18/the-republican-war-on-workers-rights/?_r=1.

7 Robert Kuttner, "The Task Rabbit Economy," *The American Prospect*, October 10, 2013. Available at: http://prospect.org/article/task-rabbit-economy.

8 Winston Maxwell and Xenia Legendre, "English Version of Proposed French Privacy Tax Report Available," HL Chronicle of Data Protection, June 24, 2013. Available at: http://www.hldataprotection.com/2013/06/articles/international-eu-privacy/proposed-french-privacy-tax-english-version-of-colin-collin-report-available/.

9 Alek Felstiner, "Working the Crowd: Employment and Labor Law in the Crowdsourcing Industry," *Berkeley Journal of Employment and Labor Law* 32, no. 1 (2011), art. 3.

10 Miriam A. Cherry, "Working for (Virtually) Minimum Wage: Applying the Fair Labor Standards Act in Cyberspace," *Alabama Law Review* 60, no. 5 (2009), 1077–1110.

11　Susan Fussell and Wayne Lutters, "Proceedings of the 17th ACM Conference on Computer Supported Cooperative Work & Social Computing" (CSCW'14 Computer Supported Cooperative Work, Baltimore, MD, 2014), 45, http://dl.acm.org/citation.cfm?id=2531602.

12　Felstiner, "Working the Crowd," 27.

13　Jacob Silverman, "The Internet Doesn't Exist," *The Baffler*, June 3, 2015. Available at: http://www.thebaffler.com/blog/internet-doesnt-exist/.

14　William Gibson, *Neuromancer* (Ace, 1984), 69.

15　John Perry Barlow, "A Declaration of the Independence of Cyberspace," February 8, 1996. Available at: https://projects.eff.org/~barlow/Declaration-Final.html.

16　Berin Szoka and Adam Marcus, eds., *The Next Digital Decade: Essays on the Future of the Internet* (TechFreedom, 2011), 165.

17　Charles J. Muhl, in his journal article "What Is an Employee? The Answer Depends on the Federal Law," gives the example of Vizcaino vs. Microsoft, a case going back to 1990 in which Microsoft had hired "freelancers" to perform work on the nearly identical circumstances as Microsoft's regular employees. The US Court of Appeals for the Ninth Circuit determined that workers were in fact employees and not independent contractors and Microsoft settled the case for $97 million 10 years later. Charles J. Muhl, "What Is an Employee? The Answer Depends on the Federal Law," *Monthly Labor Review* (January 2002), 3–11.

18　Isaac Madan et al., "The 1099 Economy Workforce Survey," *Requests for Startups*, 2015, 72. Available at: http://www.requestsforstartups.com/survey.

19　Felstiner, "Working the Crowd," 46.

20　Cherry, "Working for (Virtually) Minimum Wage," 1080.

21　US Department of Labor, "Contingent Workers," available at: http://www.dol.gov/_sec/media/reports/dunlop/section5.htm.

22　Ibid.

23　US Department of Labor, "Industrial Homework/Piecework," available at: http://www.dol.gov/dol/topic/wages/industrialhomework.htm.

24　Jeff Howe, "Crowdsourcing: Taking Measure of Mechanical Turk," November 3, 2006. Available at: http://www.crowdsourcing.com/cs/2006/11/taking_measure_.html.

25　Jonathan Zittrain, "The Internet Creates a New Kind of Sweatshop," Newsweek, December 7, 2009. Available at: http://www.newsweek.com/internet-creates-new-kind-sweatshop-75751.

26　Fiona Graham, "Crowdsourcing Work: Labour on Demand or Digital Sweatshop?," BBC News, October 22, 2010. Available at: http://www.bbc.co.uk/news/business-11600902.

27　Laura Hapke, *Sweatshop: The History of an American Idea* (Rutgers University Press, 2004), 2.

28　Felstiner, "Working the Crowd," 65.

29　Mike Isaac and Natasha Singer, "California Says Uber Driver Is Employee, Not a Contractor," *The New York Times*, June 17, 2015.

Available at: http://www.nytimes.com/2015/06/18/business/uber-con-tests-california-labor-ruling-that-says-drivers-should-be-employees. html.

30 Eric Mack, "Text of a Complaint Against Crowdflower by Christopher Otey," Crowdsourcing.org, January 4, 2013. Available at: http://www.crowdsourcing.org/document/text-of-a-complaint-against-crowdflower-by-christopher-otey/22979.

31 http://wtf.tw/ref/otey.pdf

32 "Case Docket: Lily Jeung et al v. Yelp Inc.," August 7, 2014. Available at: http://ia902302.us.archive.org/14/items/gov.uscourts.cacd.596534/gov.uscourts.cacd.596534.docket.html.

33 Dr. Amy K. Glasmeier and Massachusetts Institute of Technology, "Living Wage Calculation for New York County, New York," *Living Wage Calculator*, 2015. Available at: http://livingwage.mit.edu/counties/36061.

34 Felstiner, "Working the Crowd."

35 Ibid.

36 Ibid., 65.

37 Ibid., 64.

38 Berners-Lee did in fact refer to a Magna Carta of the Web, but I choose to discuss the proposal in the perhaps more fitting context of the Internet, also avoiding the possibly distracting comparison to the historical Magna Carta of 1215, which was a document forced onto the English king by feudal barons, aiming at limiting his powers. A Bill of Right for the Internet should be more than a political charter negotiated by various rulers.

39 Brian R. Fitzgerald, "Tim Berners-Lee: The Web Needs a Magna Carta," *Wall Street Journal*, March 12, 2014. Available at: http://blogs.wsj.com/digits/2014/03/12/tim-berners-lee-the-web-needs-a-magna-carta/.

40 "Web We Want | A Global Movement to Defend, Enhance and Celebrate the Free, Open and Universal Web," accessed April 14, 2014, https://webwewant.org/.

41 Dilma Rousseff, "General Debate of the 68th Session – Brazil," UN General Assembly, September 24, 2013. Available at: http://gadebate.un.org/68/brazil/.

42 "The Net Closes: Brazil's Magna Carta for the Web," *The Economist*, March 27, 2014. Available at: http://www.economist.com/news/americas/21599781-brazils-magna-carta-web-net-closes.

43 Passengers can refer to an Air Passenger Bill of Rights that not only makes the responsibilities of the airlines abundantly clear, but also spells out a course for action if the response by a given airline is not appropriate. The Bill details compensation rights in case of missed connecting flights and requires airlines to clearly state the total price of tickets including taxes and all other surcharges. It also grants passengers the right to be informed about the causes for delays, and much more. The Bill also offers contact numbers at the EU level to get in touch with enforcement authorities in case airlines don't follow up.

44   "Domestic Workers' Bill of Rights," New York State Department of Labor, 2010. Available at: http://www.labor.ny.gov/legal/domestic-workers-bill-of-rights.shtm.

45   Lilly Irani and M. Six Silberman, "Turkopticon: Interrupting Worker Invisibility on Amazon Mechanical Turk," *CHI 2013*, April 27–May 2, 2013, Paris. Available at: https://www.academia.edu/2413463/Turkopticon_Interrupting_Worker_Invisibility_on_Amazon_Mechanical_Turk.

46   WeAreDynamo, "Fair Payment," *WeAreDynamo Wiki*, August 21, 2014. Available at: http://wiki.wearedynamo.org/index.php?title=Fair_payment.

47   Ross Perlin, *Intern Nation: Earning Nothing and Learning Little in the Brave New Economy* (Verso, 2012), 250.

48   Electronic Frontier Foundation, "A Bill of Privacy Rights for Social Network Users," May 19, 2010. Available at: https://www.eff.org/deeplinks/2010/05/bill-privacy-rights-social-network-users.

49   Joseph Smarr, Marc Canter, Robert Scoble, and Michael Arlington led the initial meeting in 2007. The more inclusive follow-up meeting took place in 2010 at the Computers, Freedom and Privacy Conference, which resulted in the Bill of Rights of the Social Web asserting 14 fundamental rights. Joseph Smarr et al., "A Bill of Rights for Users of the Social Web," *Template*, September 2007. Available at: http://www.template.org/?page_id=599/2007/09/05/bill-of-rights/.

50   A more specific proposal than the one by Smarr et al. was made by Tim O'Reilly who responded to death threats against the blogger Kathy Sierra by calling for a Blogger's Code of Conduct. Many visible bloggers vehemently opposed the proposal. Tim O'Reilly, "Call for a Blogger's Code of Conduct," *Radar*, March 31, 2007. Available at: http://radar.oreilly.com/2007/03/call-for-a-bloggers-code-of-co.html.

51   Ari Melber, Woodrow Hartzog, and Evan Selinger, "Fighting Facebook, a Campaign for a People's Terms of Service," *The Nation*, May 22, 2013. Available at: http://www.thenation.com/article/fighting-facebook-campaign-peoples-terms-service/

52   Ibid.

53   Trebor Scholz, "What the MySpace Generation Should Know about Working for Free."

54   Kathi Weeks, *The Problem with Work: Feminism, Marxism, Antiwork Politics, and Postwork Imaginaries* (Duke University Press, 2011), 124.

55   Ibid., 129.

56   Ted Nelson, "A Thought for Your Pennies: Micropayment and the Liberation of Content," available at: http://transcopyright.org/hcoin-Remarks-D28.html.

57   David Kirkpatrick, *The Facebook Effect: The Inside Story of the Company That Is Connecting the World* (Simon & Schuster, 2011), 160.

58   Nicolas Colin, "Corporate Tax 2.0: Why France and the World Need a New Tax System for the Digital Age," *Forbes*, January 28, 2013.

Available at: http://www.forbes.com/sites/singularity/2013/01/28/corporate-tax-2-0-why-france-and-the-world-need-a-new-tax-system-for-the-digital-age/.

59 Ibid.

Chapter 6: On Tactical Refusal, Defection, and Withdrawal from Data Labor

1   In November 2013, Google reported that it patented robotic response technology, which would propose personalized responses for users of Twitter, Text, Google+, and Email. Michael Gorman, "Google Patent Takes the Social out of Social Networking: Technology Writes 'Personalized Reactions' for You," *Engadget*, November 24, 2013. Available at: http://www.engadget.com/2013/11/24/google-patent-automated-reply-social-network/.

2   There are several, fairly large-scale studies with titles like "They are Happier and Having Better Lives than I Am," which demonstrate that overall life satisfaction decreases slightly for users of Facebook. A research team at the Institute of Information Systems, Humboldt-Universität zu Berlin, Germany, conducted two independent studies with 584 Facebook users. They conclude that "users frequently perceive Facebook as a stressful environment" that provokes feelings of envy (Humboldt-Universität zu Berlin, "Facebook-Nutzung macht neidisch und unzufrieden," January 21, 2013. Available at: https://www.hu-berlin.de/de/pr/pressemitteilungen/pm1301/pm_130121_00). According to a study by University of Michigan psychologist Ethan Kross, Facebook makes us feel lonely. A Utah Valley University analysis of 40 studies confirmed the broader trend: Internet use had a small, significant detrimental effect on psychological well-being, including depression, loneliness, self-esteem, and life satisfaction. "How Facebook Makes Us Unhappy," *The New Yorker*, September 10, 2013. Available at: http://www.newyorker.com/online/blogs/elements/2013/09/the-real-reason-facebook-makes-us-unhappy.html.

3   Zizi Papacharissi, ed., *A Networked Self: Identity, Community, and Culture on Social Network Sites* (Routledge, 2010), 59.

4   Ross Barkan, "Howard Dean Says People Are Doubting Capitalism Is Good for Them," *Observer*, April 17, 2015. Available at: http://observer.com/2015/04/howard-dean-people-are-doubting-capitalism-works-for-them/.

5   David Rosen, "America's Spy State: How the Telecoms Sell Out Your Privacy," *RSN*, June 2, 2012. Available at: http://readersupported-news.org/opinion2/294-159/11729-americas-spy-state-how-the-telecoms-sell-out-your-privacy.

6   Noam Chomsky, *Powers and Prospects: Reflections on Human Nature and the Social Order* (Boston: South End Press, 1995), 70.

7   Naomi Klein, *No Logo*, 10th Anniversary Edition (Picador, 2009), 2.

8   See Matt Taibbi's work on global finance and Goldman Sachs, the giant vampire squid, in particular. Matt Taibbi, "The Vampire Squid Strikes Again: The Mega Banks' Most Devious Scam Yet," *Rolling Stone*, February 12, 2014. Available at: http://www.rollingstone.com/politics/news/the-vampire-squid-strikes-again-the-mega-banks-most-devious-scam-yet-20140212.

9   Craig McVegas, "4 Things David Harvey Thinks Anti-Capitalists Should Know," *Novara Wire*, April 6, 2014. Available at: http://wire.novaramedia.com/2014/04/4-things-david-harvey-thinks-anti-capitalists-should-know/.

10 Spencer Ackerman, "Former NSA Chief Warns of Cyber-Terror Attacks If Snowden Apprehended," *The Guardian*, August 6, 2013. Available at: http://www.theguardian.com/technology/2013/aug/06/nsa-director-cyber-terrorism-snowden.

11 Gabriella Coleman, "Weapons of the Geek," FSCONS2012, November 10, 2012. Available at: https://archive.org/details/12SAT011400-weapons-of-the-geek.

12 Discussed in an email exchange with Shah. The Centre for Internet & Society, Mumbai, India, available at: http://cis-india.org/.

13 Beatriz da Costa and Kavita Philip, eds., *Tactical Biopolitics: Art, Activism, and Technoscience* (MIT Press, 2010), 329.

14 Rupert Neate, "McDonald's Boss 'Proud' of Wages as Thousands of Workers Call for a Rise," *The Guardian*, May 21, 2015. Available at: http://www.theguardian.com/business/2015/may/21/mcdonalds-workers-protest-poverty-wages-headquarters?CMP=share_btn_link.

15 Or similarly, consider the cross-border organizing of the Wobblies and their fight for one big union.

16 PBS, "Pat Mitchell Remarks to National Press Club," *PBS*, May 24, 2005. Available at: http://www.pbs.org/aboutpbs/news/20050524_pressclubspeech.html.

17 "Welcome to Ello," *Ello*, 2014. Available at: https://ello.co/manifesto.

18 "Getting started with ownCloud," *ownCloud*, 2015. Available at: https://owncloud.org/install/.

19 "FreedomBox Foundation," available at: http://freedomboxfoundation.org/.

20 Ninety-nine percent of the free classifieds on the site are from individuals and the profits needed to pay for the technical infrastructure and for the 23 employees are generated from help-wanted listings and from brokers and apartment listings in New York City and Los Angeles.

21 Nicholas Carr, *The Big Switch: Rewiring the World, from Edison to Google*, reprint (W. W. Norton & Co., 2009), 60.

22 Julie E. Cohen, *Configuring the Networked Self: Law, Code, and the Play of Everyday Practice* (Yale University Press, 2012).

23 David Lametti, "The Cloud: Boundless Digital Potential or Enclosure 3.0?," *Virginia Journal of Law & Technology* 17, no. 3 (2012), 192–242.

24 Geert Lovink, *Networks Without a Cause* (Polity, 2012), 168.

25 Carr, *The Big Switch*, 23.

26 Introduced by Australian scholar Axel Bruns, "produsage" is a portmanteau of the words "production" and "usage."

27 There is no question that such email refusal is a sign of extreme privilege. Knuth's secretary prints out all messages addressed to his still existing e-mail address so that he can reply with written comments once every 6 months or so. Donald Knuth, "Email," Stanford University, available at: http://www-cs-faculty.stanford.edu/~knuth/email.html.

28 Equally, Stallman explains that others peruse the web for him all the time. Richard Stallman, "First Five with Richard Stallman," *New Criticals*, available at: http://www.newcriticals.com/first-five-with-richard-stallman/page-1.

29 Gary Shteyngart, *Super Sad True Love Story: A Novel* (Random House, 2010).

30 Casey N. Cep, "The Pointlessness of Unplugging," *The New Yorker*, March 19, 2014. Available at: http://www.newyorker.com/online/blogs/culture/2014/03/the-pointlessness-of-unplugging.html?utm_source=tny&utm_campaign=generalsocial&utm_medium=twitter&mbid=social_twitter.

31 Michael Seemann, *Digital Tailspin: Ten Rules for the Internet After Snowden* (Institute of Network Cultures, 2015), 42.

32 Geert Lovink, *Networks Without a Cause*, 44.

33 Gabriella Coleman, *Hacker, Hoaxer, Whistleblower, Spy: The Many Faces of Anonymous* (Verso, 2014).

34 Rebecca MacKinnon gives the example of sustained lobbying by the Electronic Frontier Foundation, the Committee to Protect Journalists and others, which led to Facebook's engineers adding new encryption and security settings that enable users to better protect themselves against surveillance of, as well as unauthorized intrusion into, their accounts. Rebecca MacKinnon, *Consent of the Networked: The Worldwide Struggle for Internet Freedom* (Basic Books, 2012), 158.

35 See Helen Nissenbaum's and Daniel C. Howe's project AdNauseam, for example. Helen Nissenbaum, Daniel C. Howe, and Mushon Zer-Aviv, "AdNauseam: Clicking Ads So You Don't Have To," *AdNauseam*, 2014. Available at: http://adnauseam.io/.

36 Email sabbaticals simply mean that you go on vacation after announcing in advance "all e-mail messages will be deleted for the duration of the holiday. The person taking the sabbatical will return to an empty inbox." danah boyd, "How to Take an Email Sabbatical," danah.org, July 7, 2011. Available at: http://www.danah.org/EmailSabbatical.html.

37 For years now, I have included an exercise in my syllabi: "A Week Without Google, Facebook, and Twitter." A whole week; students find it almost impossible to tackle. The idea, originally inspired by Mushon Zer-Aviv, is that students find alternatives for these software packages.

The exercise is complicated by the fact that like many US universities, The New School uses Gmail as its university email service. But they can still replace Twitter with identi.ca and Google search with Duckduckgo, for example.

38 "NoScript Security Suite," Add-Ons for Firefox. Available at: https://addons.mozilla.org/en-US/firefox/addon/noscript/.

39 Electronic Privacy Information Center, "Complaint, Request for Investigation, Injunction, and Other Relief Submitted by The Electronic Privacy Information Center," n.d. Available at: https://epic.org/privacy/ftc/facebook/Facebook-Study-Complaint.pdf.

40 "We're Quitting Facebook," available at: http://www.quitfacebook-day.com/.

41 Geert Lovink, ed., *Unlike Us Reader* (Institute for Network Culture, 2012), 25.

42 Douglas Rushkoff, "Why I'm Quitting Facebook," *CNN*, February 25, 2013. Available at: http://www.cnn.com/2013/02/25/opinion/rushkoff-why-im-quitting-facebook/index.html.

43 "Paul Lafargue: The Right To Be Lazy (1883)," Marxists Internet Archive, November 13, 2003. Available at: http://www.marxists.org/archive/lafargue/1883/lazy/.

44 Milena Hoegsberg and Cora Fisher, eds., *Living Labor* (Sternberg Press, 2013), 151.

45 Kathi Weeks, *The Problem with Work: Feminism, Marxism, Antiwork Politics, and Postwork Imaginaries* (Duke University Press, 2011), 13.

46 "Profile for Kevin Killian: Reviews," *Amazon*, available at: http://www.amazon.com/gp/cdp/member-reviews/A30TK6U7DNS82R/103-4091758-3020655.

47 Ibid.

Chapter 7: The Rise of Platform Cooperativism

1 Jaron Lanier, *Who Owns the Future?* (Allen Lane, 2013).

2 George A. Akerlof, "The Market for 'Lemons': Quality Uncertainty and the Market Mechanism," *The Quarterly Journal of Economics* 84, no. 3 (1970): 488–500.

3 "Review & Outlook: 'You Didn't Build That'," *The Wall Street Journal*, July 19, 2012.

4 Tom Slee, *What's Yours Is Mine* (OR Books, 2015).

5 http://platformcoop.net

6 John Duda at "Platform Cooperativism: The Internet, Ownership, Democracy," vimeo.com/149401422

7 Sascha Lobo, "Sascha Lobo: Sharing Economy wie bei Uber ist Plattform-Kapitalismus," *Spiegel Online*, March 9, 2014. Available at: http://www.spiegel.de/netzwelt/netzpolitik/sascha-lobo-sharing-economy-wie-bei-uber-ist-plattform-kapitalismus-a-989584.html.

8   Byung-Chul Han, *Müdigkeitsgesellschaft* (Matthes & Seitz Berlin, 2010).
9   livestream.com/internetsociety/platformcoop/videos/105663835.
10 McKenzie Wark, "Digital Labor and the Anthropocene," *DIS Magazine*. Available at: http://dismagazine.com/disillusioned/discussion-disillusioned/70983/mckenzie-wark-digital-labor-and-the-anthropocene/.
11 Rebecca Smith and Sarah Leberstein, *Rights on Demand: Ensuring Workplace Standards and Worker Security in the On-Demand Economy* (NELP, 2015). Available at: www.nelp.org/content/uploads/Rights-On-Demand-Report.pdf.
12 http://vimeo.com/149979122.
13 A W2 is the form that an employer must send to an employee and the Internal Revenue Service at the end of the year.
14 A 1099 form is a report of various types of income that a worker may receive throughout the year other than the salary an employer would pay. Contingent workers have to send these 1099 forms to the Internal Revenue Service.
15 Frank Pasquale, "Banana Republic.com" *Jotwell: Cyberlaw*, February 11, 2011.
16 Carmel DeAmicis, "U.S. Senator Mark Warner on Why We Need a New Class of Worker (Q&A)," *Re/code*, July 15, 2015. Available at: http://recode.net/2015/07/15/u-s-senator-mark-warner-on-why-we-need-a-new-class-of-worker-qa/
17 Seth D. Harris and Alan B. Krueger, "A Proposal for Modernizing Labor Laws for Twenty-First-Century Work: The 'Independent Worker,' " *The Hamilton Project*, December 7, 2015. Available at: http://www.hamiltonproject.org/papers/modernizing_labor_laws_for_twenty_first_century_work_independent_worker
18 Steve Randy Waldman, "1099 as Antitrust," interfluidity, September 27, 2015. Available at: http://www.interfluidity.com/v2/6165.html.
19 Starting in the late 1970s, the wages of American workers started to stagnate while their productivity consistently increased.
20 Andrew Ross, *Creditocracy: And the Case for Debt Refusal* (OR Books, 2014).
21 livestream.com/internetsociety/platformcoop/videos/105162259.
22 Frank Pasquale and Siva Vaidhyanathan, "Uber and the Lawlessness of 'Sharing Economy' Corporates," *The Guardian*, July 28, 2015.
23 Slee, *What's Yours Is Mine*.
24 Pasquale and Vaidhyanathan, "Uber and the Lawlessness of 'Sharing Economy' Corporates."
25 Harris and Krueger, "A Proposal for Modernizing Labor Laws."
26 In 2015, more than half of all Uber drivers did not stay longer than 12 months with the company. To learn more, read Steven Hill's *Raw Deal: How the "Uber Economy" and Runaway Capitalism Are Screwing American Workers* (St. Martin's Press, 2015).

27 Mike Isaac and Natasha Singer, "California Says Uber Driver Is Employee, Not a Contractor," *The New York Times*, June 17, 2015.

28 Tim Cushing, "Judge Not At All Impressed By Class Action Lawsuit Claiming Yelp Reviewers Are Really Employees," *techdirt*, August 17, 2015. Available at: https://www.techdirt.com/articles/20150815/160 91931969/judge-not-all-impressed-class-action-lawsuit-claiming-yelp-reviewers-are-really-employees.shtml.

29 Cecilia Kang, "Coalition of Start-Ups and Labor Call for Rethinking of Worker Policies," *The New York Times*, November 9, 2015. Available at: http://bits.blogs.nytimes.com/2015/11/09/coalition-of-start-ups-and-labor-call-for-rethinking-of-worker-policies/

30 Martin Di Caro, "Taxi Regulations, E-Hail App Targeted By Montgomery County Council," WAMU 88.5, June 8, 2015. Available at: http://wamu.org/news/15/06/08/taxi_regulations_e_hail_app_targeted_by_montgomery_county_council_today

31 flex.amazon.com.

32 IG Metall, "Digitale Arbeit: IG Metall Sieht Sittenverfall," *Heise Online*, September 11, 2014. Available at: http://www.heise.de/newsticker/meldung/Digitale-Arbeit-IG-Metall-sieht-Sittenverfall-2390001.html.

33 Christiane Benner, ed., *Crowd Work: Zurück in die Zukunft* (Bund Verlag, 2014).

34 Neal Gorenflo, "How Platform Coops Can Beat Death Stars Like Uber to Create a Real Sharing Economy." *Shareable*, November 3, 2015. Available at: http://www.shareable.net/blog/how-platform-coops-can-beat-death-star-platforms-to-create-a-real-sharing-economy. James Sullivan, "Home Cleaning Co-Ops in USA Get Their Own 'Uber,' " *Co-operative News*, January 28, 2016. Available at: http://www.thenews.coop/101205/news/co-operatives/home-cleaning-coops-usa-get-uber/.

35 Turkopticon is a web-browser extension that allows otherwise largely unconnected workers to jointly evaluate consignors on Amazon Mechanical Turk: https://turkopticon.ucsd.edu/.

36 Guy Standing, *A Precariat Charter: From Denizens to Citizens* (Bloomsbury Academic, 2014).

37 John Duda at "Platform Cooperativism: The Internet, Ownership, Democracy," vimeo.com/149401422.

38 Angela Johnson, "76% of Americans Are Living Paycheck-to-Paycheck," *CNN Money*, June 24, 2013.

39 Michael Snyder, "Goodbye Middle Class: 51 Percent Of All American Workers Make Less Than 30,000 Dollars A Year," *End of the American Dream*, October 20, 2015. Available at: http://endoftheamericandream.com/archives/goodbye-middle-class-51-percent-of-all-american-workers-make-less-than-30000-dollars-a-year.

40 E. G. Nadeau, *The Cooperative Solution: How the United States Can Tame Recessions, Reduce Inequality, and Protect the Environment* (Create Space Independent Publishing Platform, 2012).

41 Statistics from Marjorie Kelly's *Owning Our Future: The Emerging Ownership Revolution* (Berrett-Koehler, 2012).

42 Dave Johnson, "Bernie Sanders Proposes To Boost Worker-Ownership Of Companies," *Common Dreams*, August 18, 2015.

43 E. G. Nadeau, *The Cooperative Solution*, 37.

44 http://dept.kent.edu/oeoc/oeoclibrary/emiliaromagnalong.htm.

45 The statistics in this paragraph are taken from Marjorie Kelly's *Owning Our Future: The Emerging Ownership Revolution*.

46 www.buerger-energie-berlin.de/das-ziel.

47 http://fpwa.org/fy-2016-budget-agreement/.

48 Daniel Schlademan of OurWalmart at Platform Cooperativism: The Internet, Ownership, Democracy.

49 http://conferences.oreilly.com/nextcon/economy-us-2015/public/content/speakers.

50 "Ver.di. Innovation und Gute Arbeit – Digitale Arbeit." Available at: innovation-gute-arbeit.verdi.de/themen/digitale-arbeit.

51 Phil Gasper, "Are Workers' Cooperatives the Alternative to Capitalism?," *International Socialist Review*, 93 (2014).

52 Ibid.

53 http://vimeo.com/149516216.

54 http://vimeo.com/149540417.

55 John Curl and Ishmael Reed, *For All the People: Uncovering the Hidden History of Cooperation, Cooperative Movements, and Communalism in America* (PM Press, 2012), 378.

56 http://www.theselc.org.

57 http://loconomics.com.

58 http://ali-alkhatib.com/media/presentations/PlatformCooperativism.pdf.

59 http://seed.coop/p/V1RtF0JQe/more?wrap=true.

60 James Sullivan, "Home Cleaning Co-Ops in USA Get Their Own 'Uber.' "

61 Gar Alperovitz and Thomas M. Hanna, "Socialism, American-Style," *The New York Times*, July 23, 2015. Available at: http://www.nytimes.com/2015/07/23/opinion/socialism-american-style.html.

62 Nathan Schneider, "5 Ways to Take Back Tech," *The Nation*, May 27, 2015.

63 Axel Bruns, *Blogs, Wikipedia, Second Life and Beyond: From Production to Produsage* (Peter Lang, 2008).

64 http://resonate.io/2016/.

65 http://www.stocksy.com.

66 http://membersmedia.net

67 Jack Triplett, *The Measurement of Labor Cost* (University of Chicago Press, 1983), 101. And for a more recent discussion by the Economist: www.economist.com.

68 http://cadateamsters.org.

69 http://lazooz.org.

70 Also in Israel but not a platform co-op, Google has released the Waze app, which links up passengers who want to get to their workplaces

with drivers who have to make a similar trip. Drivers get paid depending on the distance they drive but the system is set up in such a way
that drivers cannot turn this into a business.

71   http://livestream.com/internetsociety/platformcoop/videos/104571608.

72   https://vimeo.com/149540417.

73   "Ver.di, Innovation und Gute Arbeit – Digitale Arbeit."

74   http://goodworkcode.org.

75   Over 70 percent of freelancers in the United States report that they
are frequently paid late.

76   Frank Pasquale at "Making It Work – Platform Coop 2015: Platform
Cooperativism Conference," Internet Archive, November 2015,
archive.org. See also Ramsi Woodcock, "Inconsistency in Antitrust,"
University of Miami Law Review, 68 (2013) 105–88.

77   Currently 60 million private sector workers in the US do not have
access to paid sick leave.

78   Ellen Huet, "How Uber's Shady Firing Policy Could Backfire on the
Company," Forbes, October 20, 2014. Available at: http://www.
forbes.com/sites/ellenhuet/2014/10/30/uber-driver-firing-policy/
#488c82dc8ef7.

79   For a discussion of the situation of Amazon Mechanical Turk's workers,
see Lilly Irany, "Difference and Dependence among Digital Workers:
The Case of Amazon Mechanical Turk," *The South Atlantic Quarterly*
114, no. 1 (2015) 225–34.

80   Uber requires an email from each passenger who wants to change a
rating, thereby disincentivizing accurate rating.

81   traity.com.

82   J. Galt, "Crypto Swartz Will Get You Paid for Your Great Content."
The CoinFront, June 23, 2014. Available at: http://thecoinfront.com/
crypto-swartz-will-get-you-paid-for-your-great-content/.

83   ODesk's (now Upwork's) "worker diaries" document the workflow
of workers. This includes repeated photographs of the workers with
the camera built into the computer of the worker and screenshots to
measure the progress of the work.

84   Paola Tubaro, "Discussing Platform Cooperativism," *Data Big and
Small*, December 9, 2015. Available at: https://databigandsmall.
com/2015/12/08/discussing-platform-cooperativism/.

85   Gorenflo, "How Platform Coops Can Beat Death Stars Like Uber to
Create a Real Sharing Economy."

86   http://seed.coop.

87   http://goteo.org.

88   Gorenflo, "How Platform Coops Can Beat Death Stars Like Uber to
Create a Real Sharing Economy."

89   Swarm.co

90   Nathaniel Popper, "Dream of New Kind of Credit Union Is Extinguished
by Bureaucracy," *The New York Times*, November 24, 2015.

91   http://slack.externalrevenue.us.

92   Max Dana's talk at Platform Cooperativism in November 2015.

93   http://robinhoodcoop.org
94   http://vimeo.com/149532379.
95   "Venture Communism," P2P Foundation, accessed December 11, 2015, p2pfoundation.net.
96   http://vimeo.com/149381439
97   P2P Foundation, "Commons-Based Reciprocity Licenses." Available at: http://p2pfoundation.net/Commons-Based_Reciprocity_Licenses.
98   "The Great Chain of Being Sure about Things," *The Economist*, October 31, 2015. Available at: http://www.economist.com/news/briefing/21677228-technology-behind-bitcoin-lets-people-who-do-not-know-or-trust-each-other-build-dependable; see also Rachel O'Dwyer's talk at the Platform Cooperativism event: platformcoop.net/video.
99   The nonprofit Ethereum is helping such enterprises.
100 http://vimeo.com/150040123.
101 Wikimedia Foundation's head office moved off email into Loomio, enabling collaborative decisions with 180 staff.
102 loomio.org.
103 For a discussion of blockchain technology, see Nathan Schneider and Trebor Scholz, "The Internet Needs a New Economy," The Next System Project, November 8, 2015. Available at: www.thenextsystem.org.
104 http://dcentproject.eu.
105 http://consensys.net.
106 http://vimeo.com/149541466.
107 Cameron Tonkinwise speaking at *Platform Cooperativism: The Internet, Ownership, Democracy* http://platformcoop.net
108 "Badges," MozillaWiki, December 18, 2014. Available at: https://wiki.mozilla.org/Badges.
109 "Rio de Janeiro Becomes First City in Brazil to Ban Uber," *The Guardian*, September 30, 2015.
110 http://murphyinstituteblog.org.
111 http://codesign.mit.edu.
112 Sam Kinsley, "Stiegler on Daesh and 'The Age of Disruption,'" November 26, 2015. Available at: http://www.samkinsley.com/2015/11/26/stiegler-on-daesh-and-the-age-of-disruption/.
113 Gorenflo, "How Platform Coops Can Beat Death Stars Like Uber to Create a Real Sharing Economy."
114 "Making It Work," Platform Coop 2015: Platform Cooperativism Conference.

Index